CAMBRIDGE LI

Books of end

British and Irish History, General

The books in this series are key examples of eighteenth- and nineteenth-century historiography which show how centuries of political, social and economic change were interpreted during the height of Britain's power. They shed light on the understanding of dynasty, religion and culture that shaped the domestic, foreign and colonial policy of the British empire.

Letters Written by Eminent Persons in the Seventeenth and Eighteenth Centuries

This three-volume compilation by the Oxford antiquary John Walker (1770–1831) consists mainly of manuscripts from the Bodleian Library and the Ashmolean Museum, but is significant because it contains the biographical notes on the 'lives of eminent men' furnished by John Aubrey (1626–97) to Anthony à Wood, who was at the time compiling his *Athenae Oxonienses*. Aubrey's subsequently famous 'Brief Lives' were published for the first time in this 1813 work, and, although described as the fourth appendix to it, in fact comprise slightly less than half of the second volume and the entirety of the third. Volume 2 contains letters to and from the librarian and antiquary Thomas Hearne, as well as two accounts of Hearne's travels, on foot to Whaddon Hall in Buckinghamshire in 1716, and on horseback to Reading and Silchester in 1714, and the first fifty (organised alphabetically from Aiton to Fletcher) of Aubrey's 'lives'.

Cambridge University Press has long been a pioneer in the reissuing of out-of-print titles from its own backlist, producing digital reprints of books that are still sought after by scholars and students but could not be reprinted economically using traditional technology. The Cambridge Library Collection extends this activity to a wider range of books which are still of importance to researchers and professionals, either for the source material they contain, or as landmarks in the history of their academic discipline.

Drawing from the world-renowned collections in the Cambridge University Library and other partner libraries, and guided by the advice of experts in each subject area, Cambridge University Press is using state-of-the-art scanning machines in its own Printing House to capture the content of each book selected for inclusion. The files are processed to give a consistently clear, crisp image, and the books finished to the high quality standard for which the Press is recognised around the world. The latest print-on-demand technology ensures that the books will remain available indefinitely, and that orders for single or multiple copies can quickly be supplied.

The Cambridge Library Collection brings back to life books of enduring scholarly value (including out-of-copyright works originally issued by other publishers) across a wide range of disciplines in the humanities and social sciences and in science and technology.

Letters Written by Eminent Persons in the Seventeenth and Eighteenth Centuries

To Which Are Added, Hearne's Journeys to Reading, and to Whaddon Hall, the Seat of Browne Willis, Esq., and Lives of Eminent Men

VOLUME 2 – PART 1

JOHN AUBREY
EDITED BY JOHN WALKER

CAMBRIDGE
UNIVERSITY PRESS

University Printing House, Cambridge, CB2 8BS, United Kingdom

Cambridge University Press is part of the University of Cambridge.
It furthers the University's mission by disseminating knowledge in the pursuit of education, learning and research at the highest international levels of excellence.

www.cambridge.org
Information on this title: www.cambridge.org/9781108079341

This edition first published 1813
This digitally printed version 2015

ISBN 978-1-108-07934-1 Paperback

LETTERS

WRITTEN

BY EMINENT PERSONS

IN THE

SEVENTEENTH AND EIGHTEENTH CENTURIES:

TO WHICH ARE ADDED,

HEARNE'S JOURNEYS TO READING,

AND TO

WHADDON HALL,

THE SEAT OF BROWNE WILLIS, ESQ.

AND

LIVES OF EMINENT MEN,

BY

JOHN AUBREY, ESQ.

THE WHOLE NOW FIRST PUBLISHED FROM THE ORIGINALS

IN

THE BODLEIAN LIBRARY AND ASHMOLEAN MUSEUM,

WITH

BIOGRAPHICAL AND LITERARY ILLUSTRATIONS.

IN TWO VOLUMES.

VOL. II.—PART I.

LONDON:

PRINTED FOR LONGMAN, HURST, REES, ORME, AND BROWN, PATER-NOSTER-ROW; AND MUNDAY AND SLATTER, OXFORD.

1813.

Munday and Slatter,
Oxford.

LETTER CXI.

Dr. HICKES to Mr. T. HEARNE.

On Printing MSS.

May 2, 1715.

DEAR SIR,

I HAD the favour of both your letters, and my trembling hand and other infirmities oblige me to answer them in as few words as I can. I cannot approve of your printing Tully's Works, for as I used to tell Dr. Mill, Dr. Grabe, Dr. Hudson, &c. I am for printing MSS. especially in the Universities, even the bare MSS. correctly and faithfully, though without notes and commentaries, as MSS. were at first printed, and leave posterity in after editions to refine upon them in notes, and commentaries, and what criticisms they please. Therefore I much approve of your printing that ancient copy of the Acts of the Apostles in Greek, and Latin, and in the manner you mention,* in capitals, keeping the

* Hearne did print this very valuable MS. which is supposed to have belonged to venerable Bede, and to have been written about the seventh century.

just magnitude, figure, and duct of the letters; or if you do not observe the just magnitude to have an alphabet of them cut in copper exactly to represent them as they are in the book. I saw the book, and it was from the letters of it, that in the I. Chap of my Anglo-Sax. Grammar, p. 2, I formed the opinion that the letters of the Gothic Gospels were taken partly from the Latin and partly from the Greek Letters, and for what I have said more to this purpose, and of that copy of the Acts, I refer you to the 8th page of my preface to the Saxon Grammar, which I desire you to read with part of the 9th. I am glad the "Collectanea" are so near publishing, and agree with those of your friends, who are of opinion, that it is best for you to acquiesce, and desist. Had I continued in my preferments, you had [had] the *Codex Bedæ Rushworth* printed as you mention, and Tatian's Harmony of the Gospels in Francic, as prepared by Junius, and some other Septentrional MSS. I pray God to have you always in his good keeping, and committing you to his Almighty protection, I subscribe, as I truly am,

Sir,

Your very faithful and affectionate
Friend and Servt.

GEO. HICKES.

LETTER CXII.

Dr. CHARLETT to Mr. HEARNE.

Edition of Cicero.—Old Map of Oxford.—Old Books and Ruins of Abbies.

Warwic Court, neare Grays Inne,
15 Sept. 1715.

SIR,

WITH great pleasure and satisfaction I received and read all your very kind and very curious letters, for which I must be endebted to you, not having proper opportunitys or inclinations, to give so full, or so considerate an answer, as I could wish and they deserve.

Mr. Anstis was with me some days ago, when I read to him your request about the MS. Mr. Thoresby is at present in Yorkshire, but Mr. A. undertakes to get a full answer to your query. This gentleman and Dr. Sloane, who are both very much friends to your labors and studdys, seem to lament that you should divert your application from the rough pursuit of antiquities, and withal seeme to feare, that Tully may make you weary of those other lesse polished pieces of literature. But I am not satisfyd why you should refuse yourself the pleasure and satisfaction of conversing with Tully, after so many years spent in the antiquitys of our own country, especially since I am morally sure, you never intend to be idle, and then Tully will be an excellent preparative for reprinting, correcting, and improving Camden's Latin History, whose author was so well versed in the Ciceronian dialect.

I perfectly concur with you in your opinion of reprinting the Map of old Oxford.* Dr. Wallis was exceeding zealous for it, and would not consent to the least alteration, as to the size and breadth, averring it was as record, and that he carryed two causses for the University by vertue of the old mapp, particularly one about the ground and scituation of the old schooles before the new, in relation to some way or passage, and many a controversy I have had with Mr. A. Wood about publishing the same or another with his amendments and additions, which I offered to print at my own charge when of Trinity College, but he perversely put me off with saying, it should not be done without his large History of the City and all the Churches and theyr monuments, so I could never prevail for the map alone. Mr. Anstis thinks also we do not keep Mr. Wood's MS. papers relating to the city, parishes, buildings, streets, &c. with due respect and care. I told him I was perhaps of his opinion, but I did hope Mr. Whiteside's diligence and industry would extend even to that part of his trust, so as to

* This must allude to "Aggas's Map."

make his care visible even in the particular complained of. I pray is Dr. Sloane's name ever entered in the public register of benefactors to the Bodleian Library, or any books of his, pamphlets or others lately sent thither. I agree with you entirely in viewing the ancient pictures of our colleges, and heartily wish those of Neale were republished. I thought you had reprinted some of them.* I am very glad the friend I meant is no ways concerned in the hint I gave of the inconvenience sometimes of being a member in and of a college or hall, with respect to the new register required in every college or hall by the new act.

Your advice to Mr. Bagford is equally pertinent, necessary, and usefull, and desirable, and therefore I beg him to follow it. Your wishes also are very just and desirable, as to the recovery of the printed books in Oxford, and preserving the present ruines of abbys. 'Tis great pity our friend Mr. N. did not actually survey all those remains, and take copys of them. Dr. Sloane kept an engraver and painter, 3 years in his house, to copy all his natural history that

* He reprinted the whole in Dodwell's "Dissertatio de Parma Equestri Woodwardiana." Printed at Oxford in 1713. They have been since given, from the same plates, by Nichols, in his *Progresses of Queen Elizabeth*, a work now as rare as that of Hearne.

was curious. He now employs one to describe in colours, all the monsters, raritys, &c. of Bartholomew Fair, any medals or books that he borrows. He has had copies out of the Dutch East India Books, of all plants or other raritys, natural or artificial, of which he is not master.

My surgeon gives me hopes of a good, safe, and speedy cure; nothing can be more desirable than a dish of tea with you, before day in my studdy, at Univ. Coll.

Service to all that ask for,

Your truly loving Friend

to serve you,

AR. CHARLETT.

LETTER CXIII.

Mr. BINGHAM to Dr. CHARLETT.

University College.—Headburn-Worthy.—Mr. Percival.

HOND. SIR,

I HAPPENED the other day to see Dr. Radcliff's Picture engraved by M. Burghers, where among other things I found the Rectory of King's-Worthy mentioned as given to Univ. Coll. I was much surprized at the mistake, because that is another parish in which the Dr. had no concern, for the patronage belongs to my Lady Russel. The Doctor's Will has it right, as I remember, Headborn-Worthy, al. Mortimer Worthy. And so it is called in the Valor, Mortimer Worthy, and distinguished from Worthy-Regis, and Worthy Martyris, which are different parishes. There is also Abbots-Worthy, but that is only a Tithing belonging to Kings-Worthy. The common name of our parish is Headborn-Worthy, and so I have always called it in the title page of my books, whenever I had occasion to mention it. I cannot but wonder the person who was employed in giving an account of the Doctor's benefactions should make such a mistake against so many evidences, or at least should not consult you before it was printed, who could have better informed him. We have lately had a very good Benefactor die in this place, who was pleased to make me one of his executors in trust. He gives 15*l.* per an. to a Charity School; 10*l.* per an. for reading evening prayer at St. Lawrence Church in this City; 75*l.* per an. for augmentation of poor livings throughout the nation. And the care of all these is committed in trust to the Dean and Chapter of Winton, who are to keep the 75*l.* till it amounts, by four years income, to the sum of 300*l.* and then join it to the Queen's bounty of 200*l.* to make a perpetual settlement upon each Church. He has likewise given 200*l* to Magdalen Hospital, near this place; 100*l.* to the poor of Aston, in Derbyshire, and the remainder of his estate, after debts and legacies are paid, to the poor of Winton. He gave one of his servants 200*l.* and to his two executors 50*l.* each. His name was Mr. Joseph Percival, once a Spanish merchant. He died worth about 6000*l.* and I think out of such a sum his benefactions are as considerable as most of the present age affords. I thought this short account might not be unacceptable to you, and therefore I give you the trouble of reading it, who am,

Your obliged friend,
and humble Servt.
Jos. Bingham.

Winton,
Oct. 11, 1715.

LETTER CXIV.

THOMAS WAGSTAFF to T. HEARNE.

Canterbury Cathedral.—Epitaphs on Somner and Battely.

Canterbury, Feb. 29, 1715-6.

SIR,

I ought to begin with an apology for not answering your last sooner; but I have deferred it so very long, that I am equally ashamed of my neglect, and unable to excuse it. I have not been in London this half-year, contrary to my intent, which was to have returned thither above five months ago; and had I not been prevented, I had long since returned an answer to your kind letter, and with it, a just acknowledgment for the great obligation you have laid not only upon me, but all the learned world, by your publishing of Leland, a book so long wanted, and so well known, that the vast labours of the author are not more surprising than the indolence of our own nation, in suffering a work of that extensive advantage to be so long expected by the public. However, I beg leave to take this late opportunity of returning my thanks, not only for that, but also for the very valuable and ancient copy of the "Acts of the Apostles," by which you have no less obliged the world, than by the former. Nor must I forget the favour, which Mr. Bedford tells me, you will add to all the rest, by reserving me a copy of Ross.

I cannot forbear making you partaker of the wonderful pleasure and satisfaction, which my conversation among those venerable remains of Antiquity, the many ornaments of this Cathedral Church, has afforded me; though I fear I shall interrupt you with a relation of little more, than what you have long since been informed of.

I need not repeat what Somner and Battely have observed concerning the particular monuments that lie exposed to public view, tho' that of the Black Prince is not to be omitted, whose body is made of neat brass, deposited on a pedestal of the same metal, on which is the inscription inserted in Weaver; all supported by a stone basis, to the sides of which are pinned his arms in brass. It is indeed a very glorious monument, inferior to none but that of Richard Beauchamp, Earl of Warwick, in St. Mary's, in that city, (of which we have a draught in Sir Wm. Dugdale's admirable description of the County of Warwick) and that of Henry VII. in Westminster Abbey. But nothing has made a greater impression upon me, nor given me more exalted ideas of the piety, as well as grandeur, of our forefathers, than the Lady-Chapel in the Undercroft, a building of that beauty and ornament, especially at the East end, where, I suppose, the statue of the V. M. was formerly placed, that I do not at all wonder that Erasmus was not able to describe it without transport. There is a contrivance, which is very surprizing. The cieling at the East end is painted black, and overlaid with stars of a great size, raised in a convex form, and covered over with glass, which by reflecting the rays communicated from the lights, must necessarily exhibit a very pleasing and venerable spectacle. It is a great pity Mr. Battely has not given us a draught of this chapel, as also of the three subterranean monuments erected here. He might very well have omitted (since he could not find patrons for them all) as many of those that lye above in the Church, and are not exposed to the same inconveniences with these in the Undercroft, which might then have been preserved entire to posterity, whereas they now seem hardly capable of it, being already in some measure decayed, and continually exposed to the incurious humour of a brick-layer, belonging to the Church, by whom the whole Undercroft (as it stands separated from the French congregation) is scandalously used as a repository for his tools and rubbish. However, I have procured a description of them, two of which are done accurately enough, and the third (which is that of Archbp. Moreton) though not so accurate as I could wish, is yet more than sufficient to give one an idea of its form and magnificence.

I remember, when I was at Oxford, we were lamenting that so great a man as Mr. Somner should find nobody, that had respect enough for his memory, (and at the same time capacity sufficient) to raise a monument to it; not that his established name needs any such assistance to perpetuate it, for that he has done best himself; but it is a pious and commendable veneration for our ancestors that excites in us a curiosity to know, and a desire to inform the world of, the places of their burial. This, which I was then ignorant of, was performed by Mrs. Dawson, two years after the publishing of his Life, written by Kennet, who against the North Wall of the North Isle of St. Margaret's Church, has erected a handsome table with his and her own arms, and the Inscription following:

H. S. E.
GULIELMUS SOMNERUS
Cantuarensis.
Saxonicam Literaturam,
Civitatis Cantuariæ Historiam,
(Tenebris utramque involutam)
Illustravit.
Cantii Antiquitates meditantem
Fatum intercepit.
Officium
Erga { Deum pietate severâ,
Homines probitate simplici,
Principem fide periculosâ,
Patriam scriptis immortalibus,
Indicavit.
Ita mores antiquos
Studium Antiquitatis efformat.
Cantuariæ { Natus est Martii 30, 1606,
Omnem ætatem egit,
Obiit Martii 30, 1669.

Upon the Stone that lies over him:

Eximii
Hic reponuntur cineres
SOMNERI.
Ecce Monumentum in Pariete.

Barbara, Daughter of John Dawson, of the County of Kent, Gent. and second Wife to the Deceased, did in the year 1695,

at her own charge, erect
this Monument, in memory
of her beloved Husband.

I believe you would not look upon it as impertinent should I also subjoin the Epitaph of that judicious Antiquary, Mr. Archdeacon Battely, as I transcribed it from his Monument erected against the S. E. corner of the South cross, which is as follows:

H. S. E.
Johannes Battely, S.T.P.
Buriæ Sti. Edmundi in Suffolciâ natus,
Collegii, S. Stæ. Trinitatis Cantabrigiæ socius,
A Sacris domesticis
Reverendissimo Wilhelmo Sancroft,
Archiepiscopo Cantuarensi:
A quo meritissima accepit
Præmia,
Rectoriam de Adisham prope hanc urbem,
Hujus Ecclesiæ Metropoliticæ Canonicatum,
Hujus q. Diœceseos Archi-Diaconatum,
Quæ omnia
Summa cum fide, et prudentia,
Administravit Munia.
Vir integerrimâ in Deum pietate,
Honestissimis et suavissimis Moribus,
Excellenti Divinarum et Humanarum
Literarum scientiâ,
Singulari in Egenos Beneficentiâ,
In suos Charitate,
Candore et benignitate in omnes.
Hic tot præclaris dotibus

Hanc Basilicam,
Totamque Ecclesiam Anglicanam
Insigniter ornavit,
Obiit Octob. x. Anno Dni. MDCCVIII.
Ætatis suæ LXI.

I hope you will excuse this long letter, and look upon me, as I am,

Your affectionate humble servt.

THOS. WAGSTAFFE.*

LETTER CXV.

Mr. BROWNE WILLIS to Dr. CHARLETT.

On Cardinal Wolsey's burial place, &c. and on removing his body to Christ Church.

"As to the great Cardinal Wolsey's Sepulchre, the best account I have met with is from one Mr. John Hasloe, whose grandfather Arthur Barefoot was Gardiner to the Countess of Devonshire, who lived at the Abby before the Civil Wars. He tells me that the Church stood part of it in what is now a little garden, and the east end of it, in the Orchard (which was formerly called the New Garden) where his grandfather, with others digging, found several stone coffins, the cavities of which did not lie uppermost but were inverted over the bodies. That among these he

* Probably son of the Rev. Thomas Wagstaffe, who is noticed in Nichols's Literary Anecdotes, Vol. I. 36; and Vol. IV. 171.

discovered Cardinal Wolsey's (Mr. Hasloe forgets by what means he knew it) which the Countess would not suffer to be stirred, but ordered it to be covered again, and his grandfather laid a great heap of gravel over it, that he might know the place, which still remains there."

DEAR AND HONORED DR.

I AM greatly concerned no motives, importunities, &c. will tempt you hither; I must now totally give over all thoughts, and as my health &c. is, I fear, not think of seeing you again, tho' I cannot forbear writing to you when I have opportunity, notwithstanding what I shall say must be, by the person's haste, very brief.

Anthony à Wood* has not as yet bent his course this way, and I am weary of soliciting him, and now Physic ought to take place of Antiquities; but, as Dr. Symonds says, if one is not cheerful in taking it, all aids, &c. from it are ineffectual, and such is my case, wherefore a good friend's company, who would be *Physic for Fortune,* such as yours, might prove the best Recipe. And a little antiquities intermixed might come in, which notwithstanding my indisposition I cannot forget. I am greatly pleased with the abovementioned answer to some Queries

* He means Hearne, to whom he gave the name of Anthony à Wood. Wood died in 1695.

I sent to Leicester some time ago, from which I received this answer on Tuesday, sent me by the Reverend Mr. Sam. Carte, a noted Antiquary there, amongst other things relating to that borough. I have wrote since to him concerning more particulars in relation to the discovery. In short, as I have been ever zealous concerning our founder, Cardinal Wolsey, so I cannot but [be] pleased in whatever I discover about him, and it would be a great satisfaction to me, and I should be willing to contribute thereto, if his body could be translated to Christ Church. This our College ought in gratitude to do. And, dear Sir, if you have an opportunity of speaking to any of them, as doubtless you have many, sound the thing, and see how it will agree with their notions. Methinks tho' I am but a mean person, I could gladly undergo the charge of removing the Cardinal's Body, if it was into the next parish church, rather than it should rest so obscurely there.* I desire you to write me par-

* On the place of Cardinal Wolsey's burial, the following is extracted from a letter of Dr. Tanner to Dr. Charlett.

—— "as for the place where the Cardinal himself was buried, our friend Tony from Cavendish tells us 'twas "in St. Marie's Chappel, in the Abbey of Leycester," but I don't find that ever any of those many dependents and servants that he had raised were so grateful to erect the least monument for their great master. I believe the place where his bones lay can't now be traced."

ticularly about this as soon as you can with your thoughts and sentiments, and excuse my hasty scribble, who am, with most sincere affection, gratitude, &c.

Dear and Honored Sir,

Your most devoted, obliged, &c. Fd. and Servt.

BROWNE WILLIS.

Whaddon Hall,
April 19, 1716.

And in a Letter from Dr. Tanner to Dr. Charlett, dated Norwich, Aug. 10, 1709, we find the following note:

"On the other side, is a coeval note at the end of an old MS. belonging to our Cathedral, of the odd exit of the great Cardinal Wolsey, not mentioned, I think, in Cavendish, or any of the Historians,—much like Oliver's Wind.

"Ad finem Annalium Bartholomæi Cotton MS. in Biblioth. Eccl. Cath. Norwic. habetur hæc notata.

"Anno Xti 1530 nocte immediate sequente quartum diem Novemb. vehemens ventus quasi per totam Angliam accidebat, et die proximè sequente quinto sc. die ejusdem mensis circa horam primam post meridiem captus erat Dns Thomas Wulsye Cardinalis in ædibus suis de Cahow [Cawood] infra Diocesin suam Eboracensem; et postea in itinere ejus versus Londoniam vigiliâ St. Andreæ prox. sequente apud Leycestriam moriebatur, quo die ventus quasi Gehennalis tunc fere per totam Angliam accidebat, cujus vehementia apud Leystoft infra Dioc. Norwicensem et alibi in diversis locis infra Regnum Angliæ multæ naves perierunt."

LETTER CXVI.

From the same to the same.

Mitred Abbies.—Cardinal Wolsey.

Whaddon Hall, Tuesday, May 15, 1716.

* * * * * * * *

I WAS heartily pleased with Mr. Rawlinson's good company, and concerned I had not more of it. I was really greatly troubled with the head ache one or two evenings he was here, and flattered myself he would stay till Monday or Tuesday: Anthony à Wood's* company was also very acceptable. I thought I should have never seen him here. I am glad he thinks of coming again. He would do me a great kindness if he would stay some time, and help me in the works I am about. I have two now on the stocks, or rather three; some of which you will be greatly pleased with. One is the reprinting my *Mitred Abbies*, with very large emendations, additions, &c. To which I would subjoin a like series of several other principals of Religious Houses, particularly the Monastic Cathedrals, such as were Canterbury, Rochester, Ely, Winchester, Carlisle, Worcester, Durham, Norwich, &c. which were before the Reforma-

* Hearne's. See Note p. 15.

tion governed by Priors and Monks, as were the new founded ones, as Peterborough, Gloucester, Bristol, Chester, by Abbots; the two first of which are in my first work, but Bristol and Chester must be new done, as must St. Frideswide's, Oxford [of] which I have the Priors in all 24 very complete; as I hope I have those of Dover, Southwark, Feversham, Burton-on-Trent, Leicester, &c. Abbots and Priors, with which I would swell a book to a pretty good size, and then, by way of Appendix, I would endeavour to present the reader with the names of each respective Abbot or Prior of all the Religious Houses in general with other curious observations in this respect. I hope, God willing, in about two months to adjust this undertaking, tho' I began it but this day se'nnight, having myself and Sliford collected already in this time above 40 sheets of paper, wrote on two sides, because of additions hereafter from Mr. Wharton's excellent notes lent me by Dean Kennet, which he has wonderfully improved, and I see it is from his MS. that Mr. Le Neve has taken out 11 of his Cathedrals, and the Churches of Westminster, Windsor, Provosts of Eton, &c. I am to return this book again, next week. I should by right do it this, so must work hard, and I keep home pretty close, having made but one visit, viz. to Great Brickhill on May-day last, since Mr. Hearne was here.

Another of my Works is the *Cathedral of St. David's,* which I hope soon to dispatch, only waiting for an answer to a letter or two.

The third is my *Notitia Parliamentaria,* which want of materials keep back, and may perhaps entirely defeat my intentions. * * * *

* * * * Pray when does the Bishop of Bristol come to town, I would fain know this, for I should be glad to wait on him, and talk more about our Founder Cardinal Wolsey, which I heartily thank you for communicating to him, and should think myself exceeding fortunate could I make a real discovery of the Cardinal's ashes, of which, &c. more another time, for I believe I have tired you now with my scrall, who am,

Dear Doctor,
Your most Affte. and Devoted Servt.
to command,
BROWNE WILLIS.

LETTER CXVII.

J. SOTHEBY to T. HEARNE.

Mr. Bagford's Death.

SIR,

I HAVE carefully read over *Rouse.* I find many uncommon and valuable notes, and give you my thanks for your kind mention of me. I understand *Livius** is in a manner finished; please to send a line, you will have the receipt and last payment. I now come to lament our common, and a universal, loss; Mr. Bagford is no more; after a gradual decay since he left Oxford, but very visible for a few weeks, this morning a little before six he departed this life at his lodgings at Islington, where he had been five days.† I desire our correspondence may not cease with him.

Sir,
Your faithful humble Servt.
J. SOTHEBY.

Hatton Garden,
May 5th, 1716.

LETTER CXVIII.

From the same to the same.

On the same subject.

SIR,

A LITTLE before his death Mr. Bagford told me he was either 65 or 66, he could not well say which,. and I think born in Fetter-lane; was first a shoe-maker at Turnstile, but that

* See p. 25, *infra*. † See vol. i. p. 159.

would not do; then a bookseller at the same place, and that as little; yet his genius and industry brought him to what you remember. About seven in the afternoon, Saturday, May 5th, by order of the Charter-House, the servants went with a coffin to Islington, thence bore the corpse to his chamber, and Monday following (his acquaintance Mr. Clifton, a vintner, giving four bottles of sack to be drunk at his funeral) at five o'clock, evening service, brought into the chapel, thence attended by his confreres (six of which held the pall) to the public place of interment within the precincts of the said House. Just before he died he desired to speak with me, but was dead before I knew it. He neither left will or direction about his things, so all entirely (by order of the Commons) are come into the hands of Mr. Clifton above-mentioned, his principal creditor, to whom he was indebted 70*l.* besides several years' interest in arrear. I have lately been with him, and put him in mind that the collections ought not to be separated, but carefully preserved in order to be perfected and reduced to method by some able person (which all his friends wish were yourself) both as due to Mr. Bagford's memory, and the best way to reimburse himself, which he assured me should be done. On Wednesday last I received *Livius*, &c. I am ravished with joy, I want words to express my sense of that most excellent performance.

Monday I send by Bartlet your receipt and twelve shillings, six of which I desire may be for the first payment of *Aluredus Beverlacensis** in large paper, and am with the greatest respect,

Sir,

Your most faithful humble Servt.

J. SOTHEBY.

Hatton Garden,
May 19, 1716.

LETTER CXIX.

Mr. BROWNE WILLIS to Dr. CHARLETT.

Cardinal Wolsey.

Whaddon, May 30, 1716.

* * * * * * * *

YOU may easily guess at my reason for going to Leicester, which was on account of our Founder Cardinal Wolsey, to search for his coffin. I have thoughts of having the coffin

* ALUREDI BEVERACENSIS Annales, sive Historia de Gestis Regum Britanniæ, libris IX. E Cod. pervetusto, calamo exarato, in Bibliotheca Viri Clarissimi, Thomæ Rawlinsoni, Armigeri, descripsit ediditque Tho. Hearnius, A.M. Oxoniensis. Oxon, 1716, 8vo.—One hundred and forty-eight copies were printed; large paper 12s. small paper 8s.

taken up I wrote you about, and brought to Bletchley; it may serve to hold my ashes: Pray let me knew when the Dean of Christ Church is expected at Oxon. I have reason for this inquiry on several accounts, and beg you to give me the best information you can. If he is there already, you may present him with these two catalogues of his ancient predecessors in the two famous monasteries he so very worthily presides over. Being of Christ Church, I aimed to do it in Latin, tho' I am a very poor proficient in that language, which you must excuse me in. I value myself much on these two catalogues, because they so exactly, for the most part, settle the time of the succession of the Priors and Abbots of Oxon and Bristol, and seem to be very complete. I sent the Dean before a List of the Priors of St. Frideswide's, but this has four names more than that, so I am obliged to repeat my trouble, and revoke the other; and as for the Abbots of St. Austin's, Bristol, I am induced to transmit this Catalogue to the Bishop in order to correct my friend Tom. Ford's, which he encouraged the printing of. If his Lordship will give himself the trouble to compare them, he will be well pleased with what I have done.

LETTER CXX.

T. WAGSTAFFE to T. HEARNE.

T. Livy's Hist. of Hen. V.—Preface to Rowse.

May 30, 1716.

DEAR SIR,

I HAD answered yours of April 5th before this time, but that I was willing to stay till I might return you thanks for T. Livy's much wanted History of H. V.* which I received from Mr. Deacon, to whom I have given the 2d. payment, together with 4s. for the 1st. payment of the subscription money for the book you are now printing; and now, Sir, you must give me leave to mention the great pleasure with which I read your preface to Rowse.† It discovers a wonder-

* "Titi Livii Foro-Juliensis Vita Henrici Quinti, Regis Angliæ. Accedit, Sylloge Epistolarum, a variis Angliæ Principibus scriptarum. E codicibus calamo exaratis descripsit ediditque Tho. Hearnius, A.M. Oxoniensis." Oxon, 1716, 8vo.—Of this edition one hundred and forty-eight copies were printed; large paper 12s. small paper 8s. In the Bodleian Library there is a copy which belonged to Tho. Baker, "Coll. Jo. Socius ejectus," with several notes in his hand-writing.

† Joannis Rossi Antiquarii Warwicensis Historia Regum Angliæ. E Cod. MS. in Bibliotheca Bodl. descripsit, notisque et indice adornavit Tho. Hearnius, A.M. Oxoniensis."

ful constancy and resolution in adhering to a well-settled principle, and is so pathetical a relation of your sufferings, as not only raises our pity, but makes them our own: in a word 'tis full of such sentiments as are unknown to the degeneracy of the present age, and are the peculiar affections of a soul prepared to suffer for conscience-sake.*

* * * * * *

Your obliged humble Servant,

T. WAGSTAFFE.

Oxon, 1716, 8vo.—Only sixty copies were printed; large paper 1l. 1s. small paper 16s.

* "Priusquam concludam de alia re breviter dicendum. Vicem nostram proculdubio dolebis si forsitan ad aures tuas retulerit fama, me non tantum Architypographi beneficio, quo ab Academiæ OXONIENSIS Convocatione, plaudentibus eruditis, perhonorifice ornatus fueram, cuique Bedelli superioris in Jure Civili munus inseparabiliter annexum est, spoliari, verum etiam a consuetudine bonarum litterarum in Bibliotheca BODLEIANA pene sejungi et excludi. Sed bono es animo, mi Amice, et memento Deum esse qui mundum regit. Quod sive *hic* sive *ille* fecerit id plane non est tribuendum vel Academiæ vel Convocationi. Neque re vera ulla ratio est cur ipsa graviter luat Academia quod aliena culpa contractum est. Ergo tam Academiæ quam etiam Convocationi gratiam habeo, semperque sum habiturus, ut debeo, maximam. Juxta mecum quoque fateberis contra nostram voluntatem contigisse quod quisquam e nostris vel male audiat, vel maledictis proscindatur. Nunc demum in secessu litterario mibi vivam, solutus fere ab omni cura. Immo Deo vivam, spretis divitiis, et gloria illa, quam falsa prorsus, et

LETTER CXXI.

Mr. JOHN JOHNSON to Dr. CHARLETT.

On Rogation or Perambulation Days.

Cranbrooke, Jan. 27, 1716.

——— THO' *Rogation* and *Perambulation* are words of a different signification,

inanis honorum species ostentat. A Fortuna adeo non est pendendum, ut ipsam etiam contemnant sapientes. Horum exempla mihi proponenda esse duxi. Quamvis igitur Fortuna omnia eripuerit quæ bona appellare vulgus solet, ea tamen nunquam adimet, quæ nec ipsa dedit, nec cuiquam dare potest, rectam mentem, fidem obstinatam, optima studia, pietatem in Deum patriamque. Vides, vir cl. secundum nostram opinionem (qua in sententia etiam cupio omnes alios esse) studia litteraria divino cum amore esse conjungenda; quippe sine quo nulla lætitia, nulla possit esse vera felicitas. Bona igitur fama (ad quam pervenire omnes vehementer expetunt) non in opibus aut magistratibus, principumve aulis ac palatiis quærenda est, sed a rectis cogitationibus, honestis laboribus, studioque et exercitatione virtutis re vera est exspectanda. Hæc iterum iterumque secum cogitent juvenes, memoresque sint corporis ac fortunæ dotes cito evanescere et exstingüi, et plerumque irritamenta esse nequitiæ, gloriam vero e virtute ortam perpetuo esse mansuram, nominaque ab interritu vindicaturam.

FLOREAT Ecclesia ANGLICANA, floreat Academia OXONIEN-

yet they at present signify the same time. I suppose they were called *Rogation* or *Litany-days*, from the solemn prayers used on this occasion, before the Reformation; and *Perambulation*, or *Procession-days*, from the walking round the several Parishes: and I apprehend the prayers, or litanies, were sung or said *inter ambulandum*, not in the Church, or kneeling, or standing: the best account I have met with concerning them is in Spelman's "Glossary," in the word *Litaniæ*.* We have no law or canon now obliging us to make those perambulations: they were enjoined in the rituals, or other books of public devotion in the Church of Rome; and since the use of those books is abrogated, we have had no new inforcement of this ancient, laudable practice of

sis, floreant bonæ litteræ, reslpiscant Adversarii. Vale, mi Amice, et da operam ut illa ornamenta referas in patriam, quæ nulla vis fortunæ, nulla temporum mutatio auferre possit. Volui hoc amoris ac observantiæ testimonium apud te relinquere. Sordidi et perangusti est animi ea non publice agnoscere quæ acceperim, ideoque de liberali et prolixa tua erga me voluntate gratias habeo, eamque inter summa beneficia collocandam puto. Iterum vale, et macte tua virtute et integritate. Ex Aula Edmundi, Feb. 1mo. A.D. MDCCXV." *Editoris Præfatio "ad Amicum eruditum* Thomam Rawlinsonum, Armigerum; *Virum antiquæ probitatis*." P. xxi.

* We must refer the curious reader to the original; the article being too long for a note.

going the bounds of our parishes: and we may be sure, we never shall have any, if our temporal lawyers can prevent it: for the uncertainty of our bounds brings much grist to their mill, and it can be try'd in no court, but the temporal: the ecclesiastical judges cannot oblige church-wardens, or parishioners to go their bounds; but if the churchwardens are at any expense on that account, they will allow it: and they can, I presume, go no further: this is a growing evil, and there is no remedy for it but an Act of Parliament: and this cure commonly brings some new disease along with it. A Canon will not be sufficient, because of that maxim, which our modern lawyers have invented as a clog to all Church Power, that a Canon can create no new charge.

LETTER CXXII.

T. WAGSTAFFE to T. HEARNE.

Stonesfield Pavement.

DEAR SIR,

I RECEIVED Roper* from our good friend Mr. Bedford, for which I return you my

* GULIELMI ROPERI Vita D. Thomæ Mori, Equitis Aurati,

thanks. I have paid him the remaining four shillings, and with that the first part of my subscription-money for Camden.* I have also in my hands ten shillings, which I had from Mr. Samuel Smith of the Middle Temple, a good friend of mine, who is willing to subscribe for that author, and which I will take care to return to you. I was somewhat surprized at a relation I had from Mr. Rawlinson, when in town, concerning the Stonesfield Pavement,† which he told me had been dug up by some unaccountable people, and as appears, for no other reason, but that they might be the authors of mischief, and defacers of the glory of antiquity; a strange and brutish revival of the times of the darkest ignorance! One would think that very indolence, that keeps them from improving themselves, should keep them also from being active in depriving the public of their proper advantages. It is an irrational disposition that inclines

lingua Anglicana contexta.—E Codicibus vetustis descripsit ediditque Tho. Hearnius, A.M. Oxoniensis. Oxon. 1716, 8vo.—Of this edition only one hundred and forty-eight copies were printed, large paper 16s. small paper 8s.

* Gulielmi Camdeni Annales Rerum Anglicarum et Hibernicarum regnante Elizabetha. Tribus Vol. comprehensi. Oxon. 1717, 8vo. large paper 2l. small paper 1l.

† An account of this pavement, with a print of it, is given by Hearne, in vol. viii. p. ix. of his Leland's Itinerary.

a man to admire his own times, and despise those of his ancestors, to study the benefit of the present, and not own himself obliged to passed ages. Let these modern gentlemen remember that we borrow our learning from our fathers, and fetch even our improvements of ancient learning from more ancient fountains ; and that so long since as the times of Horace, the preceding ages were preferred to the present, and the present to posterity: "Ætas parentum pejor avis tulit nos nequiores," &c. So that our improvements in vice will not be compensated by the additions we make to the treasures of learning. The most ignorant of our times value themselves upon the antiquity of their families, and thereby, with the true patrons of ancient learning, acknowledge the reverence due to it, but with this difference, that the former esteem it for no other reason but because it is *ancient*, the latter because it is useful and enlarges the compass of our knowledge. Excuse the trifles I have troubled you with, and give me leave to add, that I am sorry to hear of the usage you have met with from the University: but God will preserve you against all your enemies, and the pleasure and satisfaction that results from your own integrity will carry you through all the difficulties of the world, and render the most active malice of your adversaries but a *brutum ful-*

men, which is as little doubted, as it is greatly wished for by, Dear Sir,

Your obliged humble Servt.

T. Wagstaffe.

Dec. 15, 1716.

LETTER CXXIII.

Dr. WOOD to Dr. CHARLETT,

In which he complains of his Corpulency.

June 2, 1717,
Hardwick, Bucks.

REVEREND SIR,

I thank you heartily for your kind letter and your concern for my health, and my wife's and childrens'. I thank God I am hearty, but so corpulent that I am sure I could not walk from your lodgings to New College without resting once or twice. I ride much but find little relief from it. Fasting does not agree with my constitution, but makes me peevish, which infirmity a Judge (especially spiritual) ought in a particular manner to guard against,

I think the best remedy for your corpulency would be the gout for two or three months. But I hear you can walk up Heddington Hill, and want no such advice. An ounce of mustard seed bruised, and steep'd two or three days in a quart of white wine gives me great relief, as to my shortness of breath. A beer glass every morning fasting is an effectual cure. * * * * * * *

I am your most affectionate and
humble servt.
THO. WOOD.*

LETTER CXXIV.

ROBERT KECK to T. HEARNE.

Wickliffe's Translation of the New Testament.—Queen Elizabeth s Vanity.

SIR,

AFTER my writing to you from Bath, I did not return to town till November,

* Cousin to Anthony Wood, and fellow of New College, by which society he was presented to the Rectory of Hardwick, Bucks, in 1704. He was the author of "An Institute of the Laws of England," folio, and of an anonymous pamphlet entitled "An Appendix to the Life of Bishop Seth Ward," in answer to Dr. Walter Pope's Life of Ward, in which the author had taken some unwarrantable liberties with the Oxford Antiquary. He died in 1722. Prefixed to his "Institute," is a portrait of him by Vander Gucht.

when I found two letters from you, and though I have been again out of town once or twice since, I should not have omitted writing to you had I met with any thing worth your notice. I have received "Camden's Elizabeth," and think you have now first done the author justice, in an edition of his admirable work. I desire you will give me leave to mention a particular or two that occurred to me in reading your Preface. The first relates to the 30th Section. I have in my study a very good and correct MS. copy of Wicliff's Translation of the New Testament upon vellum, in which I doe not remember to have met with the word *Knave,* except in the 12th Chap. of the Revelation, in which it occurs twice joined with *Child,* instead of Male or Man-child, thus, verse the 5th—"And sche bare a knave child"—and again v. 13.—"He pursuede the womman that bare the knave child."*—We have likewise in our library belonging to the Royal Society, a very good copy of the same book, which I have examined and find to agree exactly with my own. When I read the 34th Section of your Preface, in which you take notice of the affectation Qu. Eliz. had to be thought handsome,† I was sorry

* It is used in this sense by Chaucer:

On hire he gat a knave childe anon.

Man of Lawes Tale, l. 5136.

† "§ XXXIV. Hoc modo quo explicuimus publicis privatisque negotiis distenta Elizabetha vitam laudabiliter agebat,

I had not formerly mentioned to you the French Memoires of one Du Maurier where you might have found several curious particulars relating to that affectation of the Queen, as likewise some that relate to the Death of the Queen of Scots. It is a book I first came acquainted with abroad, where it is had in much esteem, and indeed seems to carry with it a great air of truth throughout; it is chiefly concerned in the affairs of Holland; but what makes the particulars I have mentioned to you the more worth notice is, that the author had them all from his own father, who was sent once, if not twice, envoy from France to

spatiumque septuaginta pene annorum emensa, summo cum gemitu subditorum animam cœlo reddidit, corpore partim laboribus, partim doloribus discruciato et mire mutato, facieque rugis adeo tracta ut etiam contemptui esse cœperit. Quod quidem cum propria observatione tum aliorum indiciis quam optime sciebat, et impatienter ferebat, utpote quæ ætate etiam decrepita pro pulchra haberi voluit, vehementerque irascebatur si quis minus formosam esse prædicaret. Essexii igitur imprudentia valde inflammavit qui effutierat illam jam vetulam non minus animo quam corpore esse distorto. Imo infirmitatibus obnoxia si quando formam propriam in speculo adspiceret, indignatio idcirco illico erumpebat quod jam ætate senili laborans adolescentulæ species non compareret. Itaque quotiescunque per conclavia cubiculaque ubi specula adservabantur transitura erat, specula amovebant famulæ ne vultum forte fortuna conspiceret, et è mutationis contemplatione iracundia incenderetur." *Editoris Præfatio*, p. cxxxix.

Qu. Eliz. and was afterwards employed with that character to the States General.

I understand by Mr. Gale, that after *G Neubrigiensis*, we may expect a Scotch Chronicle from you, in both which, and all your undertakings, I heartily wish you success, and desire you to believe that in any thing that lies in my power you shall always find me ready to serve you, who am,

Sir,

Your affectionate humble Servant,

Rob. Keck.

Inner Temple,
Feb. 11, 1717-18.

LETTER CXXV.

Mr. MATTAIRE to Dr. CHARLETT.

Annales Typographici and other works.—T. Hearne.

1718, March 27.

REVEREND SIR,

I received yours, wherein you demonstrated your friendship by overlooking all the imperfections of my poor work. I wish I could find in my style that facility and felicity of language, which your great goodness flatters me with. To write Latin, is what of all the perfections of a Scholar I admire most; but I know myself so well, as to be sensible how much I fall short of it. I have herein inclosed something that will still try your patience and goodness. 'Tis a poor copy of verses,* which (after a long desuetude) I ventured to make in France, upon the occasion of presenting my last book to the King's Library; and I met with such friends, who to shew their civility to me, commanded it to be printed at the Royal Printing-house, and published their candor at the expense of exposing my faults. 'Tis ridiculous to turn poet in my old age. But you'll excuse every thing in an old friend. What you mention in your letter concerning other printers, is what I am now pursuing; the work is already begun; the name is *Annales Typographici*;† it will be three volumes in

* They are not to be found.

† "Annales Typographici ab Artis inventæ Origine ad Annum M.D. Hagæ Com." 1719, 4to.—The second volume, divided into two parts, and continued to the year MDXXXVI. was published at the Hague in 1722; the third volume, from the same press, in two parts, continued to MDLVII. and, by an Appendix, to MDCLXIV. in 1725. In 1733, was published at Amsterdam, what is usually considered as the fourth volume, under the title of "Annales Typographici ab Artis inventæ Origine ad Annum MDCLXIV. Opera Mich. Maittaire, A.M. Editio nova, auctior et emendatior, Tomi Primi Pars posterior." This volume, which appears by the title to be a new edition, is merely a revision of all the former

4to. And I hope the first will come out by next midsummer. Lucan is the next book, which is printing at Mr. Tonson's and his partner's press; but these other typographical works have made the Classics go much slower. And I find the labour growing under my hands. I own (what you hint) a *Geographia Classica* and *Astronomia Poetica* to be most useful; but they will require not only more leisure than I have at present, but also an abler undertaker.

Mr. Hearne's being prosecuted in the vice-chancellor's court, appears to most here in town, as the malice of a few persons (or may be, person in the singular) who, being unable to outdo and rival his industry, lay hold of some little exceptions (at the worst heedless, and which I grant, by a more wary man might have been left out) to bring about his ruin. We all in town have a great value for Mr. Hearne's labours; and your kindness which you expressed to me for him

volumes. The fifth and last volume, divided into two parts, was published at London, in 1741; so that the whole work may be bound either in five or nine volumes.—Maittaire was born in 1668; educated at Westminster under Dr. Busby; by the interest of Dr. South, became a Canoneer-Student of Christ Church; and in 1695 returned to Westminster-school, as second master, in which situation he continued till 1699, from which period, till his death in 1747, he lived in retirement, and dedicated all his time to his literary labours.

(when I was at Oxford) pleased me. I hope the poor suffering conscientious man has still a share in your favour. My little acquaintance with the world hinders me from having any interest. If I had, I would heartily serve him. I have, however, had an opportunity to speak of it to my Lord Pembroke and Lord Sunderland. But the business entirely dependeth on you gentlemen of the University. Give me leave, Sir, to beg the continuation of your favour to a person whose character we here take to be, conscientious, modest, inoffensive, and laborious. I am come to the end of my paper, and by this time to the end of your patience; having just room enough to subscribe myself, Worthy Sir,

Your most humble,
and most obedient Servt.
M. MAITTAIRE.

LETTER CXXVI.

From the same to the same.

Hearne.—Annales Typographici.

1718. April 21.

REVD. SIR,

I THANK you for your last, which I received from Hambledon; from which place you are now (I suppose) returned to the University, which cannot long want Dr. Charlett. I hope Mr. Hearne will find that Mr. Bridges's solicitation in his behalf has not been in vain. Your wishing Mr. Hearne had my temper, proceeds from your overkind opinion of me. But I shall never pretend to the great performances of that person, or the great applause he has met with. Nothing of what my poor pen is employed about, can ever rise to that honour of being taken notice of by an University. The most earnest of my wishes is, that

—cum transierint mei
Nullo cum strepitu dies,
Obscurus moriar senex.

* * * * * * * * *

My close attention, with which I am now wholly taken up in finishing my first volume of *Annales Typographici,* stops at present all other designs of mine. The friendly turn, which you gave to the leisure the Government has granted me, cannot intirely reconcile me to the hardships the laws have put me to. I thank God, I want no courage to go through, but courage does not exclude feeling. One thing I can boast of, that the cruelty never yet soured my looks, nor extorted any low revengeful expressions from my tongue or pen. I wish I could sometimes divert myself with an University journey. Nothing could be more acceptable and profitable, than some minutes of your conversation, to,

Revd. and worthy Sir,
Your most humble
and obedient Servt.
M. MAITTAIRE.

LETTER CXXVII.

Mr. STRYPE to Dr. CHARLETT.

Fox's Martyrology.

Low Leyton, May 24, 1718.

—— I have only cast an eye upon Mr. Hearne's new edition of "Camden's Elizabeth." I have not read his long preface. You give me one passage in it, and I humbly go along with you and your friends at Oxford, shewing your dislike of the rude character he gives of Mr. Fox's "Martyrology."* The very charge the Jesuite

* —— "agnosco Foxi Martyrologium, quod tantopere laudatur, mendaciorum magna ex parte esse farraginem.—Id quod nuperrime etiam innuit egregius Historicus Jeremias Collierus, veritatis cultor. Nimirum homines vafri, huc illuc oberrando fabularum anilium vim ingentem collegerunt, Foxoque (viro diligentia, doctrina, utinam et judicio, virtutibus, satis claro) in manus dederunt, qui illico sine ullo discrimine, ut moris est Scriptorum imprudentium, operi inservit."——

Editoris Præfatio, p. XLI.

Parsons laid upon it. It was in Q. Elizabeth's reign from the time it came forth in such esteem, that it was appointed (as you know) to be fixed in all Parish Churches with the "Great Bible," and Bishop Jewel's "Apology" and "Defence," to be read by the people. And Archbishop Whitgift in his contest with T. Cartwright, saith, that he had read it twice over. As for Fox himself, I have all his MSS. at least all that are now, I think, extant, and I find him a most diligent, exact, and elaborate searcher of Records, Registers, &c. I have said something in the vindication of his truth in the "Annals of the Reformation," Ch 21. I am very well pleased with your transcript from Camd. Elizab. MS. concerning him. That Latin Letter of his to Magdalen College when he sent his book thither, is a curiosity; and if Oxford were but 5 or 10 miles distant, I should be tempted to travel so far to see and read it. 'Tis worth transcribing.*

* Fox's Latin Letter to the President and Fellows of Magdalen College, accompanied with a Copy of his *Acts and Monuments of the Church.*

Multis magnisque dotibus Ornatissimo Viro, D. Laurentio *Collegii Magdalensis. Præsidi: pariter cum universo Choro reliquorum Juvenum, lectissimisque ejusdem Collegii Sociis Joannes Foxus, salutem et pacem in Christo sine fine.*

Etsi nihil erat in rebus meis dignum atque idoneum quod B. Mariæ Magdalenæ, veteris hospitæ ac nutricis meæ, pixidi mitterem; at Viduæ tamen Evangelicæ opulentam illam

LETTER CXXVIII.

Dr. R. MEAD to T. HEARNE.

Hearne's Preface to Camden's Elizabeth.

WORTHY SIR,

My Lord Arran came to town on Tuesday; yesterday I gave to Dr. King your

imitatus penuriam, has qualescunque Lucubrationum nostrarum minutias; pro veteri meo erga vos studio, vel officio potius, eximie idemque Doctissime Laurenti, præsidum decus, Vosque pariter universi ejusdem Sodalitatis Collegæ conjunctissimi, in publicum ærarium vestrum conjiciendas censui.— Vos in admittendo libro statuetis, pro libero arbitratu vestro, quod videbitur. Mihi, ut ingenuè fatear, indignius quiddam, ac jejunius esse videtur, quam ut in Chartophylacium vestrum recipi debeat, præsertim quum eo sermonis genere conscripta Historia nullum magnopere usum studiis vestris præstare queat. Et tamen huc me, nescio quo pacto, pertraxit, vincens pudorem et judicium meum, *Garbrandi Bibliopolæ** pellex oratio, sic ad persuadendum instructa, ut non frustra in tali tam diu Academiâ videri possit enutritus. Auxit porro nonnihil hanc mittendi fiduciam tacita quædam, et jam olim insita mihi erga Collegium istud propensio, Vestræ deinde erga me humanitatis, simulque mei vicissim erga Vos officii recordatio. Intelligo enim quid veteri Scholæ, quid charis Consodalibus, quid demum universo Magdalensium Ordini ac Cœtui, sed præcipuè quid ipsi imprimis charissimo Collegiarchæ, viro ornatissimo, D. Laurentio debeam, cui quot, quantisque sim no-

* Garbrand Herks was a native of Holland, and a bookseller living in St. Mary's parish in Oxford. See Wood's *Athenæ Oxon.* i. 241, edit, 1721.

letter to his Lordship, and the copy of that you wrote to the late Vice-Chancellor. He gave

minibus devinctus, nullo modo oblivisci aut præterire potero. Præter hos stimulos accedit denique quòd quum Historiæ hujus bona magnaque pars Oxoniensem hanc vestram attingat Academiam, unde ceu ex fonte, prima non solum initia, sed et incrementa sumpsit, ac sumit quotidie fœlix hæc et auspicata Reformatæ per Orbem Christianum Religionis propagatio; idcirco rem facturus, nec vobis ingratam, nec meo indignam officio videbar, si de rebus maxime Oxoniensibus conscriptam Historiam, ad Magdalenæum Gymnasium vestrum, hoc est, ad primarium ac nobilissimum Oxoniensis Academiæ Collegium, velut in arce quadam studiorum ac literarum, penes vos asservandam commendarem. Hoc unum dolet, Latinè non esse scriptum opus, quo vel ad plures emanare fructus historiæ, vel vobis jucundior ejus esse posset lectio. Atque equidem multo id maluissem: sed huc me adegit communis Patriæ, ac multitudinis ædificandæ respectus, cui et vos ipsos idem hoc redonare æquum est.—Habetis rationes et causas, quibus ad mittendam Historiam sum provocatus. Nunc Historiam habeto ipsam, quam, veluti pro tessera Foxianæ erga vos voluntatis, mittimus. Eam, pro candore vestro, rogo etiam atque etiam, benigne susceptam velitis. Atque ne nihil aliud quam Historiam nudam et incomitatam mittere videamur, en simul cum historia, inter cæteros, quos in hoc multiplici et numeroso Christianorum militum satellitio Oxonia vestra, tanquam fœlix mater, tum imprimis Magdalenæ fœlicissima fœcunditas, produxit, *Joscelinum* vestrum *Palmerum** e Choro vestro proximis his annis ereptum, denuo ad vos tanquam redeuntem et restitutum

* Palmer was a fellow of Magdalen College, and burnt at Newbury, in the reign of Queen Mary.

them to my lord this morning, who was pleased immediately to write a letter with his own hand to the V. Chancellor to this purpose. "That "his Lordship had received a letter from you, "in which you signified your sorrow for having "given offence to the University by what you "had printed in your preface* to Camden's Eli-

recipietis: simulque cum eo cæteros, nec paucos, nec vulgares Oxoniæ vestræ quondam alumnos, nunc illustres Christianæ militiæ Agonistas, tanquam veterem Martyrii Scholam gratis animis suscipite, et Christum in Martyribus suis glorificate. Quod superest; quoniam Chartæ arctamur angustiâ rogo, præstantissimi Juvenes, ut Dominus Jesus istum nobis Præsidem, Vos orbi et Ecclesiæ Christianæ diu servet incolumes, vestraque studia indies in majus ac melius provehat ad nominis sui gloriam.

Vester in Christo,

JOANNES FOXUS.

Londini, Maii 24 [1562.]

* The following are the objectionable passages alluded to in the above letter.

—— "Heroina igitur nostra [Elizabetha Regina] annum ætatis vicessimum octavum nondum egressa, in primis sibi cavendum esse prospiciebat, ne Collegiorum Præfecti uxores, liberos, feminas puellasque, quibus, vino ac voluptatibus deliri, se subinde delectarent, intra Collegiorum parietes vel nutrirent vel foverent." * * * "Id pro certo habeo, Elizabetham feminam castam, admirabili judicio prudentiaque, Græcisque doctam litteris et Latinis, omnibusque politioris litteraturæ deliciis expolitissimam, ad vitia connivere noluisse, sed maluisse Præfectos, bonos auctores legere, quam venari, potare largius, (ad instar Belgarum, a quibus immo-

" zabeth; that several gentlemen for whom he " could not but have regard, had applied to him " on your behalf, and that therefore he made it " his request that all prosecution against you " should be stopped, and that you may go on to " print as formerly." This letter I read, and do send it with this to the post-house; so that you may wait on the Vice-Chancellor as soon as you think convenient, and I hope in the next to give you joy of your troubles being at an end. Dr. King gives his most humble service to you, he keeps a copy of the letters. I am, your most faithful Servant,

R. MEAD.

Blomesbury, Oct. 23, 1718.

dico potu se proluere primum didicerunt Angli) ludere aleam, aliaque facere quæ indecora essent, et ad fundatorum sensum e Collegiorum Statutis eliciendum, minus congruerent.— Atque ut quid voluit clarius esset, Injunctionem transmisit ad quælibet Collegia, Statutis eorundem inserendam, et postea pro statuto habendam. An vero etiamnum exstet in Statutis, vel potius perierit illorum studio qui ab re uxoria ac venerea neutiquam abhorruerunt, videant quorum interest scire."—— *Editoris Præfatio*, p. XLVI.

LETTER CXXIX.

Dr. CLARKE to Dr. CHARLETT.

Magdalen New Building.—Dr. Radcliffe.

London, 5 March, 1719.

SIR,

I PERUSED and forwarded the two letters which came in your's of last Wednesday: the Bishop of Winchester has not yet sent me a copy of the good Bishop of Bristol's, and therefore I could neither add to, nor diminish what you enclosed to your friends. I cannot but be glad to hear that his Grace of Canterbury has sent his injunctions to our College, tho' I cannot say that I wish them exactly as they are: however, in the great points they are undoubtedly right; and if the authority of the College is supported in the execution of them, will tend to the restoring of some sort of discipline, and put an end to many unwarrantable evils. I hear of Magdalen College's talking of a New Building* by the river side, with great pleasure, because they seem to want it; I wish before they begin, that they would settle a scheme for a whole College, that they may not begin something new,

* The building, however, was not begun till 1733, fourteen years after the date of the above letter.

which may happen to stand in the way of some noble design, and be pulled down again upon better consideration.

The V. Chancellor sends me word that he intends to set out for Oxford on Tuesday. I can have the satisfaction to assure him, that the report about Brazenose ground, and all things relating to Dr. Radcliffe's benefaction, except the Linton estate, is finished, and will be forthwith given into court: what relates to that estate will be in a report by itself, when your College and the Trustees are agreed. Mr. Singleton told me this day that the Master in Chancery seems to be of opinion, that the Court of Chancery will order the buying of an advowson for the Mastership of your College, upon the deposition that Mr. Bishop has made, of Dr. Radcliffe's intentions. * * * My humble service to our friends. I am,

Sir,

Your most humble Servant,

GEO. CLARKE.

LETTER CXXX.

Mr. BEDFORD to Dr. CHARLETT.

On the Foundation of a Syriac Professorship.

Newton St. Loe, Dec. 11, 1719.

REVEREND SIR,

I INTENDED to have given you some account of the nature and usefulness of the Chaldee and Syriack Languages; but since all that I can say, and more than can be comprehended in a letter, is contained in Mr. Ockley's Introduction to the Oriental Languages, in the Appendix to the Polyglott Bible, and in the Appendix to Bishop Beveridge's Syriack Grammar, I must desire to be excused and refer you thither.

I cannot but highly approve of the design of founding a Professorship in Oxford for the Syriack language; and have reason to hope, what I heartily wish, that the pious and charitable Benefactor, who promotes the study of that language, which our Blessed Saviour spoke, when he was on earth, will hear him say, "Come, ye blessed," at his return from Heaven.

The manner how such a design may be made most useful can be better concerted among those who are skilled in those studies, in so famous an University as Oxford is. But since you were pleased to desire an account thereof from me, I shall with submission to their judgment, give you my thoughts thereof.

I believe that it would be better to settle a Professor of the Chaldee and Syriack languages, than of the Syriack alone.

For first; the Chaldee and Syriack differ very little more than the Ionick and Dorick Dialects among the Greeks; may easily be carried on by the same Professor; and he who is master of the one, may also in a month's time be master of the other.

Secondly, There being but very few books extant in the Syriack language, except the Version of the Bible, I cannot suppose, that there would be employment enough for a Professor in that single study.

Thirdly, I find a Canon in the Council of Vienna under Pope Clement the Fifth, which requires, that there should be Professors of Hebrew, Chaldee, and Arabick in the University of Oxford, and should this be settled in such a manner, it answers exactly to the design of that Council, and if the Syriack language is added to it, then the four most useful of the Oriental languages will be promoted by Professors for that purpose.

Fourthly, The Chaldee is absolutely necessary, not only for the understanding of the Paraphrase on the Bible, but also of the Jewish Commentators, the Masorites and the Talmud; so that without it, a student cannot make a much greater proficiency in the Jewish learning, than what is contained in the Hebrew Bible.

Fifthly, A Chaldee Lecture will in my opinion, encourage the Oriental Studies [more] than the Syriack alone. The natural method is to begin first with the Hebrew Bible. Now the Bible cannot be read without some understanding of the Chaldee; because a great part of Daniel and Ezra, and a verse in Jeremiah is written in that language. This done, a student will be capable of profiting by such a lecture. The affinity of these two languages will be an encouragement to proceed to the third. And every one who reads the Chaldee in the Hebrew Bible, will be in hopes of such a Professorship, which may be a greater encouragement to future industry.

Lastly, The encouragement of the Chaldee language may be the best means for the conversion of the Jews. The Jews are all skilled in the Hebrew and Chaldee, but they know nothing of the Syriack: and the best arguments against them may be taken from the Chaldee Paraphrase, for which they have a great esteem. Thus may our Divines be trained up to confute them from their own authors, and baffle them with their own weapons. We think it plain from Scripture, that a time will come, when the Jews shall be all converted to the Christian Faith; and I hope the time is near. Now the same God, who ordains the end, directs also the means, and probably such a pious Benefactor may be an instrument for such a glorious purpose, and may accordingly hope for the reward, Dan. 12. 3. of those, who turn many to Righteousness, which is, to shine as the stars for ever and ever.

As for the time, in which such Lectures should be read, if I might give my advice, it should be once a week both in term and vacation throughout the year, the holydays, Christmas, Lent, Easter, and Whitsuntide excepted. And that the Lectures should be alternately for each month in the year, one month for Chaldee, and another for Syriack. Thus all, who come to keep the Easter and Act Terms might hear Lectures for both Languages. And as the Hebrew Lectures are appointed to be read in Term time, and the Arabick in the vacation, so there might be two lectures at least weekly in the Oriental studies throughout the year, excepting the times beforementioned. I am,

Reverend Sir,

Your most humble and affectionate Servt.

Arthur Bedford.

LETTER CXXXI.

Dr. GIBSON, Bishop of Lincoln, to Dr. CHARLETT.

On the foundation of a Saxon Lectureship in Oxford.—Saxon Chronicle.—Bodleian Catalogue.—English Histories.

Duke-street, Westminster, Jan. 2, 1719-20.

DEAR SIR,

YOUR last letter from Oxford mentioned your going to the Bath, and, as I understood, with design to winter there; so that I hope I am in the right in directing thither my most hearty wishes for many happy years, and of the full benefit of the waters, in order to it. As nobody has greater obligation to wish you a full enjoyment of health and happiness than myself, so I am sure no body can wish it more cordially than I do.

I had heard nothing of an established Saxon Lecture, till I received your letter, nor do I yet know who the founder is, or what the Salary. When the present Bishop of Derry was Almoner, I have heard him speak of applying the allowance made by the late Bp. of Worcester to one or more Professors of the Oriental Languages, to a Saxon lecture, but I do not remember that he ever told me the thing was settled. My knowledge in that way is almost gone, thro' disuse; but yet I have a great desire, before I die, to make the Saxon

Chronicle a complete work ; by additions which may be had from other Manuscripts, and by reducing every piece of History whatever that has been originally written in Saxon, and may be determined to a certain year or near it, into one body of *Saxon Annals*; with proper distinctions to shew from whence every thing is taken. There are, I take it, many Saxon pieces which, tho' never parts of any formal Book of Annals, are of undoubted authority, and as truly historical as the Annals themselves ; and I think there can be no harm in casting all these into one uniform body with the Annals, so long as the Reader is told, what is, and is not, a part of the Annals properly so called ; but there will be this great benefit by it, that the reader will see at one view whatever history remains, which has been ever written in the Saxon tongue : from which circumstance, there is no doubt but all our ancient histories derive their chief authority.

Now there is a young man come into Bodley's Library, I hope the first work he will be engaged in, is a new edition of Dr. Hyde's Catalogue ; taking in all books and editions, which are in private libraries, and not in the publick. This is what I have long wanted and often spoke of ; and I think the University cannot do any thing that will be of greater service to the publick, or more for their own honour.

The way that Mr. Hearne and Mr. Hall are

got into, of publishing our English historians which have not been published before, ought to be greatly encouraged; but why so few copies to be printed of every book? Every person who is possessed of one of those books, will naturally reckon that he has a greater treasure because the copies are few; but certainly the end of printing was to multiply copies, and to spread them into many more hands, and to make learning more accessible than it was before. The notion of greater value should give way to greater use; and if it does not, you will find more and more complaints and uneasinesses upon that head; especially in London.

I am, Sir,

Your very affect. Servt.

EDM. LINCOLN.

LETTER CXXXII.

Mr. PECK to T. HEARNE.

Present of Medals.—Antiquities of Lincolnshire.

Stamford, Jan. 28, 1720.

WORTHY SIR,

ON Wednesday next our Stamford Carrier sets out for London, and will be in town on Saturday, who brings with him a parcel directed for you (to be left with Mr. Sare, bookseller, at Grey's Inn Gate, till called for, I having no correspondent at present in town, by whom I could conveniently send it as you directed) wherein you will find three score and two Roman Medals and Medalions ; seven and thirty other odd counters ; a MS. relating to Surrey and Sussex, and copies of all such pamphlets as I have hitherto published—a present, such as it is, that I hope you will not think altogether unworthy of your acceptance.

I should thank you heartily for any thing that relates to Lincolnshire, the town of Stamford, or the sufferings of K. Charles from his seizure at Holdenby to his murder. I am collecting every individual particular of that melancholy story, from our best historians, ranged in a series of time. But I shall first (and that shortly) publish proposals for printing by subscription, some Antiquities of Lincolnshire, General and Particular, in seven books, containing :

Book 1. History of the Church of Lincoln from a MS. of Bishop Sanderson.

2. Antiquities of the town of Stamford.

3. Monasteries in and about that place.

4. Churches in and about that place.

5. Hospitals in and about that place.

6. Arms and Inscriptions in the several Churches

of Lincolnshire, taken in 1604, by an eminent hand.

7. History of all the Gilds and Chanteries in the County, taken 1 Edw. VI. by order of Sir William Cecil, from the original.*

If you can oblige me with any thing relating to these matters, you will add a further obligation to your civilities shewn already to, Sir,

Your very humble Servt.

FR. PECK.

What you are at present upon does not seem to promise much for my purpose, I mean the Scotch Chronicle; when you publish any of English affairs, I shall be glad to subscribe.

* Peck's "Antiquarian Annals of Stamford" appeared seven years after the date of this letter. The laborious and ingenious author was born in 1692, completed his education at Trinity College, Cambridge, and died in 1743, as appears by the following epitaph in Godeby Church, Lincolnshire, where he was buried.

H. S. E.
FRANCISCUS PECK, A.M.
hujus ecclesiæ rector, et
prebendarius de Lincoln.
Excessit è vita nono Julii,
anno Salutis humanæ MDCCXLIII.
Illi Mors gravis incubat,
Qui notus nimis omnibus
Ignotus moritur sibi.

LETTER CXXXIII.

R. GALE to Dr. CHARLETT.

Cardinal Wolsey's Papers.

Lond. April 2, 1720.

SIR,

I HAVE ordered the bookseller to wait upon my Lord of Chester and Mr. Clarke, as you directed; he tells me he has procured a friend to get Mr. Bowles, your library-keeper, to be at the trouble of receiving subscriptions for him at Oxford. I will send for Asserius Menevensis into Yorkshire next week, but it will be this day month before he can get to town. I believe there is little of Cardinal Wolsey at York, beyond the common Acts of his time, he having never been there; when his effects were seized at Whitehall by Harry the VIIIth, all his papers were carried into the Exchequer, where, in the Tally Court, are still great bundles of them remaining, particularly letters relating to foreign affairs: this certainly would be the best place of materials for Dr. Fiddes; the Doctor is so well known at York, that upon writing thither he may know if any thing is to be had at that place for his purpose: I have not yet seen his title page, and suppose it is printed at the Theatre. Mr. Strype is so well that he preached last Sunday. I am, Sir,

Your most humble Servt.

R. GALE.

LETTER CXXXIV.

Dr. JOHN THORPE to T. HEARNE.

Textus Roffensis.

SIR,

I WAS yesterday at Mr. Barrell's house, at Sutton, near Dartford, and looked upon the "Textus Roffensis." The Title only of the 30th Chap. is in Latin, the Chapter itself is all Saxon. In the margin at the beginning of this Chapter some person has writ the following note: "Habentur fere omnia quæ sub hac rubricâ sequuntur in Chronica Jo. Brompton Latinè Hist. Angl. Scriptores X col. 852."

Mr. Barrell told me, that being lately with the Dean of Rochester, the Dean seemed apprehensive that publishing the Textus would make the Rochester MS. less valuable, and spoke as if he designed to enter a claim at Stationers' Hall in order to secure to the Dean and Chapter their property in the Copy. To obviate which Mr. Barrell wrote yesterday to the Dean, and acquainted him that it was the opinion of himself, and other Prebendaries, that printing the Textus would no ways lessen the value of their MS. that they were rather desirous that it might come abroad, and as correct and compleat as possible; and that therefore they hoped he would desist from entering any claim as he proposed, and would give leave (if you desired it) either to collate your edition with the MS. or to supply you with any thing out of it that you should have occasion for.

It is hoped that the Dean will acquiesce with this letter. However, as matters stand with us at present, Mr. Barrell advises, if you are desirous of any help from the Rochester MS. that you would please to write to the Dean for his consent. You may direct to him thus: *To the Revd. Dr. Prat, Dean of Rochester, at Windsor.* We wish your transcript had been a compleat copy of the Textus:* to make amends for which deficiency perhaps it may not be improper to print the Heads or Titles of such chapters as are wanting, with references to the Authors or Books where they are already extant in print. If it should be in my power any ways to serve you, I shall be very ready to do it.

I am, Sir,

Your very humble Servt.

Jo. Thorpe.†

Rochester, May 17, 1720.

* Hearne printed the "Textus Roffensis" from a MS. in the library of Sir Edward Dering, Bart. Oxford. 8vo. 1720.

† Dr. Thorpe communicated "The Antiquities of Oxford, by Leonard Hutten," from an original MS.

LETTER CXXXV.

Dr. GIBSON (Bishop of Lincoln) to Dr. CHARLETT.

Parish Registers.

Bugden, Aug. 13, 1720.

THE more things are entered in the Registers the better, and particularly of the kinds which you speak of in your letter; but as the Canon considers it no further than a Register of Marriages, Christenings, and Burials, we can enjoin no other entries. In the course of my parochial Visitation in Surrey, it was one special part of my care, to see that the Registers were duly kept in all respects; the titles to estates ofttimes depending on them, besides many other incidental conveniences in the course of men's lives, and it being so very reproachful to the clergy, when Registers are exhibited in the Courts of Law, with the slovenly figure and entries, which we see in so many parishes: besides that it may be a question whether they are any evidence at all, unless it appear that they have been kept and managed as the Canon directs.

LETTER CXXXVI.

Mr. PECK to T. HEARNE.

William of Wykeham.—Medals.—Collectanea Antiqua.

Cliffe,* April 28, 1721.

WORTHY SIR,

I HAD yours of the 24th instant last night, and though it will be of no service, cannot but thank you for the hint you are pleased to give of getting a sight of Sir Edm. Warcup's papers, by means of my friend the Bp. of Peterborough. The truth is, I dare not ask him to use his interest upon such an occasion; neither does he know that I was the author of that Poem,† or the Advertisement at the end of it. You need not fear my telling him that you and I have had any talk about him. I know how matters stand between you, have read wherein you have rebuked him, and (to tell you my opinion among ourselves) cannot but acknowledge that what you have said in the case of William Wickham was just, and give you my thanks for doing justice to the birth of that munificent prelate.

As to the medals I gave you; I am glad they

* King's Cliff, in Northamptonshire, of which parish he was curate.

† Probably his "Sighs on the Death of Queen Anne," which were not printed till 1719.

are like to be of some service to you. I thought that present would be the best testimony of my respect for Mr. Hearne, and the honour he hath done our church and nation in setting forth the antiquities of them both.

As to your query, I am a zealous lover of truth, and would by no means lead you into an error. I cannot say that any one of those medals, though they were most of them purchased in this neighbourhood, were dug up in it. I heard many people talk of such things being found here; but I never traced up any intelligence of this kind without a disappointment.

I was about writing to you just as I received yours.

I desire you would send me one of the Textus Roffensis, a copy of Avesbury, and so many volumes of Fordun as you have published, and direct them to Mr. Richard King, bookseller, at the Prince's Arms, in St. Paul's Church-yard, whom I will order to pay you for them.

I have been long labouring to get matters together and am now going to set up for an editor of Antiquities, in the same manner with yourself.

My Proposals are now gone to the Press at Cambridge for printing by Subscription,

Collectanea Antiqua,

A Collection of Antiquities, chiefly Monastic and Monumental, setting forth the antient estate of several Parochial, Conventual, and Cathedral

Churches of this Kingdom; and interspersed with divers other curious particulars relating to the English Story, in 6 vols. 8vo.*

Vol. 1. Academia tertia Anglicana, or the 3d University of England, at Stamford, in Lincolnshire, enquired into; with an Appendix relating to Peterborough, Burghley, Wilthorpe, and some other places in Northamptonshire, &c.

The whole collected chiefly from MSS. and Records, illustrated with copper plates, &c. at the rate of 2s. 6d. a volume the small, 5s. the large paper.

I would print 400 small, and 100 large, if I can raise so many subscriptions. I intend to trouble you with some printed proposals in a short time, and beg your assistance to promote a subscription at Oxford. I intend each volume shall consist of twelve sheets.

I beg the favour of you to give me a line what you pay for half a sheet printing at Oxon, of the letter with your Curious Discourses, and what you pay a ream for fine Genoa demy.

I hope you will not be angry with me if I should insert your name in my Proposals, and

* This work never appeared, at least not in the form above-mentioned, his "Academia Tertia Anglicana," was published in 1727, fol. and the first volume of "Desiderata Curiosa," in 1732, which was followed by a second volume in 1735.

desire such gentlemen as live at Oxford, and will please to subscribe, to pay their money to you; for, in truth, I have no acquaintance there to do such a good office for me, except you accept of the trouble, and oblige, Sir,

Your sincere Friend and Servant,

FR. PECK.

LETTER CXXXVII.

Dr. CHANDLER, Bishop of Lincoln, to the Rev. MATTHEW TATE, Vicar of Burnham.

The Earl of Nottingham's Book against Whiston.—Ecclesiastical Discipline.

Duke Street, May 11, 1721.

REVD. SIR,

I FIND by the newspapers this morning that Dr. Wild and you are deputed by the Clergy assembled at the late visitation at Beaconsfield to wait upon my Lord Nottingham* with their thanks for his book against Mr. Whiston; which book I doe also much approve and accordingly did return my own thanks to his

* Daniel Finch, son of Heneage, Earl of Nottingham. The work here commended was his "Answer to Mr. Whiston's Letter concerning the Eternity of the Son of God, and of the Holy Ghost." Printed in 1721.

Lordship in the House of Lords as soon as it was published. But I think it convenient to apprise you by the first opportunity, as well of the irregularity which you and the Clergy are committing, as of the danger in which you are involving yourselves by making a public declaration of your opinion in a matter of doctrine, which as it is a matter wholly foreign to the work of visitations, so I conceive as the law now stands it cannot be done without danger of a præmunire by any assembly of the Clergy whatsoever, except by a convocation of Bishops and Clergy legally assembled by the King's writ and the mandate of the Metropolitan. I must also add on this occasion, that tho' such a proceeding could be warranted by law, as you will find it cannot, yet I think it a great indignity to myself, and inconsistent with the oath of canonical duty, which every Incumbent takes to his Bishop, that a matter of this importance should be attempted and carried on without my privity and direction, and accordingly it is a matter which several of the Bishops have now under their consideration, as well to warn the Clergy of the danger to which they expose themselves by such illegal and unprecedented proceedings, as to put a stop to a practice which is not only a breach upon the episcopal authority, but if a timely stop be not put to it, will prove highly prejudicial to the order and government of the church. These things I thought it proper to suggest to Dr. Wild and you, that you might not, thro' surprise or inadvertency, proceed farther in an irregularity which is attended with so much danger to yourselves and the Clergy, and mischievous consequences to the peace and order of the Church.* And so not doubting but that you will sincerely weigh and consider what I have written,

I remain, Sir,
Your faithful Friend and Brother,
ED. LINCOLN.†

* The University of Oxford, in full convocation, returned "*solemn thanks* to the Earl of Nottingham for his most noble defence of the Christian Faith," &c. See Walpole's "Royal and Noble Authors," by Park, vol. iv. p. 118. And the clergy of the diocese of Peterborough waited on the Earl for the same purpose, on the very day Dr. Chandler wrote this letter. See the *Whitehall Evening Post*, May 16, 1721.

† Edward Chandler, afterwards Bishop of Durham.

LETTER CXXXVIII.

Mr. TORKINGTON to T. HEARNE.

Leland's Itinerary and Collectanea.

SIR,

I RECEIVED your letter, and Mr. Vansittart desires me to acquaint you that he will subscribe to both your books, and that he would have that set of Leland's Itinerary, and his Collectanea too, if the bookseller will not part with the one without the other. I think it a very great price, and must beg the favour of you to look them over and see they are perfect, and to get them as cheap as possibly you can, and when you have bought them for whatever you think they are really worth, please to send them directed for Mr. Vansittart, to be left at the Catharine Wheel, in Henley; at the same time favour me with a line what day they will be there, that a servant may go over for them, and let me know what they cost, and what the subscription is, and the money for both shall be paid to your order any where in London, or at Oxford if you will give directions how to send it. I am, Sir,

Your very humble Servt.

L. TORKINGTON.

Shottesbrooke,
Sept. 20, 1724.

LETTER CXXXIX.

T. HEARNE to the Rev. L. TORKINGTON.

In answer to the last.

REV. SIR,

Upon receipt of your letter yesterday in the afternoon, I immediately repaired to Mr. Wilmot. He said he would not abate any thing of twenty guineas for Leland's Itin. and Coll. Upon which I agreed with him for that price (which is not dear, considering the great scarceness of the books, and the goodness of the set) and this morning I paid him twenty guineas in full for them, and took of him a receipt, signifying what I had paid, which, for better satisfaction to Mr. Vansittart, I ordered him to put in the first volume of the Itin. The bookseller hath packed them up, and I shall send them next Tuesday morning by the Windsor carrier, directed (as you order) for Mr. Vansittart, to be left at the Catharine Wheel, in Henley. "Robert of Gloucester" is published and dispersed, so that I cannot now help Mr. Vansittart to a copy of that work; but "Peter Langtoft" is now printing, (and there is room as yet for subscription) at two guineas the large, and one guinea the small paper, as you may see by the printed paper I sent you. My money is generally returned me by carriers, but if Mr. Vansittart does not approve of that way, he may be pleased to make use of the method he shall judge most proper for remitting it. You will be pleased to let me know under what title I must enter Mr. Vansittart. I am,

Rev. Sir,
Your most humble Servant,
THO. HEARNE.

Edm. Hall, Oxon.
Sept. 23, 1724.

*** The two preceding Letters are inserted in this Collection to shew how very valuable some of Hearne's publications were esteemed even during his life-time.

LETTER CXL.

Mr. SAMUEL GALE to T. HEARNE.

A Picture of Fair Rosamond.

SIR,

PRESUMING your "Langtoft's Chronicle" is almost finished, and not being willing to lose the advantage of subscribing to your accurate works, I desire you would be pleased to insert me in the list. I shall take care to return you the whole money by the fittest opportunity. I have nothing curious at present to entertain your speculations with, but only that I have lately and accidentally purchased an ancient but fine picture of the beautiful Rosamond. It is painted on a pannel of wainscot and represents her in a three quarter proportion, dressed in the habit of the times, a straight-body'd gown of changeable red velvet, with large square sleeves of black flowered damask facings, turned up above the bend of her arms, and close sleeves of a pearl-coloured satin puffed out, but buttoned at the wrist, appearing from under the large ones; she has several rings set with precious stones on her fingers. Her breast covered with a fine flowered linen, gathered close at the neck like a ruff. Her face is charmingly fair, with a fine blush in her cheeks. Her hair of a dark brown, parted with a seam from the middle of her forehead upwards under her coifure, which is very plain, but a gold lace appears above it, and it is covered with a small cap of black silk. She is looking very intensely upon the fatal cup which she holds in one hand, and the cover in the other, as going to drink it. Before her is a table covered with black damask, on which there lies a prayer book open, writt in the ancient black character: the whole piece is extremely well preserved. I take it to have been done about Harry the 7ths time. You'll excuse this excursion which nothing but so beautiful a lady could have run me into, thus to intrench so far upon your time; but I flatter myself that you have the same value and respect for this English Venus that I have. In confidence of which favourable sentiments, I subscribe myself,

Sir,
Your most obedt. Servt.

SAML. GALE.*

London, Dec. 3, 1714.

LETTER CXLI.

J. LOVEDAY to THOMAS HEARNE.

Chapel on Caversham Bridge.

SIR,

THE gentleman who took in for me a subscription of the work you are now publishing, acquainted me with your desire to know something concerning the quondam Chapel on Caversham Bridge. I can give you but a very imperfect account of it; but such as it is, I wil-

* He died in 1754, aged 72. Several curious papers, which he communicated to the Antiquarian Society, are printed in the Archæologia.

lingly submit it to your perusal. The person who can best inform you is Mr. Brigham, of Cannon-End, in this parish, whose ancestors were once in possession of the greatest part of it, and from whose writings we might (as I am very well assured) have a satisfactory account of it. But as long as country 'squires are suspicious of every one, and especially of the curious inquirers, you must not expect any information from that quarter. The father of the present possessor I once asked about it, who told me briefly that it was dedicated to St. Ann, and that from thence the Religious went at certain times to a well now in the hedge between the field called the mount, and the lane called Priest-lane, which is supposed to have its name from their going through it to this well, which was called formerly St. Ann's well. He likewise informed me that there was in the memory of man a large ancient oak just by this well, which was also had in great veneration. This is the whole of his answer, and the son inheriting his father's suspicious temper as well as his estate, it is in vain to desire a more particular account from him. About twelve years since, an inhabitant of the parish observing what a good foundation there was still remaining of the chapel, built him an house upon it.

As pitiful as this account is, I rely upon your good nature to a young lover of Antiquities, who is far from thinking what he has said will be any satisfaction to you; but whose only motive to trouble you with this letter was the observance of your commands, though at the same time he was sure to expose himself to be an ignorant schoolboy.

Give me leave to add, that Kennett, in his "Parochial Antiquities,"* says, that the presentation to this Chapel was in the year 1258, in the

* "Parochial Antiquities, attempted in the History of Ambrosden, Burchester, and other adjacent parts, in the counties of Oxford and Bucks. By White Kennett, vicar of Ambrosden. Oxford, printed at the *Theater*, M.DC.XCV." 4to. pp. 703, exclusive of Dedication, Preface, and Index, with a glossary at the end.

As this work is now become very scarce, the following brief account of it may not be uninteresting.

The Author, after having noticed every thing he could find relating to his subject in the British, Danish, and Saxon times, proceeds regularly as an annalist from the year 1066 (1st of William the Conqueror) to the year 1460 (39th of Henry VI.) where he ends, because, as he says in the Preface, he "found the volume growing incapable to hold the remaining matter, unless he had contracted it into a compass too narrow for the projected design."

There was one Manuscript communicated to him by his "very worthy friend Mr. Blackwell, B.D. which," says he, "(tho' of modern age and no great authority) immediately relating to these parts, I thought good, with consent of the owner, to join as an Appendix to this work, under the title of "The History of All-chester, near Bircester, in Oxfordshire, &c. wrote in the year 1622."

hands of Margaret widow of Walter Mareschall, Earl of Pembroke. The same learned gentleman also mentions another Chapel in the same parish, dedicated to our Lady; but of this enough.

If you think, good Sir, that I might find out something more relating to the Chapel from some old persons in the parish, if I knew what questions to ask them; be pleased to send your queries to me at the Rev. Mr. Hiley's, in the Forebury, Reading, and they shall be faithfully executed by, Sir,

Your humble Servt.

J. LOVEDAY.*

Recd. Saturd. April 15, 1727.

T. H.

This volume contains many curious extracts from Charters, and a great number of documents relating to Consecration to Religious Uses, Appropriation of Tithes, Institution of Churches, Dependance of Chapels, Office of Rural Deans, &c. &c. The Glossary is very useful.—It likewise contains the following plates: 1. Miscellaneous Antiquities, p. 23; 2. Church and Parsonage House of Islip, p. 51; 3. House of William Glynne, Esq. at Ambrosden, p. 55; 4. Church of Ambrosden, p. 431; 5. House of Mr. John Coker, at Burcester, p. 509; 6. Church of Burcester, p. 559; 7. House of Sir John Aubrey, at Borstall, p. 679; 8. House of Sir John Walter, at Saresden, front view, p. 682; 9. Do. prospect of, p. 683.

* John Loveday, Esq. was born in 1711, and educated,

LETTER CXLII.

Mr. DRAKE to Mr. HEARNE.

History of York.

REVEREND SIR,

I PRESUME upon no other acquaintance with you, than the seeing your name prefixed to many excellent Treatises in History and Antiquity, to beg your advice and assistance in executing a design I have long formed, which is giving the Public the History and Antiquities of the truly Ancient City of York.* The subject is noble and deserves a much abler penman than

as a gentleman-commoner, at Magdalen College, Oxford, where he became M.A. June 12, 1734. In his preface to the "Liber Niger Scaccarii," printed 1728, Hearne mentions him as *optimæ spei juvenis, litterarum et litteratorum amantissimus.* Although it does not appear that Mr. Loveday actually published any work of his own, yet his collections and literary knowledge were most freely imparted to all who had occasion for his assistance. He died May 16, 1789, aged 78. For an interesting character of him see the *Gentleman's Magazine;* Obituary, May, 1789, p. 471.

* His "Eboracum; or the History and Antiquities of the City of York," was published in 1736, in a folio volume of 627 pages, besides the Dedication, Preface, a List of Subscribers, and at the end an Appendix of cx pages, and a copious Index. It is a work of much research, and has many curious plates.

I can pretend to [be], and besides requires an age to collect, digest, and deliver down to posterity, the transactions of 2000 years; during which time, allowing the British Historians to be true, there are few pauses in history, or to speak plainer, few years, in which our City cannot be traced *ab origine* to the present time. My genius and inclinations in study have a natural bent to that of History and Antiquity, and whenever the business of my profession will allow me that secess, an historian is my delight. Your learned labours in the several editions you have published of Leland, &c. have afforded me abundance of pleasure, and tho' I was never so happy as to learn when any subscription was carrying on, yet I can never want the perusal of any, whilst Dr. Richardson, you know, can furnish me. Thus you may guess, Sir, that what you have already printed I am no stranger to; but I am told there are several things much to my purpose in Mr. Dodsworth's Collections in the Bodleian Library, which I can never come at, unless assisted by you: these and whatever else you think worthy to communicate to me, shall meet with the most grateful acknowledgement. Dr. Richardson will, in a short time give you a Testimonial of me, as also I shall claim it from another hand, the Reverend Mr. Fothergill, at London, who married my aunt, and whose principles of conscience, honour, and integrity, I am told, you do not disrespect.

I have by me large collections, deduced in the course of my reading, from British and Roman Historians, as well as all the monkish writers; the best editions of which, by Savil, Twisden, and Gale, are to be met with in our Church library, and above all Leland's Collectanea are an inexhaustible fund for me, tho' I am surprized the Itinerary has so little to my purpose to be found in it, the traveller having, by an unfortunate turn out of the way for me, not touched upon York, or very little, at all. I have besides, the perusal of a copy of the MS. History of this City by Sir Thomas Widdrington, sometime Recorder here, which will be of vast help to my design in law affairs; that gentleman having taken the pains to draw out of Year-books, Acts of Parliament, Public Records, and City-books, all that is proper to insert about the several charters, privileges, and customs of the city, which I confess I had neither leisure nor inclination to do; but as to the historical part, I must say I can go beyond him, both in connection and facts, a great way. You have, inclosed, a draught, hastily drawn, of the whole building I propose, and as I know you capable to furnish me with many materials for it, I hope you will consult your vast magazine of this kind of learning for some proper supports to the fabrick. As I intend no interest in the affair, but resolve to publish it, if God sends me life and health, your generous way, it may be some inducement to you to lend a helping hand to one, who, swayed by no thirst of interest or vain glory, undertakes to deliver down to posterity the transactions of this famous City; which if you consent to do, the warmest acknowledgments, that either my tongue or pen can testify to the world, shall be justly and faithfully paid you.

In which pleasing thought give me leave to subscribe myself,

Your much obliged humble Servant,

F. DRAKE.

York, 8r. 27th, 1729.

LETTER CXLIII.

J. WORTHINGTON to Mr. T. HEARNE.

Herbert's Country Parson. — Barnabas Oley. — Curious Legacies.

WORTHY SIR,

IN answer to your inquiries on July 14, these are to let you know that I cannot tell from whence my father transcribed the account I sent you of Mr. Ferrar's first years; nor do I see any thing to the contrary, but that it may be proper to refer to my Father's MS. for its authority. As for the other matter you want to know, viz. who was the author of the prefatory account of Mr. Herbert's life printed in his little book called the Country Parson, the following lines in his Life written by Walton will fully satisfy you.

"At the death of Mr. Herbert this book fell into the hands of his friend Mr. Woodnot; and he commended it into the trusty hands of Mr. Bar. Oley; who published it with a most conscientious and excellent Preface."

No doubt, Mr. Wood* has given some account of Mr. Barnabas Oley; whom you could not but acknowledge to be a person of very great worth, if you knew no more than what I shall add by way of postscript.

That your work is in such forwardness is very welcome news to,

Sir,

Your most humble Servant,

J. W[ORTHINGTON].

London,
July 23, 1730.

From a mural inscription within the Church of Great Gransden, in the County of Huntingdon, transcribed by me, Nov. 2, 1699.

* Wood does mention him certainly, but Oley was a Cambridge, not an Oxford, man.

The Reverend Mr. Barnabas Oley, Archdeacon of Ely, Prebendary of the Cathedral Church of Worcester, and Vicar of Great Gransden 53 yeares, gave the pulpit 1633. gave the wainscot seates in the Chancell 1621. and in 1664 Mr. Oley was the first contriver and chief benefactor of the brick-school-house. And he built brick houses for six poor people upon his own freehold land, and did lease them for one thousand yeares to the Church-Wardens and their successors at the yearly rent of one pepper corn, if lawfully demanded upon Christmas day. He gave one acre of freehold land for ever, to enlarge the herd commons at Hanginton-Layes in this parish. He gave six godly books, named the Whole Duty of Man, for the benefit of poor people that can read English: and the present vicar of this church is to lend them six moneths together to six several persons, and then call for them, and deliver them to six other persons; that the whole parish in time may have the benefit of reading them. He gave six leather-buckets to prevent casual fires in this town. He also built a strong and large vicarage-house with barns, stables, and out-houses, and a brick wall next the highway or town-street, and against the church-yard.

LETTER CXLIV.

EDWARD, Earl of Oxford, to T. HEARNE.

Durandi Rationale Divinorum Officiorum.—Catholicon Joan. Januensis.—Caxton.—Cottonian Library.—Benedictus Abbas.—Mr. T. Baker.

Wimpole, Dec. 25, 1731.

SIR,

I ASSURE you I am very sorry I have not answered your letters which you was so kind as to send me. I tell you truly it proceeded not from any neglect of you, or any unwillingness to communicate to you any thing in my power, for whenever I have any opportunity to pleasure you with any thing I have, it is a very great satisfaction to me. As to your letter in relation to *Durandus,* I could not for some time come at the book to answer your question fully, at least to go as far as I could [wish.] There is a "Durandus's Rationale Divinorum Officiorum" in All Souls' Library, very imperfect.* I

* On this book we find the following note in Hearne's "Walteri Hemingford Historia de rebus gestis Edvardi I. Edv. II. et E. III." Præfat. p. cx.

"They have in All-Souls College-Library a noble folio Book printed on vellum, of Durantus's Rationale Divinorum, but then it hath been horridly abused, several leaves being cut out. Nor does the date when printed appear,

believe it was discovered to be that book by Dr. Tanner. I have been so told. I have some rea-

tho' it was very early, as may appear from the following M.S. Note at the beginning of the Book: *Liber Collegii omnium animarum Oxon, quem Reverendus pater Jacobus Goldwell, Episcopus Norwicensis, emit in civitate Hamburgensi, dum erat missus in ambassiatam a Christianissimo principe Edwardo Rege Angliæ, &c. ad illustrissimum principem Regem Daniæ, voluitque dictus Reverendus pater, ut cathanetur in choro dicti Collegii, ad utilitatem studencium. Et si quis eum alienaverit, vel contra hanc disposicionem fecerit, anathema sit. Et hæc disposicio erat per præfatum Reverendum patrem anno Domini millimo* CCCCLXXXXVIII.

"This book is even imperfect at the end, where, in all likelyhood, was the date.

* * * It is, as it is, a Book of great value, but were it perfect, it would be look'd upon as worth about an hundred pounds among curious men.

"Licet fortasse non desint, qui ex hac nota conjicient, nos esse stultos pretii librorum existimatores, haudquaquam tamen hercle nos inepte sensisse judicabunt alii, simul atque cognoverint, suam cuique rem esse carissimam, virumque quendam, his in rebus longe versatissimum, Baronetti prænobilis* (quem supra innuimus) Codicem centum plus minus valere libras nobis indicasse." Præfat. cx, cxi.

Hearne afterwards alludes to this letter from the Earl of Oxford:—"In Præfatione mentionem feci *Durandi Rationalis Divinorum Officiorum* Moguntiæ excusi M.CCCC.LIX. Nunc tandem intellexi, exemplar ejusdem editionis penes se habere Comitem nobilissimum Oxoniensem, Edvardum Harleium, idque etiam membraneum et perquam nitidum. Me

* Tho. Sebright.

son to think that this was the only copy in England of that book till the year 1715, when the copy came over which I have; it is printed in folio upon vellum, and very fair. It contains 319 pages. At the end is printed in red ink, what I have here inclosed. I have had it done for you in as exact a way as any one I have could do it here in the country. I will take notice to you of a great mistake of Mentelius in his book "De vera Typographiæ origine," in quarto. I think it is plain he did not see the book page 68. If you have not the book I will have the place transcribed for you. The next book that I have is the "Catholicon Joan. Januensis," upon vellum, in two vol. in folio, illuminated, printed in 1460. I have had transcribed what is printed at the beginning of the first volume of the vellum, as also what is printed at the end of the work. I have this printed also upon paper the same year, this is only bound in one vol. I will take notice to you that greater care was taken in illuminating

per litteras, docte et candide propria sua manu scriptas, certiorem fecit ipse Comes. conatuum nostrorum litterariorum fautor eximius." p. 731. Operum Catalog.

With respect to the "Catholicon" mentioned in the above letter, we find the following notice in the same work.

"—— cujus bina [unum membraneum, alterum chartaceum] exemplaria in bibliotheca sua, libris omnibus instructissima, habet Comes quem diximus, præstantissimus Oxoniensis." p. 733.

the vellum books than the paper ones, as appears from this work, both printed in one year. I have a great number of old printed books, which I think if they were considered, something [more] would come out as to printing, and the history of it, than has yet been taken notice of, though perhaps I may be mistaken.

I have a great number of books printed by Caxton, and in very good condition, except a very few. I think the number is forty-two. Have you any notes relating to that good honest man? I think he deserves those titles, and I may add industrious too. I have several very curious books printed by those that succeeded him in that work, I mean that business. Pray what is your opinion of that book said to be printed at Oxford in 1468?* The signatures stare one in the face. I do not know how to get off of that affair as yet. I hope you will help me, that only sticks with me. The Register of ABp. Bourchier is I think not in being.

As to what you desire in your letter of Nov. 17, that I would send you Mr. Wanley's transcript of "Benedictus Abbas Petroburgensis de Vita et Gestis Henrici 2d."† This brings into

* For some account of "Expositio in Symbolum Apostolorum," the book above alluded to, see vol. i. p. 160.

† "Benedictus Abbas Petroburgensis, de Vita et Gestis Henrici II. et Ricardi I. e Cod. MS. in Bibl. Har-

my mind the terrible calamity that has befallen the Cottonian Library through the villainy of that monster in nature, Bentley * He must be detested by all human creatures. I mean the civilized part of them. I think the man that stole

leiana descripsit, et nunc primus edidit Thomas Hearnius." Oxon. 1735, 8vo. 2 tom.—This was the last of Hearne's publications.

* He alludes to the fire which happened about two months before the date of this letter, and which is thus noticed in the first volume of the *Gentleman's Magazine,* Oct. p. 451.

" Oct. 23. A Fire broke out in the House of Mr. Bentley, adjoining to the King's School near Westminster Abbey, which burnt down that part of the House that contained the King's and Cottonian Libraries; almost all the printed Books were consumed and part of the Manuscripts. Among the latter, those which Dr. Bentley had been collecting for his Greek Testament, for these last ten years, valued at 2000l."

This account, however, is exaggerated; it afterwards appeared that one hundred and eleven books were lost, burnt, or entirely defaced, and ninety-nine rendered imperfect.

Hearne speaks feelingly of this unfortunate accident in the Preface to his " Benedictus Abbas," in which he deplores the loss of a valuable MS.

————————" incendio illo acerbo, quo nuper perplura itidem alia antiquitatis monumenta, in illa Bibliotheca, per totum orbem terrarum litterarium celeberrima, reposita, absumpta fuerunt, hominibus sane doctis, aliisque etiam bonis, miserum in modum eo nomine lugentibus, quippe qui optime viderunt, quanta inde perturbatio, quanta confusio jacturaque antiquarum litterarum consecutura fuit." Præfat, xvi.

the books at Cambridge by much the honester man. I beg pardon for this, but I have not yet been able to bring myself either to write or speak on this subject with any sort of temper or patience. I believe I never shall.—All my MSS. are in London; as soon as I go to town I will send you the MS. of Benedict the Abbat, and also that other MS. the "Annales Dunstapliæ."* You shall have them both together, if you do not contradict me in your next.

There are those that set a very great value upon "Benedict," and give him the preference to any of his cotemporaries. Of this you will be the best judge when you come to look into him. This, I know, was Mr. Wanley's opinion, which was one reason of transcribing him for the press.

I have had the pleasure when I went to Cambridge, of waiting upon Mr. Baker of St. John's, that reverend and most worthy man. I saw him about a fortnight since. He told me he had heard from you, and mentioned you as he always does, with great respect. I had the pleasure to see him look very well. He is an example to the whole University, but I fear few will follow him. At his age† he is up by four o'clock in the morn-

* "Chronicon sive Annales Prioratus de Dunstaple, una cum Excerptis e Chartulario ejusdem Prioratus, e Codicibus MSS. in Bibl. Harleiana descripsit, primusque vulgavit Thomas Hearnius." Oxon. 1733, 8vo.

† He was at that time 75; he died in 1740, aged 84.

ing, goes constantly to chapel at five, and this he does without any regard to the season.

I am happy at home with the company of Mr. George Harbin and Dr. Middleton. Both desire you will accept of their hearty service. My Lord Dupplin desires you will not forget him nor think he has forgot you. He is your servant. My Lord has given me all the books printed at Constantinople. Mr. William Thomas desires to be remembered to you.

I have been very busy in furnishing a new room I built last year for books, and it is quite full, it is in length 47 feet, in breadth 21 feet.*

I am now to make my retreat, for it is not reasonable to take up so much of your time, that know so well how to employ it. I wish you a merry Christmas and a happy new year, and many of them. I am with true respect, Sir,

Your most humble Servant,

OXFORD.†

* Of this wonderful private collection of books, government purchased the MSS. for 10,000l. and placed them in the British Museum. The printed books, (on the binding part of which alone, Lord Oxford expended more than 18,000l.) were sold to Osborne, the bookseller, for only 13,000l. For an excellent Analysis of the Harleian Catalogue published in 1743-4, we refer the curious reader to Dibdin's Bibliomania, p. 463. edit. 1811.

† In the Collection from which these letters are taken, there are many others from the Earl of Oxford to Hearne,

I am sorry to hear that Dr. Tanner's books and papers have suffered by water.*

LETTER CXLV.

Mr. GEORGE BALLARD to Mr. T. HEARNE.

Dr. John Dee.

SIR,

I HAVE at last sent the fragment of the Manuscript Bible and Testament I promised you, having but lately received it from my friend that gave it me; whose character of it was such that I thought to have had an extraordinary present; but when I received it I found it so strangely imperfect, and of so small value, that I should not have troubled you with it but that I love to be as good as my word; therefore such as it is I would beg your acceptance of. Among other bookes that I lately purchased (as Colvile,

on literary subjects. They all express the greatest kindness, but contain no important anecdotes or information.

* Bishop Tanner's printed books were sunk in the river on their voyage to Oxford, and remained under water for many hours. They are in sad condition from this circumstance, and many have received so much injury as to be perfectly useless, crumbling into pieces on the slightest touch.

or Coldewel's Translation of Boetius de Con. Philo. printed anno 1556, Lanquet and Cooper's Chronicle, printed anno 1560, Bp: Kennet's Parochial Antiq. &c.) I bought Heming's Chart. of the Church of Worcester, Rob. of Gloucester, and John of Glastonbury's Chronicles, in the latter of which I was mightily pleased (though strangely surprised) with the account I met with concerning Dr. John Dee;* from

* John Dee, a most extraordinary character of the sixteenth century, was celebrated for his extensive learning, and excessive credulity. He was born at London, in 1527, and after some time spent at school there, and at Chelmsford, in Essex, he was sent to St. John's College, Cambridge, and was afterwards chosen one of the fellows of Trinity College, on its erection by Henry VIII. In 1548 he left England, in consequence, as has been hinted, of some reports prejudicial to his character, but in all probability to increase his mathematical and astronomical knowledge, since we find that he read lectures in Paris, with such applause, that the greatest offers were in vain made to retain him there. At his return to England he was introduced to King Edward, who granted him a pension. In the next reign he was indicted for treason in the star-chamber, but was acquitted, and obtained his liberty, when he presented a memorial to the Queen "for the recovery and preservation of ancient writers and monuments," a design, which, had it taken effect, would have been truly beneficial to literature. When Elizabeth came to the throne, Dee was immediately taken into favour, and was even honoured with a visit from his royal scholar (which that Princess had been;) and in 1578

which account may be seen the wonderfull variableness of Fortune, and that no dependency is to be made upon the flattering promises of great ones; nor upon any abilities or deserts of our own, be 'em never so extraordinary He being a person that had made such surprising acquisitions in several parts of learning, that he was justly accounted one of the greatest learned men of that age; and yet for all his valuable and

was sent to Germany to confer with some physicians of that country upon the Queen's ill-health; an evident proof of the high estimation in which his talents and services were then held. Dee's ambition to surpass all men in knowledge, led him now to a desire of being acquainted with things beyond the bounds of human faculties, as he conceived by certain invocations, an intercourse with spirits could be obtained; this persuasion was his subsequent ruin, for he squandered immense sums in the attempt, and so exasperated the common people, that, at his departure to Poland, with the palatine of Siradia, they destroyed his valuable library, mathematical instruments, and other curiosities at his house at Mortlake. In 1596 he obtained the wardenship of Manchester college, which was his last preferment, and which proved so unpleasant a residence, that he returned in 1604 to Mortlake, very old, infirm, and destitute of friends and patrons. His infatuation, however, continued to his death, which happened in 1608, in the eighty-first year of his age; and to this may be attributed the occasional poverty alluded to by Ballard, although he still appears to have retained his situation at Manchester. He left behind him a numerous family, of whom his eldest son was afterwards physician to Charles the First.

wonderfull partes, and the fair promises that were made him by the prime nobilitie of the kingdome; without all which, to any ones thinking, his own merits would undoubtedly have been a patron good enough to have presented him to some noble benefit. But, to the great scandal of the English nation, he was neglected, and necessitated to the last extremity, being forced oftentimes (saith Lilly in his Life and Times,) to sell one book or other to buy himself a meal of victuals; one of which (that perhaps was parted with in that way), I have seen; it was a very fine copy of John Harding's Chronicle, having his name (wrote with his own hand) upon the top of the title.

My brother presents his humble service, and begs pardon for not calling upon you according to his word, being forced unexpectedly to go out of Oxford, on the morrow morning, upon a very urgent occasion; which, with my most kind respects, is all, in great haste, from

Sir,

Your most devoted humble Servant,

George Ballard.*

Campden, Nov. ye 15th, 1732.

* Mr. Ballard was born at Campden, in Gloucestershire, and being of a weakly constitution was placed with a habit-maker; in this situation, impelled by the strongest love for literature, and antiquities in particular, he acquired the

LETTER CXLVI

Mr. T. HEARNE to Dr. R. RAWLINSON.

Ludus Carparum.

DEAR SIR,

On the 5th I received yours of the 3d, together with your present of little books, for both which I thank you. Among these things is part of your catalogue of my late friend your brother Thomas's MSS. I shall be glad to have the remaining sheets to complete it.* I am well

Saxon language, which he mastered by stealing a few hours from sleep, after the business of the day was over. Lord Chedworth, and the gentlemen of his hunt, who spent annually a month of the season at Campden, hearing of his fame, generously offered him an annuity of one hundred pounds; but he modestly told them that sixty pounds were fully sufficient to satisfy his wants and wishes. Upon this he retired to Oxford, for the benefit of the Bodleian Library, where Dr. Jenner, president of Magdalen, made him one of the clerks of that college. He afterwards became one of the university bedels, but died young in 1755, owing, as was supposed, to too intense application to literary pursuits His only publication was "Memoirs of learned British Ladies," 4to. 1752, a work of much merit, and containing a variety of curious and interesting information.

* For an account of the numerous Catalogues of Mr. T. Rawlinson's very extensive Library, "which continued, for nine succeeding years, to meet the public eye," see Dibdin's Bibliomania, p. 455, edit. 1811. A complete collection of

pleased with the drawing it. Pag. 56, numb. 482, is mention of *Ludus Scaccarum*, as one of the MSS. Pray does it contain an account of any other games or plays, besides that of Chess? I ask, because I am inquiring what sort of a play *Ludus Carparum** was. 'Tis prohibited in some Statutes, and is joined with *cards*, and reckoned as a kind of *alea*, but the word is so very uncommon, that I am at present uncertain what game or play it really was. Nor can I find, that Dr. Thomas Hyde (who hath been particular, and hath divers curious observations on the Oriental Games, from whence our Western ones generally came) hath said any thing about it. The word, as I remember, is mentioned by Dr. Nathaniel Johnston (who, I believe, I cannot be positive, was a Non-Juror) in his book about the King's Visitatorial Power, which, I think, is scarce (I am sure I have it not); but then he was altogether in the dark about it. 'Twas, without doubt, call'd *carps* in English, and perhaps, might be a sort of Back-Gammon. The

these Catalogues with the prices, is among Mr. Crynes's books in the Bodleian.

* Mr. Baker, in a letter to T. Hearne, dated Cambridge, Jan. 5th, 1733, says—" the word *carparum* I do not remember to have met with in any of our old statutes, or in Merton or Lincoln College statutes with you, nor do I know its meaning, unless it be another word for *cartarum*, explaining it."

play was used in Oxford much; but being not mentioned in New College Statutes, I take it to have been brought up here since the foundation of that College, as I believe *cards* were also; cards being not begun to be printed till Hen. VIth's time, unless I am mistaken.

* * * * * * * *

Jan. 7, 1733.

LETTER CXLVII.

Mr. BROME to Mr. RAWLINS.

Urry's Chaucer.—Christ Church New Quadrangle.

June 23, 1733.

* * * I FIND you a very curious person (inter alia) about books, for I see your name among Mr. Hearne's subscribers; and if your acquaintance be much among the Litterati, as I suppose it is, you may do me a kindness. One Mr. Urry, student of Christ Church, was engaged to put out a new edition of Chaucer with a Glossary, &c.* Before he had finished it, he dies, and leaves me executor with an in-

* The Works of Geoffrey Chaucer.—By John Urry, student of Christ Church, Oxon, deceased. London, 1721, fol.

tention that some of the profits arising from the impression, should go towards building the new Quadrangle. The College, myself, and Mr. Lintot, the bookseller, enter into a tripartite agreement upon these terms. The College and myself to get the copy of Chaucer, with Prefaces, Indexes, Glossary, &c. for Mr. Lintot.* Mr. Lintot to be at the expense of printing and paper: and the copies were to be equally divided in three parts between us. The College oblige scholars upon their entrance to take off a copy; and by their acquaintance dispose of their share. Mr.

* Mr. Tyrwhitt informs us that the charge of publishing Chaucer devolved, or rather was imposed, after Mr. Urry's death, on Mr. Timothy Thomas. "I learn this," says he, "from a MS. note in an interleaved copy of Urry's Chaucer, presented to the British Museum by Mr. William Thomas, a brother, as I apprehend, of Mr. T. Thomas. T. Thomas was of Christ Church, Oxford, and died in 1751, aged lix. In another note, Mr. W. Thomas informs us, that the *Life of Chaucer*, in that edition, was very uncorrectly drawn up by Mr. Dart, and corrected and enlarged by W. T. (i.e. himself.)" Chaucer's *Canterbury Tales*, edited by Tyrwhitt, Oxford, 1798, 4to. Appendix to the Preface, p. xiii. Mr. Tyrwhitt's opinion of Urry's *Chaucer* should be added: "The strange licence, in which Mr. Urry appears to have indulged himself, of lengthening and shortening Chaucer's words according to his own fancy, and of even adding words of his own, without giving his readers the least notice, has made the text of Chaucer in his edition, by far the worst that was ever published." *Ibid.*

Lintot is in the way of business, and sells off his; but mine lie upon hand, so that I am like to be a great sufferer. By our articles we are not to sell a copy under the subscription price, which is, large paper fifty shillings, small paper thirty shillings, in sheets: the book is adorned with copper plates before each tale. If any friend of yours wants such a book, I can supply him at London: but by no means I would have you importunate with any person on my account.

LETTER CXLVIII.

T. HEARNE to Dr. R. RAWLINSON.

Urry's Edition of Chaucer.—Re-printing Books in the Old English Character, or Black Letter.

DEAR SIR,

I THANK you for the large parcel of books I received from you on Saturday last, the 15th inst. Several of them are old Chaucer's, such as what you mentioned some time since. The more I look upon such old black-lettered editions, the more I wish that the late edition had been printed in the black letter, which was what my friend Mr. Urry intirely designed, as I have often heard him say, tho' the managers afterwards, for frivolous reasons, acted contrary to it. Curious men begin to esteem the old editions more than the new one, partly upon account of the letter, and partly upon account of the change that hath been made in the new edition, without giving the various lections, which would have been of great satisfaction to critical men. John Stowe was an honest man, and knowing in these affairs, and would never have taken such a liberty, and I have reason to think Mr. Urry would (what I used often to tell him to do) have accounted for the alterations with a particular nicety, had he lived to have printed the book himself. * * * * * * *

March 18,
1734.

LETTER CXLIX.

Mr. BAKER to Mr. HEARNE.

* * * YOUR speaking of old editions, puts me in mind of a discovery made by Mr. Palmer in his *History of Printing*, Append. Pag. 299, 300, of a book printed by Guttenburg, an. 1458, viz. St. Gregories Dialogues, with this Colophon:

Explicit* liber quartus
Dialogorū Gregorii.

Then follows in red letters;

Presens hoc opus factum est per Johan.
Guttenburgium apud Argentinam,
Anno Millesimo CCCCLVIII.

And yet after all, I am told, it is a mistake,† and that mistake corrected in a separate sheet, or

* The word *explicit*, generally used at the end of MSS. and early printed books, is a contraction of *explicitus*. The ancient books were nothing but rolls of parchment, (hence the Latin word *Volumen*, and our *Volume*) which were unfolded by the reader in his progress through them. When they were quite *unfolded*, they were of course *finished*; and the word *explicitus*, which properly conveys the former sense, was afterwards used in the latter, when the books assumed a different form, to signify that they were *finished* or *ended*.

† In a subsequent letter, dated Nov. 12, 1734, he says, * * * I think I once told you of a discovery made by Mr. Palmer, of a book printed by Guttenburgh. I have since received the half sheet, shewing it to be a mistake or rather a cheat. They have long made a trade of counterfeiting medals, and now are beginning with prints, at least with the Colophons.

For
The worthy Mr. Hearne
at Edmund-Hall
Oxford.

half-sheet, which I have not yet met with. Have you, Sir, seen or heard of it? If it be genuine, it is the only book [that] yet appears with the name of Guttenburg. If it be a mistake, it is a very strange one, especially from a printer.

Cambridge, Aug. ult. 1734.

LETTER CL.

Mr. BROME to Mr. RAWLINS.

On the Vicar of Bray.

June 14, 1735.

* * * I HAVE had a long chase after the Vicar of Bray, on whom the proverb. Mr. Hearne, tho' born in that neighbourhood, and should have mentioned him, Leland, *Itin.* vol. v. p. 114, knew not who he was, but in his *last letter* desired me if I found him out to let him know it. Dr. Fuller, in his *Worthies*, and Mr. Ray from him, takes no notice of him in his *Proverbs.* I suppose neither knew his name. But I am informed it is Simon Aleyn or Allen, who was Vicar of Bray about 1540, and died 1588, so was Vicar of Bray near 50 years.*

* The writer of the well-known song of *The Vicar of Bray,*

You now partake of the sport, that has cost me some pains to take. And if the pursuit after such game seems mean, one Mr. Vernon followed a butter-fly nine miles before he could catch him. But this apology will take this turn; I excuse my folly by a greater folly in another.

LETTER CLI.

Mr. BAKER to THOMAS RAWLINS, I

Death of T. Hearne.—Athenæ Cantab.

WORTHY SIR,

I HAVE the favour of your letter, and am to thank you for your account of the loss of our common friend,* and heartily condole with you upon that melancholy occasion, and for the common loss, not only to you and me, but more to the public. I often cautioned him against fatiguing himself too much, and over-

has changed the date of the original story, applying it to the seventeenth century, and making the Vicar's versatility shew itself by the frequent variation of his *political* principles.

* T. Hearne, who died June 10th, 1735, aged 57 years, of a fever brought on by a violent cold. The inscription, written by himself, on his tomb-stone in the Church-yard of St. Peter's in the East, Oxford, is well-known.

loading his constitution, but he was not to be advised, and so he died a Martyr to Antiquities. For this reason, I was the less surprized, especially having heard both from Mr. Bedford and Mr. Loveday, the former of whom has been at Oxford to receive his legacy, but tho' he has brought it off with him to London, yet he has not yet found time or room to open and dispose of his cargo, having lately married a young lady, and the days of rejoicing being not yet over, which, I am told, is commonly for a month or longer. Mr. Bedford is a very worthy man, my good friend, and very deserving the Degree of M.D. and I wish him that, and all other happiness.

To your enquiry concerning *Athenæ Cantab.* I can give you no sure account, only it is certain Mr. Richardson* is making collections towards such a work, and I have furnished him with somewhat towards this College.† It is a work, I was well inclined to myself: but our Registers are so imperfect, that as far as I understand such things, it is hardly possible to give a perfect account, or any thing near to what Mr. Wood has done for Oxford.‡ If Mr. R. finds it otherwise,

* William Richardson was editor of the new edition of "Godwin de Præsulibus." He died in 1775, Master of Emanuel College, Cambridge, of which society he had previously been only an independent member.

† St. John's.

‡ The design was afterwards carried on by Mr. William

I shall be glad of his success. I am, Worthy Sir,

Your most ob. humble Servt.

THO. BAKER.

Cambridge,
Aug. 23, 1735.

LETTER CLII.

Dr. TANNER (Bishop of St. Asaph) to Dr. RAWLINSON.

Peter Le Neve.—Blomefield's History of Norfolk.—Newcourt's Repertorium.—Oxford Writers.—Notitia Monastica.

Ch. Ch. Oct. 2, 1735.

GOOD DR.

I am very much obliged to you for your late letters, and the like curiosities you were so kind as to inclose in the same. * * * *
If Peter Le Neve's Epitaph be printed, it is very

Cole, of Milton, and of King's college, Cambridge. After plodding for many years, and collecting sufficient materials to fill a vast number of volumes in MS. (now deposited in the British Museum,) Mr. Cole sunk under the weight of his undertaking, and the task yet remains for some more fortunate Cantabrigian, who, with Baker's judgment, Cole's diligence, and the fidelity of Anthony à Wood, combines youth, and health, and speculation, sufficient to bring so desirable a project to maturity.

abominable. It was spread about by a clerk (whom he had turned off) from a copy filched out of his scrutoire. I fear that poor gentleman was too far gone in the modern ways of thinking about Religion, but I must do him the justice to declare that I never heard him say an Atheistical or unchristian expression; he perhaps was more upon his guard before me. He was indefatigable in his Collections about Antiquities and Genealogies, especially relating to Norfolk, and exceedingly communicative in lending and communicating his MSS.* As I remember, there is nothing amiss in his will. There was an ugly Codicil made a few days before his death in favour of his wife, upon which she set up a claim for several of his Norfolk Collections, and has hindered the execution of that part of his will, which relates to the putting those papers into some public library in Norwich. But I have

* Peter Le Neve, Norroy King at Arms, spent above forty years in amassing, at much expence and trouble, the greatest fund of Antiquities for his native county that ever was collected for any single one in the kingdom, which came into the possession of that industrious antiquary Mr. Thomas Martin, of Palgrave, Suffolk, who married his widow, and spared no pains to continue and augment the collection. After Mr. Martin's death, which happened in 1771, the collection passed through several hands, and it is greatly to be lamented, that at last it was entirely dispersed. See Gough's *British Topography*, vol. ii. p. 2.

hopes given me that she is coming into better temper, and will let us perform our trust without entering into a Chancery suit. In the mean time there is a very industrious young clergyman, one Mr. Blomefield, who, by the help of these Collections and his own is about a Civil History of Norfolk. He has sent me up what he has done as to our Hundred, which I am mightily pleased with, and hope he will be encouraged to proceed thro' the whole county.* I think as to the account of Manors and Estates and their possessions, he is as exact as Dugdale or Thoroton, and in some other things more so. I will give him a plate, and assist him what I can out of my own Collections, which were chiefly as to the ecclesiastical state; for having a little fee out of every institution while I was Chancellor there, I

* Francis Blomefield, Rector of Fersfield, in Norfolk, began to print his History of that county, at his own press, in his house at Fersfield, in 1739, by subscription, and intended to publish a list of his subscribers when the whole was finished. During his life, it came out in monthly folio numbers; but he died when he had proceeded only to page 678 of the third volume. This volume was completed by Charles Parkin, Rector of Oxburgh, Suffolk, and after his death, was printed in 1769, by Mr. Whittingham, bookseller at Lynn, by whom the Continuation, which is very inferior to the former part, was published, in two volumes more, in 1777, making in the whole 5 vols. fol. Another edition has since appeared in 11 vols. 8vo. Lond. 1810.

thought to earn it, by going thro' the Registers, and making a series of the incumbents and patrons in the manner of Mr. Newcourt's *Repertorium.** Mr. Blomefield will take in all that. That way I helped you formerly to the incumbents in the patronage of King's and Eton Colleges, and have now sent down to the Registry for a continuation. I have herewith sent you up a Catalogue of the Fellows of Eton, which I took formerly out of Bp. Fleetwood's Collection, with some little hints of their other preferments. Probably there is little or nothing but what you have before, however I thought you would not dislike to see it; when you have run it over, please to return it to me again.

If your leisure and health would permit you to continue your design as to the OXFORD WRITERS, in which you shall have all the assistance that either my own observations and collections, or my correspondents can furnish you out with, and

* The "Repertorium Ecclesiasticum Parochiale Londinense," &c. by Richard Newcourt, Notary Publick, was published in two volumes, at separate times, in folio. Lond. 1708 and 1710. It contains a complete History of the Diocese of London, &c. and is a book of great authenticity and use. If a work of this nature could be undertaken, embracing all the Dioceses of England and Wales, its value would be incalculable to the antiquary, the historian, and to all who are connected with ecclesiastical government or church property.

I doubt not but that Dr. Bedford would communicate to you T. Hearne's Collectanea, which, tho' a strange farrago, yet a discreet man would get out thence many good materials. Such a paper of quæries will be very serviceable, but I never saw any thing like it among A. Wood's papers.

What I can recollect about the Non-jurors in the diocese of Norwich (who were most of them personally known to me, and acknowledged my tenderness to them) you shall have as soon as I can get Dr. Lee's Catalogue.

I am very glad my present book to Dr. Finch is fallen into your hands; there were but ten printed in that royal paper, all which I gave away, but none of them bound as that was. I am not unmindful of the scarcity of that little book, compiled when I was scarce 20 years old, and am, as fast as my leisure will permit, preparing for a new edition, to which end I have fairly transcribed as far as the middle of Yorkshire, and want only the remainder of that county, and Wales, to revise and transcribe, which if it please God to allow me health and give me no avocations, I hope to finish by the spring, and then put it to the press, which I was not willing to do before all was ready, knowing the tormenting of devils, printers, and booksellers for copy, &c. Tho' I keep to the old method, yet in my new way, I believe it will amount to 200 sheets and upwards, and must be in small folio.*

I thank you for your papers of the dimensions of St. Peter's, and St. Paul's, London, and for the judicious observations of Mr. Durns, of Balliol (whom I well remember, and have met often at Dr. Charlet's) on the *Parma,* and for poor old Tony's† persecution, which I shall put into my ATHENÆ. The point of law upon which that hard sentence is founded is discussed by his nephew T. Wood, in his *Observations on Dr. Pope's Life of Seth. Ward.* The Vindication prefixed to the last edition of the *Ath. Oxon.* was drawn up by A. W. himself, but licked over and some spirit put into it by Wh. Kennet, whose the last paragraph (which bears so hard on his after patron) is entirely.

I have by this time almost tired you I fear, but as things occur you may be further troubled with me, and if I live to come again to town, with

* The bishop here alludes to his "Notitia Monastica," first published in 8vo. Lond. 1695;—and republished in folio, in 1744, with additions, by his brother the Rev. John Tanner. The third and improved edition, was printed under the care of the Rev. James Nasmith, at Cambridge, folio, 1787; the greater part of which impression was consumed at the fire in Mr. Nichols's printing-house, on the night of Monday, the 8th of February, 1808.

† Anthony à Wood.

my company at London-House (where I have not been since I subscribed for Deacon's Orders, Dec. 1694) and shall be glad to see you in New Palace Yard, being,

Sir,

Your very faithful friend,

and humble Servt.

THOM. ASAPH.

LETTER CLIII.

Bp. TANNER to Dr. RAWLINSON.

List of the Provost and Fellows of Eton, and of the Canoneer Students of Christ Church.—Bodleian Speech.—T. Hearne.

Ch. Ch. Oct. xi. 1735.

GOOD SIR,

I HAVE received your kind letters of the 8th and 9th instant, and what was inclosed in them, particularly Bp. Fleetwood's List of the Provosts and Fellows of Eton. I take the dates to be the years on which every Fellow's name continued upon the Bursar's books or rolls of the College accounts; and those with the mark + were new names which the Bp. found out and added to the old Catalogue from whence he took the rest. I think there is a Charge of Bp. Weston's printed, but have it not. You know that he took his Doctor of Divinity's Degree here at Oxford, as member of New College, to qualify him to stand for Provost of King's. It will be a very acceptable and useful work for the public to have your papers concerning that College and School digested and published. I will look as soon as I have leisure among my papers, and perhaps may find some further things relating thereunto; if I do you shall have notice. I will put the sheets of Proceedings against A. Wood, which you favoured me with, into the Library Book.

I inclose the names of such Canoneer students since 1668, which stand upon a matricula begun by Bp. Fell, but I have reason to think it is not perfect; but if it please God I live it shall be made [so.] This begins only in 1660; they had before no lists but only of those elected from Westminster since Qu. Elizabeth's reign. I have this and the last year rumaged among the old Buttery books and Treasurer's accounts, and Chapter books, in order to make a list of all the Canons, Students, Chaplains, Noblemen, Gent. Com. and Commoners, who ever were of the society; when they came in, how long they staid, and, where I can, what preferment they went off to, if they did not die in the College. And as far as the books we have left will furnish, I have recovered most of the members from the year of the foundation 1546 to 1660, and shall as I go down, correct and supply several since that time. But my pains herein are as yet but in rough loose papers. When I can run over the Matriculation books of the University, I hope to be able to lick them into some form, and make them of some use to those who are willing to know who went before them in this royal and ample foundation.

You shall have the remainder of the Canoneer students in a post or two; but I shall not, I fear, be able to recover their several patrons, the rolls on which they were nominated not being preserved nor entered in the Chapter book as of late; besides, when a roll is made, many do not put down the scholars, and others change them with other scholars. As many as I meet with, you have at the side of this list.

As to the makers of the Bodleian Speech, I will inquire them out, if I can: but their names are no way entered on our books, because they are not named or appointed by the Chapter, but privately either by the Dean or the Hebrew Professor, and are paid by the Vice-Chancellor, in whose accounts, if one could see them, probably their names are entered. This gives me an opportunity to wipe off a reflection which A. Wood (Ath. Oxon. last edition, col. 385.)* makes on Bp. Fell, and our Ch. Ch. Deans, as if they unfairly kept the making that speech to their own Members, without regard to All Souls, or other Colleges; whereas it is expressly ordered in Dr. Morris's Will, that the speech should be made by a Ch. Ch. man.

The Case of the Provost of Queen's upon the death of Dr. Halton, was in my absence from Oxford; but there was one pamphlet writ on that

* The passage alluded to, is as follows:

"The Reader may be pleased now to understand that Dr. Joh. Morris, Canon of Ch. Ch. did bequeath to the University of Oxon. a rent-charge of 5l. per an. to be given to a Master of Arts that shall make and speak a Speech in praise of Sir Tho. Bodley, every year on the 8th of Nov. (on which day the Visitation of his Library is commonly made,) to be nominated by the Dean of Ch. Ch. and confirmed by the Vice-Chancellor for the time being. But the said gift was not to take place till the death of his widow. At length upon her decease, which was at Great Wolford, in Warwickshire, 11 Nov. 1681. (she being then the wife of Tho. Keyt of that place, Gent.) the said annuity fell to the University. Whereupon the year following, Dr. Fell, Dean of Ch. Ch. nominating one of his own house, (Tho. Sparke, M.A.) there was a solemn speech made by him in the *Schola Linguarum*, on the 8 Nov. 1682. Which speech is yet continued by Ch. Ch. men, *without any regard had to those of* All Souls *Coll. wherein Dr.* Morris *had most of his education, and had been chaplain thereof, or to any Master of another Coll. or Hall.*"

occasion by Mr. Francis Thomson, then Fellow, now Vicar of Burgh on Stanmore, who opposed Dr. Lancaster, assisted by Dr. Crosthwait.

Bp. Kennet's Life was neither writ by his son, nor by Mr. Russel, but by a Clergyman, near Peterborough, whose name I have been told, but now quite forget.

The Winchester Converts writ against Bp. H. on the Sacrament, is generally ascribed to Dr. Tovey, Principal of New Inn Hall, and the answer (said to be [by] Mr. Ayskue of Corpus Christi) thinks so by describing him as plain almost as if he [had] named him. But that book and subject ought not to be treated in a ludicrous way; it is to be hoped that it will be examined in a more serious manner by some wise and good man.

I was very glad, by a letter this day received from Mr. Loveday, to have the story of the Popish Priest's being with our friend T. Hearne *in extremis,* cleared up, so as in great measure to clear him from the imputation of dying a papist. I am,

Sir,

Your faithful friend and Servt.

THOM. ASAPH.

*** In another letter, dated Ch. Ch. Oct. 20, 1735, he says—" I now send the remainder of the Canoneers to the last year; as to their Patrons, as near as I can remember,

LETTER CLIV.

Mr. WHEATLY to Dr. RAWLINSON.

Common Prayer Book.—Bishop Fleetwood.—Godwin de Prœsulibus.—Milton's Monument.

DEAR SIR,

In examining my letter case, I find myself indebted to you for two. Your two other letters for enquiry of Dr. Astry and Dr. Waterland I keep safe by me: but have been very unfortunately disappointed of seeing either of those

since my time, I have set them down right; but there is no certainty to be had from the rolls we have left, the Canons changing their turns often one with another, one's scholar perhaps not being old enough to come in, and another's wanting the vacant place. It has cost me some pains to recover the Christian names of many of the members of this foundation, but I have now got most of them down to 1660, which you shall have, and the rest as I get through the books since. These are amusements, in which I hope innocently, if not usefully, I have employed and do employ the time and health, God is so good as to allow me, with as much satisfaction to myself, as others do in play, hunting, or other diversions. Whatever be the event of one's pains this way, herein I imagine I in some measure discharge a duty one owes to the noble foundation he is a member of, and to the worthy men that have gone before us, to save them from the curse of the Psalmist, that in the next generation their names be not clean put out."

gentlemen, the two or three last times of my being in town. In March next, if well, I hope to make another attempt.

At present I thank you for your communication of the Com. Pr. Book, which I herewith return: I find the name of Fleetwood at the end of it, which you tell me is Bp. Fleetwood's: and very likely it may be so; for he was a very curious man. By some calculations in the book, I perceive that his notes, and very probably his collation of this book with the sealed ones, must have been made in the year 1685, when I apprehend the Bishop must have been very young, tho' he has collated the sealed book, I believe, pretty exactly; for I find but very few things which differ from my own.* For I have a book of the same edition; which I compared very diligently with a sealed book (stolen, I suppose, from some Cathedral, but now) in the library of Balliol College, Oxford. From thence I noted all the variations between that sealed book, and the present printed ones: and sometime afterwards I again compared those collations with the sealed book in the Tower, and found very few and insignificant, if any, differences between them. If you have any curiosity to see it, I will send it up to you;

* Now in St. John's College library, where also is a copy of Wheatley "On the Common Prayer," with MS. notes and additions by the author.

tho' it will only confirm that the bishop and myself had the same inquisitiveness, and pretty nearly the same accuracy.

Of Godwin " de Præsulibus," I have both the English and the Latin edition. Does Dr. Richardson design any additions to it, or continuation of it? If he does, I hope he will take in better helps than our poor friend Dr. Salmon will afford him. Law's Regeneration, nor the 2d answer to his Christian Perfection, I have not yet seen. Any thoughts that occur to me as to Oxford Authors, you may depend upon being communicated. Sam. Parker's* son, I had heard before was apprenticed to Mr. Clements; but the account you give me of his extraordinary proficiency is new. If it be true also, I hope some generous patron of learning will recall him from the Bookseller's Shop, and place him in his father's seat, the Bodleian Library. Benson's Monument is erected to the Author of Paradise lost: and in a *poetical* corner I believe his busto will disturb none that lie near him. Even Dryden or Butler, I believe, would give him room; as I do myself, who, tho' detesting all regicides,

* Son of the Bishop of Oxford. See Noble's Continuation of Granger, vol. iii. 321. His son, Sackville Parker, who is mentioned above, was a bookseller in Oxford, and honoured with the friendship of Dr. Johnson. See Boswell's Life of Johnson, vol. iii. 572, edit. 1793.

can, after South has ruffled me with indignation against them, calm and compose myself with a few lines of Milton. Campbell I have not seen a long time, nor since he has so thoroughly discovered his temper do I enquire after him. From our Friend Dr. Brett* I had a letter last week, which promises me another very speedily.

I am, Dear Dr.
Very sincerely and heartily,
yr. humble Servt.
C. Wheatly.

Pelham, 5 Dec. 1739.

LETTER CLV.

Mr. BROME to Mr. BALLARD.

Mr. Wanley.—Mr. Thwaites.

Jan. ye 19, 1739-40.

DEAR SIR,

I have received yours with the A. S. Dict. and Cædmon,† and am not a little

* Author of a great variety of Tracts. He died in 1743. See Nichols's *Literary Anecdotes*, vol. I. p. 407.

† CÆDMONIS MONACHI Paraphrasis Poetica Genesios ac præcipuarum Sacræ paginæ Historiarum, abhinc annos M.LXX. Anglo-Saxonice conscripta, et nunc primum edita a Francisco Junio F. F. Amstelodami, apud Christo-

pleased, that they afforded you any entertainment. Mr. Wanley, you know, began his studies with transcribing Somner's Dict.* which was the foundation of his learning, and proved the advancement of him in the world by the assistance of Dr. Hickes, who knew his value, and recommended him as he deserved; all which I was privy to.

Mr. Thwaites I was most intimately acquainted with, and have by me several of his letters, but cannot find you much account of his life. He was certainly one of the greatest geniuses of the age; much a gentleman, a good-natured man. His patience and magnanimity in his sufferings by lameness was beyond compare; so great that it was not impertinent in Serjeant Bernard,† his

phorum Cunradi, typis et sumptibus Editoris. CIↃ IↃC LV. 4to. Of this uncommonly rare and valuable book, a few copies were discovered in a ware-house at Oxford in the year 1752. The notes written in the learned editor's own hand in the printed copy bequeathed to the University of Oxford, and now in the Bodleian, were printed and added to these copies. The original MS. preserved in that library, contains a variety of very curious drawings.

* Ballard, it seems, followed the example of Mr. Wanley, for a very beautiful transcript of Somner's Dictionary, with Thwaites's additions, is now among Ballard's MSS. in the Bodleian, written by himself, with the greatest accuracy and neatness. It is probable that Mr. Brome lent him the original, which he here mentions, for this purpose.

† Charles Bernard, serjeant-surgeon to Queen Anne.

surgeon, to acquaint Queen Anne therewith, who ordered him 100*l.* and made him Greek Professor in Oxford, &c. He went from Oxford to London to have his leg cut off above the knee by Ser. Bernard, who being afraid to perform the operation, would have declined it; whereupon he told him, if he would not do it, if he would give him his instruments, he would do it himself; to which Bernard replied, he thought he could do it better. He would not suffer himself to be held, &c. and without shewing the least sign of pain went thro' the operation. Laid in bed, and the Surgeon gone out about other business, the arteries feel a bleeding. He took a bedstaff and with his handkerchief screwed the end of the stump, ran his fingers into the orifices, like spickets, of the arteries, and then knockt for his surgeon, who soon came back to him, and staunched the bleeding. By too spare a diet, 'tis believed he shortened his life.*

WM. BROME.

* See another letter, from the same person, on this subject, in Nichols's *Literary Anecdotes*, vol. iv. p. 148. This, however differs slightly from the present, as it states Queen Anne's donation to have been two, instead of one, hundred pounds. Thwaites, fellow of Queen's College, died in 1711, and was buried in the Church of Iffley, near Oxford.

LETTER CLVI.

Mr. BROME to Mr. RAWLINS

Pine's Horace.—Athenæ Cantabrigienses.

* * * * * *

I LIKED Mr. Pine's Horace so well that I purchased it. The first Vol. come out cost a guinea in sheets, and the second will cost as much when published, and I have subscribed half-a-guinea towards it. Mr. Pine had formerly from me three guineas for a set of Magna Chartas engraved exactly like the original. These are my running horses, and extravagances I cannot sometimes avoid. 'Tis very laudable in you to transmit to posterity the memory of that great and good man Dr. Pocock, whom I remember when I was of Christ Church. I have some impatience to see his life and works. One Mr. Richardson of Emanuel College* is collecting for an *Athenæ Catabrigienses*; and is, as the great Mr. Baker of St. John's says, well qualified for it.† I have no other news from the

* See p. 102. Besides these foundations for a history of Cambridge writers, he left in MS. many collections relative to the constitution of that University. See Gough's "British Topography," vol. i. p. [250.*]

† Mr. Baker himself made great collections for the same purpose. Twenty-three folio volumes of these MSS. were

Republic of letters. When I have leisure I will transcribe some matters and send you for your diversion. If I could see you here, I promise you, I would celebrate a Jubilee.

I am, Dear Sir,
Your most obliged,
and most obedient servant,
W. B.

LETTER CLVII.

Mr. G. RUSSEL to Mr. G. BALLARD.

Isaac Walton's Lives.—Ballard's Learned Ladies.

St. Mary Hall, May 15, 1749.

DEAR SIR,

I RETURN you by the bearer with many thanks, Isaac Walton's "Lives of Donne, Hooker, Wotton, and Herbert,"* and cannot

given by the author to his great friend, the Earl of Oxford, and are now among the Harleian collection in the British Museum, and sixteen folio and three quarto volumes were bequeathed to the University of Cambridge. The work was afterwards undertaken by the Rev. William Cole, see p. 102, *note*.

* Of these lives, that of Donne was originally prefixed to his "Sermons," folio, Lond. 1640; that of Wotton, to the "Reliquiæ Wottonianæ," 8vo. Lond. 1651; and that of

part with the book without gratefully acknowledging the pleasure I received in the perusal of it. An integrity of heart shines, in my opinion, through every page; the author seems delighted with the goodness he treats of, and to look on the virtues of these great men as peculiar advantages to himself. It is a great pity that lives of so eminent and exemplary a conduct, are not in like manner, transmitted to posterity; but it is an observation too justly made by foreigners, that the English are the most desirous of perpetuating the memory of their villains, and the most negligent of recording their virtuous persons, of any nation on earth: perhaps it may be the same perverse turn which makes us build palaces for our beggars, and alms-houses for our Kings. There might be an inconceivable benefit derived from faithful accounts of private virtue. I am as much pleased with them as with Histories of a more

Hooker appeared in a small vol. Lond. 1665. These, with the Life of Herbert, were afterwards collected and printed in 8vo. Lond. 1670. Walton wrote also a biographical account of Dr. Sanderson, Bishop of Lincoln, first printed in 1678, with four tracts written by the bishop. A valuable edition of all Walton's "Lives," with notes, and an account of the author by Thomas Zouch, appeared at York in 1796, 4to. and 1807, 8vo. and a reprint of the Lives only has issued from the Clarendon Press, in two small volumes. Oxford, 1806. See some account of Walton in Wood's "Athenæ Oxonienses," by Bliss, vol i. col. 698.

public nature, nor can I see any reason why it should not afford a Christian Reader as much useful entertainment to observe the steps and gradual advances by which a religious man conquered his passions, as to follow Alexander or Marlborough in the reduction of the Eastern or Gallic Monarchies. Matters of so specious a kind as these last are seldom (says the judicious and elegant Dr. Sprat) related with fidelity, and even when they are, serve but for the imitation of very few. They make more for the ostentation than real benefit of human life. It is from the practice of our equals we are taught to command our passions, regulate our knowledge, and govern our actions. The work you are now engaged in,* will I hope rescue us in a great mea-

* "Memoirs of Several Ladies of Great Britain, who have been celebrated for their writings, or skill in the learned Languages, Arts, and Sciences. By George Ballard, of Magd. Coll. Oxon." 4to. Oxford. 1752, and again in 8vo. 1775. A copy of the first edition of this work, now in the Bodleian, contains several MS. notes in the hand-writing of the author. (D. D. 1. Jur.) Perhaps the following alphabetical list of the lives contained in this accurate work may not be unacceptable to the reader.

Arundel, Mary countess of
Ascham, Margaret
Askew, Anne
Astell, Mary
Bacon, Anne lady
Barnes, Juliana
Baynard, Anne
Bland, Elizabeth
Bovey, Catherine
Bridgwater, Eliz. countess of

sure from the too just accusation our neglect in Biography has occasioned, and you have this additional satisfaction in prospect, that as the Fair Sex are the subject, so they will be the Protectresses

Burnet, Elizabeth
Bury, Elizabeth
Burleigh, Mildred lady
Catherine, queen
Chidley, Katherine
Chudleigh, Mary lady
Clement, Margaret
Dancy, Elizabeth
Davies, lady Eleanor
Elizabeth, queen
Fane, lady Elizabeth
Gethin, Grace lady
Gray, lady Jane
Grierson, Constantia
Halket, Anne lady
Heron, Cecilia
Hopton, Susanna
Howard, lady Mary
Inglis, Esther
Juliana, anchoret of Norwich
Kempe, Margery
Killigrew, Anne
Killigrew, Catherine
Legge, Elizabeth
Lincoln, Elizabeth countess of
Lucar, Elizabeth
Lumley, Joanna lady
Mary, queen of England
Mary, queen of Scotland
Masham, Damaris lady
Monk, honourable Mrs.
Newcastle, Margaret dutchess of
North, Dudleya
Norton, Frances lady
Pakington, Dorothy lady
Parr, queen Katherine
Parry, Blanch
Pembroke, Anne countess of
Pembroke, Mary countess of
Philips, Katherine
Richmond and Derby, Margaret countess of
Roper, Margaret
Roper, Mary
Russel, Elizabeth lady
Seymour, lady Anne
Seymour, lady Arabella
Seymour, lady Jane
Seymour, lady Margaret
Tishem, Catherine
Walker, Elizabeth
Westmoreland, Jane countess of

and Guardians of your performance. Their smiles, like a benign planet, will gradually ripen it to perfection, and their breath embalm it to posterity. * * *

GEORGE RUSSEL.

LETTER CLVIII.

Mr. PARRY to THOMAS RAWLINS, Esq. at Pophills.

On the author of the Whole Duty of Man.

Shipston, Dec. 4, 1749.

DEAR SIR,

MR. Hen. Owen, M.B. a friend of mine, paying me a visit about two months ago, among several other interrogatories asked me whether I had learned from any hand the name of the author of The Whole Duty of Man; I told him that Dean Hickes, Mrs. Elstob, and others, gave the honour of that performance to Lady Packington; and that our friend Mr. G. Ballard had been assured by a letter from the late

Sir Herbert Packington, that the original (or at least a copy) of that performance, written by the aforesaid lady, was now to be seen in the archives of that family. To which Mr. Owen replied, he had received a different but more probable account from a gentleman of his acquaintance at Broadwell, near Stow, whom he would consult with once more upon this matter, and then he would oblige me with a more satisfactory answer than he could give me at that present time.—And this was the occasion and foundation of the following letters.

Broadwell, Oct. 12, 1749.

DEAR SIR,

THE account which I promised to procure you, in relation to the author of The Whole Duty of Man, is as follows.

A certain gentleman of figure and fortune (name unknown) embarked so deeply in the King's cause, that he was either ruined in his circumstances, and so affected with his misfortunes, that he died; or else was so closely pursued by the opposite party, that he was obliged to fly his country;—which, my author is not certain.—His family, however, was reduced very low, and his lady was forced (for the support of herself and children) to keep a sort of boarding house; and for this purpose she rented a large old house (since demolished) called Barrows-Hedges, situated upon the side of Banstead-Downs, about two miles beyond Epsom, in Surry. To this place many of the lady's friends, (women chiefly) who were attached to the King's cause, retired; insomuch, that the family consisted ordinarily of about 24 persons in number; occasionally of perhaps twice as many.—Now there was a certain clergyman in this family, who officiated as chaplain, and to whom several persons (who were for the Church and Constitution) brought their children to be baptized, and also came themselves at proper times to partake regularly of the Lord's Supper. But all this you are to understand was performed in a clandestine manner, and among friends; for the clergyman's real name was not known to any of the Sisterhood itself, the Lady of the House and some few of her most intimate friends excepted.

This Clergyman, during the time of his residence in this place, preached a course of lectures to his congregation, wherein he insisted chiefly upon the Necessity of Good Works to Salvation; and that, as he said, for this reason, viz. *Because the Fanatics were shamefully regardless of good works, and preached up Faith as all-sufficient.*

Now while he preached these lectures, it was the custom of a select club of the ladies who were his hearers, to meet immediately after the Sermon, and to pen down all that they could conjointly remember of it in a book. This common Note-Book (if I may so call it) each one afterwards copied out at her leisure for her own private use.—And here I must observe to you, that the Sisterhood remarked that the Lady of the House made (at this time) frequent and stated journeys to London; and that whenever she went, she took a bundle of paper along with her, which they all concluded among themselves was written by this gentleman, and meant for the press.

Sometime after, one of these ladies removed to a relation's house, where she exhibited those Notes she had made of the fore-mentioned Lectures, which were highly esteemed by that family.

Soon after this, came out that noted book, entituled "The Whole Duty of Man." The character it bore, soon determined the Master of this last-mentioned Family to procure it.—I mean, to buy it. But he had no sooner begun to read it, but, to his great surprise, he found it to be the original from whence the Lady must have taken her Notes, as agreeing thereto, upon comparison, both in order, argument, and diction. —Upon this, the Lady was put to enquire *who* the forementioned Clergyman *really was*; and upon application to the Lady with whom she had boarded, she was assured that the Gentleman's *true* name (for he had assumed a *false* one for fear of being discovered) was *Praise God* or *Accepted* (my author knows not which of the *two* his Christian name was) *Frewen,* afterwards Bishop of Lichfield and Coventry, and at last Archbishop of York.

He, indeed, never owned himself to be the author of it, (viz. The Whole Duty of Man) nor yet ever disowned it. And how far the foregoing account will determine it to be his, let the reader judge.

Your's,

HENRY OWEN

An Appendix to the foregoing Letter.

My informer, or author, perused and approved the foregoing account, and desired me to add to it the following remarks: viz.

1°. The Place is now called Barrow's Hedges, but that was not the name of the old House.

2°. The Clergyman, whilst he lived in this House, was supposed to be beyond sea.

3°. This account my author had from Mr. John Hodges, a gentleman of great piety and probity, who was formerly Treasurer to the So ciety for propagating the Gospel, &c.—who told my author, that the Society having (upon a time when he was Treasurer) ordered "The Necessity of Caring for the Soul" to be translated into some foreign language, (my author forgot which) thought fit at that time to make enquiry after the Author of The Whole Duty of Man. Accordingly several of the Members did make enquiry, and brought in their several accounts. The foregoing was the best grounded, and accordingly was that in which the Society acquiesced.

The account is indeed at present a little obscured by the omission of names, which my author has forgot: but as to the facts in general he is absolutely positive.

If you have any queries to make, my author is ready to answer you.

Let this question be proposed to Mr. Ballard, viz. Is not the pretended original in the Packington Family, one of the Note-Books mentioned above, or a copy of one of them?

Your's,

H. Owen.

Oct. 19, 1749.

Having sent the originals of these Letters to Mr. Ballard, together with an account of the occasion of writing them, he was pleased to favour me with the following answer.

REVD. SIR,

I HAVE received the favour of yours, and am very much obliged to you for so kindly communicating that which you imagined might be serviceable towards determining who was the real author of that excellent treatise "The Whole Duty of Man;" a desirable Truth, which most people would gladly know. But those who will examine this last pretension to it with any exactness or care, will not easily be induced to believe that Archbishop Frewen was the author of that incomparable work, &c. His character will by no means correspond with it. For 1°. though the Abp. was a man of considerable learning and abilities, yet I cannot find that he had any knowledge of the Oriental languages, which the author of those books was undoubtedly skilled in. 2dly, I do not find that the Abp. had the least tincture of that self-denial and great modesty, for which the author of that excellent treatise is so justly celebrated, and so consequently would not have concealed his name, when so much honour was lost by it. 3°. Those who are acquainted with the several accounts of him which have been handed to the public by Mr. Wood, Mr. Willis, Mr. Drake, and others, will hardly be induced to think he had true piety enough to suggest to him the many admirable precepts and primitive doctrine contained in those valuable books. 4thly, that which puts the thing beyond all dispute is, that it fully appears from "The Causes of the Decay of Christian Piety," that the Author of "The Whole Duty of Man" was living in the year 1667. Now, as Archbishop Frewen died in the beginning of the year 1664, it is impossible that he should be the author.*

I would not have said thus much of this Bishop, had I not been led to it by the subject you have furnished me with, in order to shew you the improbability of his being the author of The Whole Duty of Man. And if the Arguments in favour of his being the author of that book were not already sufficiently confuted by the last article, I could produce others which would very much shake the credit of such an assertion, but I be-

* It seems pretty clear from Ballard's "Learned Ladies," that Dorothy lady Packington, wife of Sir John Packington, knight and baronet, and daughter of Thomas lord Coventry, was the author of *The Whole Duty of Man.* For Mr. Ballard's arguments in support of this opinion, we must refer to his work, in which he notices the preceding letter as written by "an ingenious clergyman," but he considers his correspondent's reasons, in support of the Archbishop's claim to the production in question, "not important enough to need a particular refutation." *Mem. of Learned Ladies,* p. 320, edit. 4to. 1752.

lieve you will think enough has been said already upon this subject, by

Your most obliged, &c.

GEORGE BALLARD.

Oxford, Nov. 15, 1749.

If what has been offered does not prove satisfactory, be pleased to let me know your objections, for I assure you, Sir, there is not any thing gives me greater pleasure than the discovery of truth.

I have not hitherto received from Mr. Owen any reply to Mr. B.'s answer; nor have I any news to impart to you, but that Dr. King has at last published his speech, which he delivered at the opening of Dr. Radcliffe's Library.

* * * * * * * *

I am, with respect, Sir,

Your obliged humble Servt.

W. P.*

* Mr. Parry was fellow of Jesus College, and presented by that society to the living of Shipston-upon-Stowre, Warwickshire. He was famous for caligraphy; several specimens of his skill are extant in the Bodleian library. A beautiful transcript which he made of the Statutes of his college, is preserved with care among its Archives.

*** On the subject of the above letter, the following is extracted from one of T. Hearne to Dr. Smith.

"There is given to the Public Library the Original MS. of the *Decay of Christian Piety*, written by the excellent author

LETTER CLIX.

Mr. T. CARTE to Mr. G. BALLARD.

On the Death of Henry VI.

Dean's Yard, Westminster,
May 4, 1751.

SIR,

I HAD a letter in the beginning of this week from Mr. Monkhouse, and inclosed in it, a relation of the design of murdering K. James II. at *Warminster:* it agrees with one

of *The Whole Duty of Man.* Dr. Aldrich has been shewed it, to know whether he could discover the hand. He replied, 'twas not the author's own hand he believed, but copy'd with a disguised hand by Bp. Fell. I saw a paper a week since written by Archbp. Sancroft's own hand. I compared it with this MS. and the hand in divers respects appeared the same, as much as can be supposed, when a hand is disguised. Some of the letters exactly of the same make, the same distance of lines, &c. what confirms it is that some years since Dr. Holbeach, Master of Emanuel College, Cambridge, making a visit to Dr. Sancroft, of the same Coll. he saw certain papers lying on the table, written by the said Dr. Sancroft, which he afterwards told one of his friends he would swear were part of what was printed under the title of *The Whole Duty of Man.* This was before the Restoration. But I cannot tell how very well to depend upon it, and it may be 'tis not fair to be inquisitive."

"Oxon. Aug. 17, 1706."

which I had from the late learned Mr. G. Harbin, who had it from Dr. Sheridan, Bp. of Kilmore, who assisted Sir G. Hewet at his death, when he expressed his repentance of having been engaged in that design. Mr. Monkhouse mentioned to me a passage in my History relating to the death of *Henry* VI. upon consulting which, I find my printer left out the MS. Authority to which I referred, perhaps for want of understanding the reference, or for haste. It was *Scala* Mund. MS. inter MSS. Norfolc. in Off. Armor. N. S. The late Mr. Anstis paid a great deference to this Author, who lived in the reign of E. IV. and in his Criticisms on Sandford's "General Hist." prefers his accounts of the births, deaths, &c. of our princes to any others: and indeed they are much more exact. His words that I copied are—"Post bellum de *Tewksburi,* Henricus nuper Rex Angliæ repositus in Turri London. in Vigilia Ascensionis Domini ibidem *feliciter moriens* per Thamesin navicula usque ad Abbatiam de Chertsey deductus, ibi sepultus est." I want to know where the original MS. is, whence the Continuation of the Prior of Croyland was printed; because I am fully persuaded that the words which follow his speaking of Hen. 6, being found dead or dying suddenly in the Tower, were added after Hen. 7. formed the design of getting him canonized. It was proper for this purpose to represent H. 6 as murdered, and I don't believe, that before that time you will find any enemy of R. III. suggesting either that H. 6 was murdered, or murdered by R. III. I wish you could inform me of the original MS. that I might examine it.

I am, Sir,

Yr. very obliged and obedt. humble Servt.

THO. CARTE.

LETTER CLX.

From the same to the same.

Historical Memoranda.

Dean's Yard, Westminster,
May 18, 1751.

SIR,

I RECEIVED the favour of your's in due time, but the hurry I have been in, to prepare for my leaving this place next Tuesday, when I shall set out with Mr. Bertie or Mr. Hill for Yattendun, in Berkshire, hath hindered me from acknowledging it till now. I shall be obliged to you likewise for supplying the deficient reference in the Bodleian copy. I knew the late Mr. Brome very well, and I believe I have the late K. James's dying words among my papers: but not the diverting conversation, which passed in Mr. Harbin's presence, between Sir Godfrey Kneller and Dr. Wallis, about the birth of that K.'s Son, nor did I ever see it. I wonder my friend Mr. Harbin never mentioned it to me, and I shall be much obliged to you for a copy thereof.*

* The following account is transcribed from one of Dr. Rawlinson's MSS. in the Bodleian. "A. Alsop (Anthony Alsop, of Christ Church) has been wth one of Corpus who came from Dr. Wallis, where had been some talk of the F. Kgs proclaiming ye P. of W James ye 3d. And ye Dr. told this gentleman how many original letters he had seen under the queen's own hand, ye bricklayer's wife, and others concern'd in the matter, and a long letter also in cypher, wch cost him some pains, all wch made it out clear to him, and he thought 'twould to any body, yt twas all cheats and imposture. It chanc'd at this time yt. Sr. G. K.* coming down to draw ye Drs. picture by Sir Sam. Pepys' order, was present. "Wat de devil (says he) de Prince Wales te son of a brickbat woman, begot it is a ly. I am not of his party, nor shall not be for him, I am satisfiet wit wat ye parliamt has done, but I must tell you wat I am sure of, and in wat I cannot be mistaken. His fader and moder have sate to me about 36 time a piece, and I know every line and bit in their faces. Be got I could paint K. James just now by memory. I say the child is so like both, yt there is not a feature in his face but wat belongs either to fader or moder; this I 'm sure of, and, be got, I cannot be mistaken. Nay

* Sir Godfrey Kneller. The portrait of Dr. Wallis, which is one of his best pictures, was given by Sir Samuel Pepys to the University of Oxford, and is now in the gallery of the Bodleian Library.

The passage you mean about Q. Elizabeth's incapacity to bear children, is found in the Notes of the famous Du Plessis Mornay upon the History of Thuanus; and is published in the 7th volume of my edition of Thuanus;* else I would

ye nails of his fingers are his moders ye Qn yt was. Dr. you may be out in yr. *letters*, but be got I cant be out in my *lines*."

Hearne corroborates this account in his *Diary*, vol. v. page 137. "When Sir Godfrey Kneller (as Dr. Hudson informs me) came to Oxon. by Mr. Pepys's order, to draw Dr. Wallis's picture, he, at dinner with Dr. Wallis, was pleased to say, upon the Dr.'s questioning the legitimacy of the Prince of Wales, that he did not in the least doubt but he was the son of K. James and Q. Mary: and to evince this, he added, that upon the sight of ye picture of ye Prince of Wales sent from Paris into England, he was fully satisfyd of what others seemed to doubt so much of: for, as he farther said, he had manifest lines and features of both their faces, which he knew very well, having drawn them both several times. When this was said, were present at dinner with Dr. Wallis the following persons; Dr. Aldrich, dean of Ch. Ch. Dr. Charlett, master of University College; Dr. Hudson, head library-keeper, and Dr. Gregory (the Scotchman) one of the Savilian professors."

* It is to be found in the following note of M. Plessis de Mornay, on that part of the LXXIVth book of De Thou's History, which gives an account of the negotiations of marriage, for some time carried on between Queen Elizabeth and the Duke of Anjou. See Thuani Hist. vol. vii. c. vi. p. 97. Lond. edit. 1733.

"Monsieur le Prince d' Orange estoit lors à Gand où je

search among my papers, and transcribe it for you. This incapacity was ascribed to poison given her, which affected her womb: and though she got over it, she was in a dangerous state of body for several years, so that every body despaired of her recovery (as I find in the Letters of Messrs. de Noailles, the French Embrs. in England in Q. Mary's time) till almost the very end of her sister's reign: but M. Du Plessis (who was highly esteemed by Q. Eliz. and very inti-

l'avois suivi, lequel ayant cette nouvelle m' envoya aussi tost les Lettres de Monsieur de Saincte Aldegonde; m' appellant incredule, parce que j' avois toujours contesté, pour le connoissance que je pensois avoir de l' humeur de la Reyne, que le mariage ne se feroit point. Le lendemain s' en rendirent graces à Dieu en la grande Eglise, qui devoient estre suivies de coups d' Artillerie et de feux de joye. Sur le milieu de l' action luy vinrent contraires Lettres de Monsieur de Saincte Aldegonde, sur lesquelles, assis que j' estois auprés de luy, je luy vis changer de visage, et lors me les bailla, me disant que j' avois dit trop vray. Surquoy fut arresté le surplus de la joye. Il en fort marry, pour ce qu' il avoit fait grand état au peuple des utilités qui luy viendroient de là pour luy faire plus aisement accepter Monsieur. Disoit la Lettre que comme la Reyne eut la plume en la main pour signer, tremblant de colere elle l' avoit jettée; et tournée vers les Seigneurs de son Conseil, elle leur avoit dit, "Malheureux, étes vous si aveugles, que vous ne voyez qu' apres ma mort vous vous entrecouperes la gorge, et ne scavez vous pas que me mariant, je ne la feray pas longue?" Ce qu' on interpretoit de quelque defaut naturel connu de peu."

mate with her) doth not mention the reason of her incapacity.

I hope to wait on you at Oxford in the summer, and am with great respect, Sir,

Your very obliged and obedt. humble Servt.

THO. CARTE.

LETTER CLXI.

Mr. BALLARD to Dr. LYTTELTON, Dean of Exeter.

A Defence of the History of Learned Ladies.

REVD. AND HOND. SIR,

MY best acknowledgments are due for the favour of two epistles; the first of which I received a few minutes after my last set forward for Exeter. I would have answered it immediately, but that I thought a little respite might be agreeable, before I gave you the trouble of another long letter.

The day before I received your first epistle, a Gent. of my acquaintance brought me the *Monthly Review** for February, that I might see what the candid and genteel authors of that work had said of mine. They observe to the publick, that *I have said* C. Tishem was so skilled in the

* Vol. viii. p. 124.

Greek Tongue, that she could read Galen in its original, which very few Physicians are able to do. Whether this was done maliciously, in order to bring the wrath of the Æsculapians upon me, or inadvertently, I cannot say: but I may justly affirm, that they have used me very ill in that affair; since if they had read with attention, which they ought to have done before they attempted to give a character of the Book, they must have known that the whole account of that lady (which is but one page) is not mine, but borrowed with due acknowledgment, from the *General Dictionary*. They are likewise pleased to inform the world that I have been rather too industrious in the undertaking, having introduced several women who hardly deserved a place in the work. I did not do this for want of materials; neither did I do it rashly, without advising with others of superior judgment in those affairs, of which number Mr. Professor Ward was one. But those pragmatical Censors seem to have but little acquaintance with those studies, or otherwise they might have observed that all our general Biographers, as Leland, Bale, Pits, Wood, and Tanner, have trod the very same steps; and have given an account of all the authors they could meet with, good and bad, just as they found them: and yet, I have never heard of any one that had courage or ill-nature enough, to endeavour to expose them for it. While I was ruminating on these affairs, three or four letters came to my hands, and perceiving one of them come from my worthy friend the Dean of Exeter, I eagerly broke it open, and was perfectly astonished to find myself charged with *party zeal* in my book; and that from thence the most candid reader might conclude the author to be both a Church and State Tory. But after having thoroughly considered all the passages objected to, and not finding the least tincture of either Whig or Tory principles contained in them, I began to chear up my drooping spirits, in hopes that I might possibly out-live my supposed crime; but, alas! to my still greater confusion! when I opened my next letter from a Tory acquaintance, I was like one thunder-struck at the contents of it. He discharges his passionate but ill-grounded resentment upon me most furiously. He tells me, he did not imagine Magdalen College could have produced such a rank Whig. He reproaches me with want of due esteem for the Stuart Family, to whom he says I have shewn a deadly hatred, and he gives me, as he imagines, three flagrant instances of it. 1. That I have unseasonably and maliciously printed a letter of Queen Elizabeth's, in order to blacken the memory of Mary Queen of Scots, and that to, at a time when her character began to shine as bright as the Sun. 2dly. That I have endeavoured to make her memory odious, by representing her as wanting natural affection to her only son, in my note at p. 162, where he says I have printed part of a Will, &c. And 3dly, tho' she was cut off in such a barbarous and unprecedented manner, yet she has fallen unlamented by me. I am likewise charged with having an affection to Puritanism; the reasons for which are, my giving the Life of a Puritan Bishop's Lady, which it seems need not have been done by me, had I not had a particular regard for her, since it had been done before by Goodwin who reprinted her Devotions. And not content with this, I have blemished my book with the memoirs of a Dissenting teacher's wife, and have been kind enough to heighten even the character given her by her indulgent husband: and that I am very fond of quoting Fox and Burnet upon all occasions. These are thought strong indications of the above-mentioned charge. It may be thought entirely unnecessary to answer any of the objections from Exeter, after having given you this Summary of my kind Friend's Candid Epistle; but to you, Sir, to whom I could disclose the very secrets of my soul, I will endeavour to say a word or two upon this subject, and make you my Confessor upon this occasion; and I will do it with as much sincerity, as if I lay on my death-bed. Before I was fourteen years old, I read over Fox's Acts and Monuments of the Church, and several of the best books of Polemical Divinity, which strongly fortified me in the Protestant Religion; and gave me the greatest abhorrence to Popery. And soon after I perused Mercurius Rusticus, The Eleventh Persecution, Lloyd, Walker's Sufferings of the Clergy, and many others, which gave me almost as bad an opinion of the Dissenters. But then I learned in my childhood *to live in Charity with all Men*, and I have used my best endeavours to put this doctrine in practice all my life long I never thought ill, or quarrelled with any man merely because he had been educated in principles different to mine; and yet I have been acquainted with many papists, dissenters, &c. and if I found any of them learned, ingenuous, and modest, I always found my heart well disposed for contracting a firm friendship with them: and notwithstanding that, I dare believe that all those people will, with joint consent, vouch for me, that I have ever been steady in my own principles.

I can truly affirm that never any one engaged in such a work, with an honester heart, or executed it with more unbiassed integrity, than I have done. And indeed, I take the unkind censures passed upon me by the furious uncharitable zealots of both parties, to be the strongest proof of it. And after all, I dare challenge any man, whether Protestant, Papist, or Dissenter, Whig or Tory, (and I have drawn up and published memoirs of women who professed all those principles) to prove me guilty of partiality, or to shew that I have made any uncharitable reflections on any person, and whenever that is done, I will faithfully promise to make a public recantation. I wish, Sir, you would point out to me any one unbecoming word or expression which has fell from me on Bishop Burnet. Had I had the least inclination to have lessened his character, I did not want proper materials to have done it. I have in my possession two original letters from Bishop Gibson and Mr. Norris of Bemerton,* to Dr. Charlett, which, if published, would lessen your too great esteem for him. And what, I beseech you, Sir, have I said in praise of Mrs. Hopton and her pious and useful labours, which they do not well deserve, and which can possibly give any just offence to any good man? I dare not censure or condemn a good thing merely because it borders upon the Church of Rome. I rather rejoice that she retains any thing I can fairly approve. Should I attempt to do this, might I not condemn the greater part of our Liturgy, &c.? and should I not stand self-condemned for so doing? I cannot for my life perceive that I have said any thing of that excellent woman, which she does not merit; and I must beg leave to say that I think her letter to F. Tur-

* See vol. i. p. 157.

beville deserves to be wrote in letters of gold, and ought to be carefully read and preserved by all Protestants. Mary Queen of Scots fell under my notice, no otherwise than as a learned woman. The affairs you mention would by no means suit my peaceable temper. I was too well acquainted with the warm disputes, and fierce engagement both of domestic and foreign writers on that head, once to touch upon the subject. And indeed, unless I had been the happy discoverer of some secret springs of action which would have given new information to the public, it would have been excessive folly in me to intermeddle in an affair of so tender a nature, and of so great importance.

I have often blamed my dear friend Mr. Brome for destroying his valuable collections, but I now cease to wonder at it. He spent his leisure hours pleasantly and inoffensively, and when old age came on, which not only abates the thirst, but oftentimes gives a disrelish to these and almost all other things, which do not help to make our passage into eternity more easy, he then destroyed them (I dare believe) in order to prevent the malicious reflections of an ill-natured world.

I have always been a passionate lover of History and Antiquity, Biography, and Northern Literature: and as I have ever hated idleness, so I have in my time filled many hundred sheets with my useless scribble, the greater part of which I will commit to the flames shortly, to prevent their giving me any uneasiness in my last moments.*

[May 22, 1753.]

LETTER CLXII.

Dr. LYTTELTON to Mr. BALLARD.

In Answer to the last.

SIR,

THE pleasure I generally receive in reading a letter from you was much lessened when I was favoured with your last of the 22d ult. as I perceived by it you was sensibly affected by some passages in a former letter of mine relating to your Lives of the Learned Ladies. The objections I then made were not my own, but those of other people, and you have given so satisfactory an answer to them that must

* Ballard left a very large collection of original letters, including copies of several of his own writing, and a complete Index to the whole, to the Bodleian, where they are now preserved with great care. The original Manuscript of his "Learned Ladies" was in the possession of the late Mr. Gough, and was sold with the rest of his books, in 1811.

at once stop the mouths of *candid* critics; and as for others, it is of no consequence to endeavour to refute them. As to what you observe of Mr. Brome's burning his papers long before his death, I am fully persuaded he was so far from passing the remainder of his life the more quietly for such a hasty action, that he must have a thousand times repented of it in his cooler hours, and consequently have suffered much uneasiness on that account. Let me advise you therefore not to follow such an example, but remember that no works are faultless, any more than their authors; and if there are more readers who approve than condemn, 'tis as much as any author should expect.

June 11, 1753.

APPENDIX.

APPENDIX.

No. I.

LETTERS FROM THE ASHMOLEAN MUSEUM.

LETTER I.

R. KNIGHT to WILLIAM LILLY,* the Astrologer.

Consultation relative to the probability of a Marriage.

September ye 8th, at half an hour after
4 in the afternoon.

SIR,

HAVINGE been with you divers times, as upon the 24 of December, 1647, and upon the 27 of Sept. 1648, and twise in the latter end of Aprill last, at all which times I made bould to desire your judgement concerninge some

* William Lilly was born at Diseworth, in Leicestershire. in 1602, and died in 1681. His " History of his Life and Times," affords many curious instances of credulity and imposture. A portrait of him is preserved in the Ashmolean Museum.

thinges I then propounded unto you, wherein you were pleased to give me some satisfaction. You may happily remember me by this character: I was borne three weekes before my time, neare Newberry, on the 16th of August, 1619; but what houre I cannot learne, I am very tall of stature, goeing stoopinge a little at the shoulders, I am leane, havinge thinne flaxen haire, of a longish visage and a pale complexion, gray eyed, havinge some impediment in my upper lippe, which hath a small mole on the right side thereof: I have allsoe on the right side of my forehead an other little mole, I am of a mellancholly disposition, havinge beene all the course of my life in an unsetled condition. When I was last with you I was very desirous to knowe your judgment about what time you did thinke I might be setled, and I did then acquaint you that there was a match propounded unto my father for me unto a gentlewoman who lived south from the place of my usuall residence; she was borne neare Worcester, in May, 1613, but for the most part of her life had lived south or southwest from me. She is an Ayresse, of a reasonable tall stature, of a brownish haire, of an ovall visage, and a saturnine complexion, very discreete, and excellent well spoken, all which when I was with you, you described unto me, and told me that possibly I might succeed in the businesse, if she were not preingaged which I should knowe before the 10th of Maye then followeinge, and in case it did come to any thinge, it should notwithstandinge goe but slowely on at the first, and that I should have many rubbs and delayes, duringe the time of Mercury his beinge retrograde, but at his comming to be direct all thinges should goe fairely on; but however this business did succeed you did assure me that I should be settled before the 20th of November next. Nowe, Sir, to acquaint you howe much of your judgement proved true, I refrained to make any addresse unto her untill those aspects were over in the 9th of May, but afterwards I went unto her, when with some difficulty I obtained leave to waite on her, and at last procured of her to thinke of a treaty of marriage, which she did, and appointed it three several times, duringe the time of Mercury, his last beinge R. but still by severall accidents unexpectedly put of, yet at last it was appointed to be the 22cond or 23d of August, soe my father, with my selfe and some other friends set out towards the place appointed for the treaty, (which was southwest from us, and west from the gentlewoman) on Munday the 20th of August, at halfe an houre after twelve, and on Thursday, at the place appointed, the treaty beganne between 2 and 3 of clocke, P.M. at which time they could not come to an agreement, but proposalls were tendered by my father, the which were by her commissioner to be delivered, or sent unto her, and after she a little had deliberated upon them, I should goe to knowe her answere, and soe I went on the 30th of Aug. but it was 31, about 2 of the clocke, before I came to her, where, after an houres stay, I demanded her resolution, but before she delivered her answere we were interrupted, and soe continued all that day, but the next day after a great deale of arguinge upon the proposalls, she told me that she wold not accept of those termes proffered, upon which we broke of. Nowe, Sir, beinge not a little trowbled, that having revolved the Ephemerides, where finding soe many of the planets neere the places they were in at the time of my birth, this businesse should goe soe crossely, and being by this meanes for a long time likely to continue in an unsetled condition, my desire unto you is that you will be pleased to resolve me, or at least to lend me your opinion in some of these ensuinge questions. First, whether or noe you wold advise me to make another attempt to endeavour the bringinge about the businesse I have here mentioned unto you, if soe what possibility I have to be likely to speede in my desires, and by what meanes I am likely to doe any good in it, and at what times I were best to make any newe addresses unto her, or secondly whether or noe you are of the same judgement still as formerly, that I shall assuredly be setled about the middle of November next, if soe, by what meanes it is likely to come to passe, and lastly, if neither of these thinges should come to passe, whether or noe there be any probability for me to travell beyond seas as I very much desire, of which let me desire your speedy answere and judgement, by which, if I receive any good, I shall be thankful unto you: let me allsoe desire you to let me knowe whether or noe, you can resolve a question without seeinge of the party, in case they acquaint you with theire desires as I have done, for heere are divers whoe have had experience of your art, whoe can not conveniently come to London, that doe intend to trouble you. Thus hopinge to receive a speedy and satisfactory answere from you, I rest,

Your humble Servant,

ROGER KNIGHT, Jun.

I pray send your letter by the Bristoll post, and direct it to Mr. Roger Knight, jun. at Greenham, neare Newberry, to be left with the post master of Speenhamland, to be conveighed unto me.

I have sent here inclosed a 11s. peece for your present paines.

To his ever honored
Friende Mr. Lilly
att the corner house
over against Strand
Bridge in
London.
post paid.

LETTER II.

VINCENT WING to WILLIAM LILLY.

Consultation on a Rubbery.—" Harmonicon Cœleste."

HONRED. MR. LILLY,

A WORTHY gentlewoman of this towne hath requested me to write a line unto you, concerning a great number of fine linnings, that was stolne in the night time, the last weeke, out of a private garden close under her house. And because shee much fancies Astrologie, I would desire you to give her your advise therein, and to write a line or two back, whether you thinke they bee recoverable, or not. I set one figure for the 1st question, but I forebore to give judgment, and the rather, because shee hath (not undeservedly) so good a confidence of you, and your writings, for which (I must say) we are all obliged to you. Good Sir, at her request, be pleased to honour her with a line, and shee protesteth to make you pl. of satisfaction, if ever it be in her power. Her husband is a Member of this Parliament, and one (I suppose) well knowne to you, and is a man that highly esteemes of your singular parts.

Sir, I have a little Tract of Astronomy now in the presse, printing in folio, under the title of "Harmonicon Cœleste." If you please in your Anglicus, 1651, to write a line in comendacon of it, I shall take it as no small kindeness, but because you know not before perusall, whether it deserve your notice, I shall procure some printed sheets for you, if I can, which I hope wili gaine your approbation and liking. Nay, I hope my Antagonist (your friend Mr. Shakerley) will give a better character of it, then hee did of V. P. I am already confident it will please his humor. The man, I verily thinke is well grounded in the fundamentalls of Astronomy, but for his Anatomy of V. P. there is in it more malice than matter, and nothing but what I well knew before Mr. Shakerley, and I hope my future endeavours will manifest what I am, yet I am sorrie time was so short with me at that time wee sent abroad Ens fictum Shakerlæi, but I hope his ingenuity is such hee tooke it not unkindly. But I wish him well, and should bee glad to heare from him now and then, yet which way to send I know not, in regard his place of residence is far remote from hence. Sir, being loath to trouble you further, I take leave and rest

Your very reall freind and servant,

VINCENT WING.*

* He was born in 1619, and is supposed to have died in 1668. Mr. Grainger, in his Biographical History, observes that the name of WING, though he has been so long dead, continues as fresh as ever at the head of our sheet almanacks, and advises that this motto should be affixed to his almanack, after his name:—

Illum aget *Penna* metuente solvi
Fama superstes. HOR.

Good Sir, bee not forgetfull of the former business.

North-Luffenham, in Rutland,
28° Julii, 1650.

For his honred freind Mr. Willm.
Lilly, at the Corner house over
against Strand-Bridge,
London, theise.

LETTER III.

Mr. RAY to Mr. JOHN AUBREY.*

Aubrey's History of Wiltshire.—And on several Subjects of Natural History.

Black Notley, 7ber 22, [16]91.

SIR,

THESE are to acquaint you that I have received not only your letter, dated at

* John Aubrey was a gentleman-commoner of Trinity College, Oxford. He procured a drawing of the Remains of Oseney Abbey, (which was etched by Hollar,) for Dugdale's "Monasticon," to which he contributed considerable assistance. The "Natural History of the North Division of Wiltshire," the work mentioned in this letter, was never finished. It appears from some MS. notes, written by himself, and now in the Bodleian Library, that he was born at

Oxford, 7br. 15, by post, but also your Manuscript History of Wiltshire, by Carrier which I read over with great pleasure and satisfaction. You doe so mingle *utile dulci*, that the book cannot but take with all sorts of readers; and it's pity it should be suppressed; which though you make a countenance of, I cannot persuade myself you really intend to do. I find but one thing that may give any just offence, and that is the Hypothesis of the Terraqueous globe, wherewith I must confesse my self not to be satisfied. But that is but a digression, and aliene from your subject, and so may very well be left out. I find little in the phrase or expression to except against. I am not critick enough to censure any man's writings. Some words I have noted, that doe not sound well to my ears. You are not ignorant how Mr. Boyle hath been κωμωδȣμενος for some new-coyned words, such as *ignore* and *opine*. Cæsar, I think, saith that *verbum insolens tanquam scopulum fugiendum est.* I'll name you one or two, to *apricate, suscepted, vesicate, continently* put as opposite to *incontinently.* I observed some particulars to be repeated, but that is excusable in such a work, and there may be reason enough to warrant it. A great number of *lacunæ* there are which you must endeavour to

Easton Piers, Wilts, March 12, 1625-6. Hearne says that he died, "as nearly as can be conjectured, in 1700."

fill up as far as you can before it be published. Two things I desire satisfaction from you in. 1. Where Signor Cassini makes mention of the consummation of one of Jupiter's Satellites, whether in any printed book; and whether there is really any losse of one of those Satellites, or remarkable change of it into a Comet observed by any other? 2. What authority you have for fishes not being found in the deep seas? That fish will live a long time with water alone, and grow to a great bulk is clear by the experiment of Rondeletius. These particulars I may make use of, and therefore desire a full confirmation of them.

Please to return my service to Mr. Bobart,* and my very good friend Mr. Lloyd. They can

* Son of old Jacob Bobart, who succeeded his father as keeper of the Physic-garden, at Oxford. The following curious anecdote is told of him in one of Grey's notes on Hudibras, vol. i. p. 125. "He made a dead rat resemble the common picture of dragons, by altering its head and tail, and thrusting in taper sharp sticks, which distended the skin on each side till it mimicked wings. He let it dry as hard as possible. The learned immediately pronounced it a dragon; and one of them sent an accurate description of it to Dr. Magliabechi, librarian to the grand duke of Tuscany; several fine copies of verses were wrote on so rare a subject; but at last Mr. Bobart owned the cheat; however, it was looked upon as a master-piece of art; and, as such, deposited in the Museum."

satisfy you, that *Tilia vulgaris platyphyllos,* and *Tilia folio minore* are two really distinct species. *Sed vulgus non distinguit.* This latter, whatever those gentlemen you mention say, I believe, is to be found wild in England. The trees at Newhall are of the first kind, and were, I have heard, brought out of Holland.

I am very glad that Mr. Bobart hath been so diligent in observing and making a collection of Insects, he may give me much assistance in my intended Synopsis of our English Animals and Fossils, and contribute much to the perfecting of it. But this will be still a work of some years, and God knows whether I shall live to finish it. I rest

Sir,
Yours in all offices of love
and service,

JOHN RAY.

For Mr. John Aubrey
at Mr. White's the
Chymist in Holywell
in
Oxford.

LETTER IV.

From the same to the same.

Aubrey's Adversaria Physica,—and several subjects of Natural History.

SIR,

I RECEIVED your kind letter and generous present, for which I return you many thanks. Your reception and entertainment heer, was such as my meanenesse could afford, not such as your merit did exact, and were you not a philosopher, would rather need excuse, than deserve thanks. The best of it was a hearty welcome. Indeed, I think my self obliged to you, for honouring me so far as to be at the pains and expense of such a journey to see me, who could contribute so little to you.

Your *Adversaria Physica* I have read over once, but the variety and curiosity of the matter and observations is such that I cannot satisfy my self with a single reading. As for the Catts heads, all that I know of them I learn'd of you, and therefore can give you no light or information concerning them. But my ingenious friend and neighbour Mr. Allen, whom you saw heer, intends very suddainly to make a journey to Epsham* on purpose to inquire into, and examine all the ingredients of those waters. I understand, that in the earth about those wells of Epsham are found of the Selenites Rhomboides, which may communicate some quality to the waters. When he returns again and brings with him of those minerals and stones, I may be able to give you a better account.

The information concerning the Darters and Vultures, if it come not before Michaelmas, will come too late to be inserted in my *Synopsis Animal. Britann.* I never heard of any Vulture seen in England, I meane wild and at liberty. They tell of Eagles about Tiptree heath, that come over in summer time, and sometimes have bred thereabouts; and I understand that Totham is not far from thence.

Mr. Dale returns his humble service to you, so doth my wife and young girls, who are indeed much pleased with the glasse microscope. We shall be careful to inquire concerning ancient coyns or medals found hereabouts, though they are but rarely met with in this country.

I am very glad that so ingenious a person as Mr. Doody is made Keeper of the Garden at Chelsey. I doubt not but he will answer the expectation men have of him, and much promote botanicks.

* Epsom.

I thank you for your good wishes, and rest, Sir,

Your obliged friend and humble
Servant,

JOHN RAY.

Black Notley,
Aug. 24, [16]92.

LETTER V.

Mr. TANNER to Mr. J. AUBREY.

Posthumous Works.—History of Wiltshire.

WORTHY SIR,

I GIVE you many thanks for your kind letter, which I received about a week since, but being extraordinary busy in performing some exercise required by the Colledge for my Batchelor's degree (which I take next term) I could not answer you sooner. I was heartily sorry to hear of your affliction by that tormenting disease the gout; but was more troubled at that you told me at the bottom of your letter, viz. that you were so far stricken in years. I have seen, heard, and read of the notorious misfortunes that usually attend posthumous papers, so that I hope you will make haste, and yourself communicate the greatest and best part of your laborious collections to the world; I'll assure you there shall no industry be lacking on my part, if you please to command it in any thing whatsoever. I highly approve and commend your thoughts of sending your Natural History of Wilts hither. I shall long to see it, and will do the utmost of my endeavours to get it printed; and dare engage for Mr. Lloyd's assistance therein, whom you know to be excellent in that part of learning. I hope you will be as good as your word about your *Remains of Gentilism,* I liked the subject, from the first time I heard of it, and I promise you if we get it among us, we will quickly put it into a method. One thing I must beg of you on my own account; which is, that you would be pleased to let me have your *Wiltshire Antiquities* (if it be but for a month) seeing they will be of extraordinary use in guiding me in the gathering of my Collections, which I intend to fall to with all the diligence and speed imaginable. I have not spoke with Mr. Clements of late; he told me about 3 weeks since, that he would subscribe for 14 himself; he will be at London at Whitsuntide, so that I suppose it will be convenient for you to talk with him about it: you may hear if he is in town of Mr. Smith, or any of the Booksellers; I will also acquaint him where you lodge. I was desired by a particular friend to enquire of you whether you have, or where you have seen any coins, or any other antiquities relating to the kingdom of the Northumbers, for there is a reverend person eminent for his skill in Antiquities, (Mr. Nicholson, Archdeacon of Carlisle,) that hath made great progress in illustrating the History of that Country: so that if you would be so kind as to acquaint me with any such thing, you will in an extraordinary manner oblige my friend, and that worthy person the Undertaker (he is Mr. Archer's uncle) who (I do not question) would be very ready to communicate any thing of the like nature to you. All your friends at Queen's give their service to you. So wishing you health and good success, I rest,

Sir,

Your most affectionate friend to serve you in all practicable commands,

THO. TANNER.

Qu. Coll. Oxon.
May 10, 1693.

I desire you to let me hear from you as soon as you can about your Wiltshire Antiquities. If you can spare them, I will order the Waggoner to call for them in a short time. I shall scorn to be like Ant. Wood, viz. make use of your papers and acquaintance and at last not afford you a good word: your entire originalls shall be deposited hereafter in the Musæum according to your desire, that posterity may see how just we have been to the memory of your pains.

LETTER VI.

Mr. BYROM to Mr. AUBREY.

On the custom of Salting at Eton.

Stanton, Nov. 15, [16]93.

HONOURED SIR,

I THANK you for the favour of yours of the 8th of this instant. I could send you a long answer to your Quæres, but have not the confidence to do it, for all that I can say was only heard from others, when I was at school at Eaton, and if I should depend upon that, perhaps, I should make too bold with truth. 'Twas then commonly said, that the college held some lands by the custome of salting, but having never since examined it, I know not how to answer for it. One would think at first view, considering the foundation was designed for a nursery of the Christian Religion, and has not bin in being much above 250 years, that it is not likely any remain of the Gentils relating to their sacrifices should in so public a manner be suffered in it; however, I cannot but own with those that understand any thing of antiquity, that the Christians very early assumed some rites of the Heathens; and probably it might be done with this design, that the nations seeing a religion which in its outward shape was something like their own, might be the sooner persuaded to embrace it. To be free, Sir, with you, I am apt to believe, for the honour of that society of which I was once an unworthy member, that the annual custome of salting alludes to that saying of our Saviour to his disciples, *ye are the salt of the earth,* for as salt drys up all that matter that tends to putrefaction, so it is a symbol of our doing the like in a spiritual state, by taking away all natural corruption. I might enlarge here, but I know to whom I write. However, if this will not please, why may it not denote that wit and knowledge, by which boys dedicated to learning ought to distinguish themselves?* You know what *Sal* sometimes signifyes among the best Roman authors. *Publius Scipio omnes sale facetiisque superabat.* Cic. and Terent. *Qui habet salem qui in te est.* I will not trouble you

* There have been various conjectures relative to the origin of this custom. Some have supposed that it arose from an ancient practice among the friars of selling consecrated salt; and others, with more probability, from the ceremony of the *bairn* or *boy*-bishop, as it is said to have been formerly a part of the montem-celebration for prayers to be read by a boy dressed in the clerical habit.

with more at present, but when I have better considered your Quæres, you may, if you please, have a particular answer to them. I cannot, Sir, but commend your design, which looks back into the ruins of ancient time, and would willingly have a sight of truth, which lyes buried under it.

I am, Sir,
Your most humble Servt.
J. BYROM.

LETTER VII.

Mr. TANNER to Mr. J. AUBREY.

Monumenta Britannica.—History of Wiltshire.—Camden.

WORTHY SIR,

I RECEIVED yours of Nov. 8th which I could not then possibly answer (having a country stranger in town, on whom I was forced to attend) and not long after I heard that you were gone to London, where I could not tell whither to direct it for you. But having heard lately from my brother, he told me my father gave you the trouble of a letter to him, so that I have sent this to him, hoping that it may come safe to your hands.

I have spent some thoughts upon your business of printing the first part of your *Monumenta Britannica,** and I must crave leave to tell you, that it will be more for your interest (which I heartily wish I could promote in this, or in any thing else) and every jot as honourable for you to abridge it all, and print it in about 40 sheets, which will make a very fair octavo or quarto And indeed I cannot apprehend, except the other parts be a great deal larger than this I have by me, how the whole can amount to the number of sheets promised in the proposalls. But this I take to be the cheapest way for your self, and if so, you may afford it at a lower price, and the cheaper a book is, the more buyers it will have. In a second impression you may encrease it to what bulk you please. These are my own private thoughts, what Mr. Gibson's sentiments in this matter are, I do not know; he is a great judge in these matters, and a well wisher to all good designs. When you print it in this, or any other method, if I can serve you in any thing I hope you know that you may command my time.

You promised to send me your other parts of your Monumenta, and your Natural History of Wilts, as soon as you came to London, but I

* Monumenta Britannica, or a Discourse concerning Stone-henge; and the Rollrich-stones, in Oxfordshire. This was never printed.

suppose you have altered your mind on hearing that I am engaged in Camden; which I confess is true, and I should not have conceal'd it so long from you if I had thought (which I did not a month since) it would have gone on, or at least that I should have [any] thing to do in it. But since it is so, you need not fear my playing the plagiary with your MSS. tho' I must excuse your jealousy of such a thing, Antony Wood having dealt so ungenteely by you.* Yet if you will take the word of him that hath done all that led in his power since he hath had the honour to be known to you, to approve himself your true friend, there shall be no injustice done you upon the perusall of your papers. Nay, farther, suppose I should prove never so false (of which I hope you will not entertain the least thought) what great harm can I do you in one single sheet, for that will be all I shall have in that volume. And I think nothing can raise the expectation of the world more, than to quote two or three curious

* Aubrey, in a very friendly letter to Wood, dated Sept. 2, 1694, and preserved in the Bodleian Library, reproaches him for having "cut out a matter of forty pages out of one of his volumes, as also the Index." He concludes—"I thought you so dear a friend, that I might have entrusted my life in your hands; and now your unkindness doth almost break my heart. You cannot imagine how much your unkindness vext and discomposed me, So God bless you. Tuissimus, A."

remarks out of a book with respect to the author. But this is not my business with your MSS. only I thought that I must prevent this objection which you might naturally raise, for indeed I have by me at present (beside your Wiltshire Antiquities) above 100 sheets relating to the History of Wilts, (which indeed I have collected toward the completing your Antiquities) so that I shall not want materials to fill four pages. But tho' there be some things in your books which I would willingly see, yet the principal reason why I send for them, is to pleasure you more than my self. For I am now going through a course of all our English Historians (a public design of which you shall hear farther, when it is come to greater maturity) so that if I knew the particulars you treat of, I might be capable of collecting a great many things, which might be very pertinently added to your book. If upon this or any other consideration you can venture to trust your papers in my hands, I would desire you to send them as soon as you can, and in so doing you will mightily oblige

Your faithful Servant,

THO. TANNER.

Qu. Coll. Oxon.
Dec. 26, [16]93.

LETTER VIII.

From the same to the same.

Natural History of Wiltshire.

WORTHY SIR,

I RECEIVED your letter of the 5th instant in due time, and your Natural History of Wiltshire on Saturday last I return you a thousand thanks, for that I have the favour and trust to peruse them I hope you never had the least reason to suspect my integritie and love to you, ever since I had the honour to be known to you, and I shall take care to preserve the good opinion you have of me, by making no use of your MSS. but to your honour. In your letter you mention a box, wherein were besides your Natural History other MSS. and things, but I received nothing but your Natural History of Wiltshire, and a sheet or two containing printed proposals concerning a general fishery, on the back of which is written with your own hand, *For the Musæum.* There were some printed books came down in the box you sent me (of your other MSS.) which I carefully keep for your use. As for your Natural History of Wiltshire you shall have it return'd you again in a fortnight's time if you please. I have already read over the first part with incredible satisfaction, and have taken the boldness to add some remarks of my own. There [is] one thing that I thought fit to acquaint you with, that is, there is now printing here a Catalogue of all the MSS. belonging to the University, and all private Colleges, in which will be a Catalogue of the MSS. in the Museum, so that you may consider whether it would not be for your greater honour to give your MSS. before the Catalogue is printed, they will make a more honourable mention of you.

This is all at present from (in haste)

Your most affectionate friend
and oblig'd Servant,

TH. TANNER.

Qu. Coll. Oxon.
Feb. 15, [16]93-4.

No. II.

AN ACCOUNT OF MY JOURNEY TO WHADDON-HALL, IN BUCKS, Ao. 1716.*

From HEARNE's MS. DIARIES, in the Bodleian Library, Vol. 61, Page 59.

HAVING for many years been importuned by my excellent friend, Browne Willis, Esq. (who is Grandson to the famous Physician Dr. Thomas Willis) to come over to his Seat of Whaddon Hall, near Fenny-Stratford, in the County of Bucks, I at last came to a Resolution of making a journey thither, and accordingly I set out on foot on Friday morning, somewhat before five o'clock, being May the fourth, in the year one thousand, seven hundred, and sixteen, and I look upon this Journey as one of the happy occurrences of my Life, as I afterw[ds] upon my return home, acquainted this Gentleman's Lady

* See Page 18, of this Volume.

the virtuous and ingenious Mrs. Katharine Willis.

Just after I set out, beyond St. Clement's Church, Oxford, I overtook an old man, one whom I have often seen before, and who is a very great Admirer of Antiquities. He went part of the way with me, and took occasion to talk of Aldworth, near Ilsley, in Berks, which is a very old Church, but small, in which are many ancient monuments, bigger than the life, without inscriptions. They are commonly called Gyants, tho' they are only monuments of some of the De la Beaches, a knightly family, exstinct before Edw. IIId's. time. So the Church must be very old. They had a Castle here. I have not yet seen the place. The old man talked much about them. And he was so pleased with what I remark'd that he would have went on with me much farther, if business would have permitted.

Having never been in the Church of Stanton St. Johns, 3 miles from Oxford, I took occasion to view it now. There is nothing of Antiquity in it. I saw in the Chancell a monument of white marble erected on the wall to the memory of Mr. Lawrence Squibb, Bach. of the Civ. Law and fellow of New Coll. and Rector of this Church. There is a long Epitaph on it in Latin in praise of his learning and virtues. He died on the 21st of Sept. an. 1710, æt. 68. Twas put up by his grand daughters Mrs. Ann and Agatha

Squibb. I saw also in the Chancell three other white marble monuments, namely, one to the memory of Mrs. Judith Price, who died Oct. 7, 1709, æt. 62, another to the memory of Mrs. Frances Squibb, mother of the said Mrs. Judith Price, and wife of Mr. Rob. Squibb. She was mother of 12 children, and was widow above 28 years. She died Oct. 7, 1695, æt. 82. The third of the said white marble monum^{ts} is to the memory of Mrs. Anne Mann, sister of John White, Esqr She died Sept. 30, an. 1703, æt. 35. Besides wch monum^{ts} I saw a brass plate fixed in a wall of the Chancell to the memory of Wm. Pudsey, Gent. who died Feb. 14, 1658, æt. 56. This Stanton is a pleasant place, and very healthy. The famous Robt Boyle, Esq. preferr'd the air of Garsington and Stanton to any other.

From Stanton I went through a fine common, called Stanton Common, on each side of which are very pleasant Woods, to Brill, or Burgh on the Hill, very pleasantly situated. It is a very pretty village. There is a great house much in decay. Here was a Castle, as 'tis supposed in the Roman times. Many Roman Coyns have been found here. Mr. Willis shew'd me one of Commodus found at Ashenton, near this place. It is of the bigger sort, and is of Brass, on the reverse is figura muliebris stans, sinistra clypeum. It relates to a battle.

Leaving Brill I pass'd by Wotton, through

the Common, where is a very fine new house of the Greenvils, in which is very curious painting done by one Thornhill, a good artist, now living. This is the same Thornhill that hath done the fine Altar Piece, in All Souls Coll. Chapell, and the Painting in the new Chapell at Queen's Coll. This house at Wotton is badly situated; but as well as could be in such a place. There are good fish ponds belonging to it.

After I had left Wotton, I went on towards Winslow, and observed many fine woods by the way I did not keep the direct road, but went some miles about on the left hand. Winslow is a pretty good markett town, and is tolerably well situated. I did not stop to see any thing, but went on to Whaddon, passing through pt. of the chace. I read most pt. of the way from Oxford to Whaddon the *Scriptores Historiæ Augustæ*, it being my custom in my walks to read some book.

Whaddon is very pleasantly situated upon an hill, from whence there is a fine prospect. Mr. Willis's house is a little without the town on the north side. He happened to be from home, about two miles off, when I came thither, but his Lady was extraordinary kind, and took particular care that I should be received with all possible civility. She is a fine ingenious woman; but being indisposed, and thereby confined to her chamber, she could not stir down herself. However she took effectual method that I should be entertained in as decent a manner as if she had been present herself.

Mr. Richard Rawlinson, of St. John's College, in Oxford, happened to be at Whaddon at the same time I took my journey. He went over the Monday before, and went away upon Saturday morning, the day after I came. He went on purpose to visit Mr. Willis, and to extract some things out of Mr. Willis's Collections, in order to improve a design about the History of Eton College. He found several things to his purpose.

The next day, being Saturday, after I came to Whaddon I walk'd over to Blechley, two miles from Whaddon, which is a rectory of about 300lbs. per annum, and is in the presentation of Mr. Willis. He hath built a large fine house here of brick, which cost him several* thousand pounds. The Church is very neat and handsome, and hath a ring of eight very good bells. These bells were founded at Mr. Willis's own charge, who likewise laid much out in adorning and repairing the Church, in all, to the value of about twelve hundred pounds. Mr. Willis ordered the bells to be rung at my coming to Blechley. They rung two good peals. He told them it was

* Hearne had originally written "about *three* thousand pounds," which he afterwards altered to *several*.

because the Oxford Antiquary was come. Such is his affection to me.

Whaddon, as well as Blechley, is within Whaddon Chace, which is reckoned to be about 10 miles in circuit. There are some other villages within it. About two furlongs on the east side of Mr. Willis's house at Whaddon, are the Ruins of the Priory of Snelshall, which was a very small thing, being valued for no more, according to Dugdale, (at the Dissolution) than 18*l*. 1*s*. 11*d*. per an. but according to Speed at 24*l*.

The said Priory was of Black Monks, and was founded in the 12th year of K. Hen. IIId. as I gather from Mr. Willis's Collections. The founder was Ralph Martell, and it was dedicated to St. Leonard. The Surrender at the Dissolution was signed only by 3 Monks. The last Prior was Nich. Maltby.

It had a church, whereof none of the Ruins now remain. For the four* Arches in the south wall of the farm house (which three Arches are the only remains of the Priory) do not seem to have been part of the Chapell, but either of some Cloysters, or at least of the Buttery or Kitchen. But conjectures are very uncertain.

Mr. Willis's MS. Collections are very consi-

* Hearne had originally written *three*, and probably forgot to correct the number in the next line.

derable, and much surpass my expectation. He hath been at a great charge on that account. I am of opinion, that he hath rather too much than too little for the Antiquities of Bucks, which is an undertaking he hath been engaged in several years, though diverted from so vigorous a prosecution as I could wish by other affairs.

Among other pictures, I saw at his house these following, which I took particular notice of, viz. (1) Archbp. Dolben, by Sir P. Lilly, a most excellent piece. (2) An old Picture done upon wood, found at Snelshall Priory, above mentioned. This picture, which is a very great curiosity, represents our Saviour, St. John, and St. Peter. (3) A large Draught of Ipswich, by Ogilby, which I do not remember to have seen before. (4) A large Draught of the South Prospect of York Cathedral, done with a Pen. (5) A Picture of Bp. Fell. (6) Mr. Willis's own Picture, done excellently well by Daul, and by it is his Lady's also, done some years since, I do not know by what hand; but it is a good picture.

As I cursorily run over Mr. Willis's Collections I found a note in one of them, that not one of the Monks of Snelshall was found incontinent at y[e] Dissolution, and that there were at that time 8 servants there, besides the Prior's Father and Mother, who brought all their goods to the said Priory, in hopes of having their living there. At the same time I also met with another note, signifying, that it does not appear at the Dissolution that (so far as we have surveys) there were any of the Religious found incontinent, in the County of Bucks, excepting one Nun at Ankerwike; which is a very considerable argument to me of the virtues of the Religious.

I saw only two old MSS. at Mr. Willis's. The first of which is a Folio Bible in Vellum of the vulgar Latin Translation, towards the beginning of which is this Note: *Hunc librum dedit magister* Johannes Rudyng, *archidiaconus* Lincoln. *cathenand.̃ in principali disco infra cancellum ecclesiæ suæ præbendal.̄ de* Buckyngham *ad usum Capellanorum & aliorum ibidem in eodem studere volencium quam diu duraverit.* Just by is another Note in Capitals, viz. FVNDATOR CANCELLORUM, signifying that he was founder of the Chancell where the Library was built, which consisted of several Stalls or Desks of Books, the word *discus* being the same in signification in this place with *pluteus.* There is also another Note written likewise in a later hand, which shews y[t] the said Rudyng was y[e] founder of y[e] said Chancell, & withall it points out to us the time in wch he lived. It is this: *Johannes Rudyng collatus fuit ad Archi-diaconatum Lincoln̄ & Præbendam de Sutton cum Buckingham Aug.* 6. 1471. *Moriebatur* 1481. In another

Leaf of the Book are the s[d] Rudyng's Arms.*

And 'tis remarkable, that there are Escallops and a Crescent to be seen at this time in the Windows of the Church, and they are also carved in Stone on the outside of the wall.

[As Hearne has left nearly ten pages blank in his MS. volume, it is probable that he intended to continue this account of his Whaddon Journey.]

* Hearne has drawn the Arms with a pen, in a very rough manner. They consist of six escalops and a crescent, with the Motto—" May God All Amend."

No. III.

AN ACCOUNT OF T. HEARNE's JOURNEY TO READING AND SILCHESTER, 1714.

From HEARNE's MS. DIARIES. in the Bodleian Library. Vol. 50, Page 104.

1714, May 22, Saturday.

On Sunday morning last, being Whitsunday, I rode over very early in the morning to Reading, and taking with me the 2d. volume of Leland's Itinerary, I examined many particulars that that excellent antiquary hath noted, and found every thing to be so exact, that I have every day a much better opinion of his great industry, care, learning, and judgment. He tells us "that at the north end of Causham Bridge, as we come from Reading, there stondith a fair old Chapelle of stone on the right hand, piled in the foundation for the rage of the Tamise." I could find nothing of this Chapelle, but was told that there was lately built a new house (which I saw) where it stood, and that remains of an old building were taken up where the said house was erected.* I went to Reading on purpose to renew my acquaintance with the Ruins of the Abbey. I took particular notice of all the Remains of it, and am inclined to think that the old Castle certainly stood where this Abbey was afterwards placed, for tho' from the name of Castle Street, some would imagine that it stood in that street somewhere, yet I believe that street was so denominated from some inn of note, that carried the sign of the Castle.

Mr. Leland also observes that there is a Park coming into Reading town, belonging to the late Monasterie there. I made enquiry after this Park, but they told me there was no other Park now than Whitley Park, (commonly called Whitley Farm) about a mile south from the town.

The town of Reading is very pleasantly situated, and it is large, but nothing near so famous now for cloathing as it was formerly. The houses are very mean, and the streets, tho' pretty large, unpaved. The occasion of the houses being so mean is this. The greatest part of them belong to one Blagrave, and his interest in them being only for lives, there is no likelihood of their being rebuilt as yet. The names of the

* See Page 72 of this Volume.

streets are Broad Street, London Street, Fryers Street, Castle Street, and Minster Street.

At the north end of Castle Street, as Mr. Leland observes, is the Grey Fryers. A good part of the Chapel is now standing. It serves as a Bridewell. 'Twas built cross-ways, tho the east and north wings of the cross are wanting.

The Ruins of the Abbey (to which Minster Street leads) are very large and many. One part of them they call the Hall, which was the place where they dined; and by it was the Church. They lately dug up bones in the Ruins, a broad piece, and some other money. The Church was built in form of a cross, and it had a spire.

From Reading the next morning I rode over to Silchester, in Hampshire, being about eight miles from Reading, Leland says [Itin. Vol. viii. Part i. p. 19.] a VI miles or more. When I came there, I had the curiosity to walk quite round the walls, which they there say are about three miles in compass, tho' Leland says they are about 2 miles only, and he is followed by Camden. [Brit. Ed. opt. p. 195.] and Stowe [Annals. ed. fol. p. 53.] both which have transcribed Leland's account, as they have in several other particulars. Indeed Mr. Camden (to do him justice) hath improved his account with some learned observations, but Stowe hath not added any thing, but taken the very words of Leland in his relation of

Silchester, yet without the least acknowledgment, and as little acknowledgment does he make in a great many other places, which are nevertheless wholly owing to Leland, tho' the greatest piece of his ingratitude was shewed by him in his Survey of London, a very great part of which, I am really persuaded, is to be ascribed to Leland, particularly such things and observations as concern the most ancient state thereof, and what was chiefly translated before Stowe's time, who had not learning enough to extract and make use of any ancient Latin Records.

The Walls are still about four yards in thickness. They are so intire that there is hardly any breach, excepting where the four gates were. They are still in height, in some places, six or seven yards, Leland says only six or seven foot, and so Stowe. But I believe this is a mistake in Mr. Stowe's transcript for yards, and I had only the use of Mr. Stowe's transcript in that particular, the original in that place being wanting The upper part of the walls which contained the battlements and the towers, is quite wanting, having been beat down I suppose at the same time when the City was destroyed. The walls are built of slates and flint, which are so wrought in and fastened with the mortar, that it is a thing almost impossible to pull or beat the walls down, the mortar being as firm as the flints themselves. Now and then a free stone appears in the walls, but that is seldom. The ground within the walls lyes even with the walls themselves, having been filled up so by the rubble and ruins of the city, but withoutside the ground is very much lower, insomuch that the walls are in height in some places six or seven yards, as I said before. There was a very deep ditch or trench that went all round the walls, which is now very visible, and a great part of it is still full of water. It was about 40 yards in breadth. Among the rubble very often appear Roman and British bricks. I say British as well as Roman, because the Britains made the same sort of bricks, having learned the art from the Romans, and especially in this place, which was a defence to the Britains against the Saxons, after the Romans were gone.

Before the west gate, there is at a considerable distance an Agger, or raised work, that was made for defence of the city, when it was beseiged on that side, as there is another raised work or mount on the north-east side, made also upon the same account when the seige happened from the enemy that lay on Mortimer's heath. It is very certain, that considering the strength of the walls, the city must have been impregnable during the stay of the Romans, who built this place about the time of Constantine the Great.

* * * * * * * *

[Some of the narrative is here omitted, as being particularly dry and uninteresting.]

And as I take the honorary monument to Constantius to have stood on the south side of the wall, so I believe the south part of the city was the most principal and considerable of the whole, and that the Emperors, and Princes, and Generals, and other great men used to lodge in that part whenever they had occasion to reside here for any time, and that which makes me guess so chiefly is, that not far from the south gate, in the south field, as they term it, they found not long ago a tesselated pavement, very large, but miserably broken, which I suppose was an ornament of the principal room of the palace. Whether there were any figures upon it, as there are on that of Stunsfield, I cannot learn; but whether there were or not, I believe it was hardly so curious in all respects, tho' being done much about the same time, we are to imagine that the manner of laying the tessellæ, and the tempering the mortar, was the same in both. So that the palace being in this part of the city, 'tis probable that King Arthur, after the city fell to the Britains, was crowned in the same place; for that he was crowned at Silchester we have the authority of some of our historians, and there is no reason to doubt but, that as the Britains after the Romans held this place and preserved it, so they made use of the same part of it that they did for a court or palace.

I say, as the Britains held this place after the Romans; for tho' the Romans had deserted the Isle, yet they had thoughts of returning again, and therefore, tho' they destroyed several of their buildings, such, I mean, as were of a less consideration, and hid their coyns, yet such cities and towns as were very strong and remarkable they did not demolish, but left them in possession of the Britains, who had a great honour for the Romans, and were extremely sorry when they relinquished the Isle, and left them exposed to the insults and invasions of the Saxons. The Romans were willing to trust the Britains, and therefore they left them in possession of their fortifications, not doubting but that they would willingly resign them if ever they returned again. They knew withall the strength and power of the Saxons and their other enemies, and that the Britains would be easily subdued, unless they were defended by such strong places as Silchester. So that the Britains being now to play their own part, they laid in provisions in all the cities, towns, and castles that were of chiefest note, and particularly here at Silchester, which was of such extraordinary strength, that 'twas impossible almost to force it, or to make a breach in the walls.

Now, as 'tis plain to me, that the Britains had possession of this extraordinary place after the Isle had been deserted by the Romans, so I cannot but think that they built and repaired many of the houses after it came into their own hands. And I am, withall, of opinion, that even whilst the Romans themselves had it, the Britains were also employed in those buildings as were judged necessary either for convenience and pleasure, or for an additional strength to the place, in order the better to keep off the enemy. For these reasons many of the bricks found up and down here are to be called British, tho' I know that some will not allow any of this kind of bricks found in England to be British, as if the Britains were not capable of making such kind of bricks. I will indeed allow that when the Romans came first hither, the Britains led such a life as did not require such works as were made use of by the Romans, nor had they therefore learned the art of building. But after the Isle had been conquered and subdued by the Romans, there is no reason to think that they continued as ignorant during this period of time as they were before. No, we are to imagine that as the Britains were ingenious, so they learned of the Romans, and that many of them were excellent architects, and could work as well as many of the Romans themselves, and that therefore Leland, Somner, and the best antiquaries have not erred in calling many of these old bricks, British bricks.

I am farther of opinion, that several expert Britains amongst the Romans were made use of when the city was first begun by Constantine, and afterwards finished by his son Constantius, and that the Romans pitched upon this place, surrounded with woods, for erecting a city on, purely out of regard to the Britains, who, like the Gauls, delighted to have their buildings seated within woods, as I have lately observed in my letter to Mr. Thoresby, at the end of the 1st Vol. of Leland's Itin. § 3. And to what else can we attribute the great oaks growing upon the walls of Silchester, but the Britains taking pleasure in woods and groves? They thought there was something extraordinary in the oak, and that this tree had power to protect and defend them. Yet after all I can[not] say and affirm, that the oaks were first of all planted upon the walls, but it seems rather to have been merely accidental after the city was destroyed, and the rubble and dirt scattered and laid upon the remains of the walls, after the battlements and pinnacles of them had been beat and thrown down. But that which seems most strange is, that young oaks should continually spring and grow up upon the walls, as they certainly do, even when one would think it was impossible for any thing whatsoever to grow. Many of the oldest oaks were lately cut down, but then there is a vast number of young ones coming up in their stead, as I observed particularly when I was there, to my great astonishment.

How long this city continued before 'twas demolished, after the Romans had left the Isle, is very uncertain. Mr. Camden is of opinion (Brit. p. 195) that 'twas not destroyed till after the year 900, and that the person that did it was Adelwolf, or Adhelwold, brother to Edward the Elder. This Adelwolf had revolted from his brother, and had taken part with the Danes, and had committed strange disorders with him, by ravaging the country and burning and throwing down many places, particularly in Hampshire, as well as elsewhere. But I must here dissent from this great man, and beg leave to think that it was demolished much sooner. How comes it otherwise to pass that we hear nothing of it in the Saxon Chronicle, and other authors? Is it likely that had this place stood so long, that it should not be noted in these old Annals and other Records? Methinks a place of such strength and of such considerable note (it having been once a Bishoprick, as I should have noted before, as well as very eminent under the Romans and Britains) could not have been passed over by the Saxons, and be looked upon as a mean inconsiderable place, when on the contrary Kings-cleare, not far off, and a town of much less account, was much regarded by them, and was one of the seats of the Saxon Kings, as Mr. Camden himself hath observed.

Upon this account I believe this city was destroyed by the Saxons, and not by the Danes, and this happened, in my opinion, soon after the death of K. Arthur. For tho' this great King vanquished the Saxons in divers set battles, and kept them under as long as he lived, yet after his death they strangely prevailed, having always fresh supplies from their own country, and they got Silchester, and a great many other strong holds into their hands. And after they had made these conquests, for fear the Britains should recover them again, they quite demolished them, and built others in other places in a much slighter manner, which were more agreeable to their own rude and unpolished education. Yet tho' they destroyed the city of Silchester, they did not think fit entirely to demolish the walls, thinking that 'twas enough that by the rubbish, they had made the ground within equal to what of them remained, and that they could not afterwards be any better security to the Britains, than any other ground that is raised by art, and afterwards fortifyed with a trench, of which there is much in England. But leaving this point, I must now observe, that notwithstanding the vast quantities of rubbish buried within the walls, towards harvest, when the corn is almost ripe, it is not difficult to discover the very traces of the streets of the city, by the different condition of the corn; that which stands where the streets were, quite decaying as it were, and the other continuing in good case. And the way for the Rampart on the west side quite to the west gate may be discovered by the same circumstances. As I' was walking on the east side of the wall in the trench, just under the wall, I came to a tumulus or barrow, in one part of which as they were digging in the year 1713, they found the head, skull, and bones of a man, 9 feet in length, which they think there (as is usual with the vulgar on such occasions) to have been the bones of a gyant

The Church of Silchester stands just within the wall, and by it is a farm-house (being the only house within the walls) and here it was that the East gate of the city was. I went into the church, but found only one piece of antiquity in it (excepting a little painted glass) and that is the figure of a lady lying at full length in the south wall, being the effigies, as I take it, of one of the Blueths, to whom the Manor of Silchester some years after the Conquest belonged. The Manor now belongs to the Lord Blesington, an Irish peer, being purchased by him of the Lady Draper, Relict of Sir Tho. Draper, Kt. and Bart.

And as there are no old inscriptions in the Church, so there is only one modern one, and that is on a monument of white marble erected in the north wall of the chancel, and is as follows:

This Monument was erected by the Lord | and Lady Blesinton in Memory of their dear and | much beloved Grandson IAMES BUTLER Lord Viscount | IKERRIN, who died at London on the 19th day of July | 1712, aged 13 years and 7 months. | His Piety, Virtue, Goodness, and Knowledge in Religion | and Learning did infinitely exceed his years and rendered | his Quality the least part of his Character. He lyes | interred near this Stone, and was the only child of | PIERCE Lord Viscount IKERRIN by ALICIA BOYLE | Lady Viscountess IKERRIN, both deceased and | buried in Ireland. |

Immodicis brevis est ætas, et sera senectus.

No. IV.

LIVES OF EMINENT MEN,

BY JOHN AUBREY.

Selected, and now first published, from the original Manuscripts in the ASHMOLEAN MUSEUM.

To my worthy friend Mr. ANTHONIE à WOOD,
Antiquarie of Oxford.

SR.

I HAVE, according to your desire, putt in writing these Minutes of LIVES tumultuarily, as they occur'd to my thoughts: or as occasionally I had information of them. They may easily be reduced into order at yr. leisure by numbring them with red figures, according to time and place, &c. 'Tis a taske that I never thought to have undertaken till you imposed it upon me, sayeing that I was fitt for it, by reason of my generall acquaintance, having now not only lived above halfe a centurie of yeares in ye world, but have also been much tumbled up and downe in it; wch hath made me so well knowne. Besides the moderne advantage of coffee-howses in this great citie; before which men knew not how to be acquainted, but with their owne relations, or societies: I might add, that I come of a longævous race, by which meanes I have wiped some feathers off the wings of time for severall generations, wch does reach high. When I first began I did not thinke I could have drawne it out to so long a thread. I here lay downe to you (out of the conjunct* friendship between us) the trueth, the naked and plaine trueth, which is here exposed so bare that the very pudenda are not covered, and affords many passages that would raise a blush in a young virgin's cheeke. So that after your perusall, I must desire you to make a castration (as readers to Martial) and to

* Utrumque nostrûm incredibili modo
Consentit astrum.

HORAT. *Lib.* 2, *Od.* 17.

Nescio quod certe est, quod me tibi temperat, astrum.

PERS. *Satyr.* V. *v.* 51.

sowe on some figge leaves (i.e.) to be my *Index expurgatorius.*

What uncertainty doe we find in printed histories! They either treading too neer on the heeles of trueth, that they dare not speake plaine; or els for want of intelligence (things being antiquated) become too obscure and darke! I doe not here repeat any thing already published (to the best of my remembrance) and I fancy my selfe all along discourseing with you; alledgeing those of my relations and acquaintances (as either you knew or have heard of) *ad faciendam Fidem*: So that you make me to renew my acquaintance with my old and deceased friends, and to *rejuvenescere* (as it were) which is the pleasure of old men. 'Tis pitty that such minutes had not been taken 100 yeares since or more: for want wherof many worthy men's names and notions are swallow'd up in oblivion; as much of these also would, had it not been through your instigation: and perhaps this is one of the usefullest peeces that I have scribbled.

I remember one sayeing of Generall Lambert's, "*That the best of men are but men at the best*:" of this you will meet with divers examples in this rude and hastie collection. Now these *Arcana* are not fitt to lett flie abroad, till about 30 yeares hence; for the author and the persons (like medlars) ought to be rotten first. But in whose hands must they be deposited in the mean time? Advise me, who am,

Sr.

Your very affectionate friend

to serve you,

JOHN AUBREY.

London,
June 15,
1680.

SIR ROBERT AITON, KNIGHT.

He lies buried in the south aisle of the Choir of Westminster Abbey, where there is erected to his memory an elegant marble and copper monument.

His bust is of copper curiously cast with a laurell held over it by two fig. of white marble.

That Sr. Rob. was one of the best poets of his time: Mr. Jo. Dryden says he has seen verses of his, some of the best of that age, printed with some other verses.

He was acquainted with all the witts of his time in England. He was a great acquaintance of Mr. Thos. Hobbes, of Malmsbury, whom Mr. Hobbes told me he made use of (together with Ben Jonson) for an Aristarchus, when he made his Epistle dedicatory, for his translation of Thucydides. I have been told (I think by Sr. John himself) that he was eldest son to Sr. John Ayton, Master of the Black Rod, who was also an excellent scholar.

MR. THOMAS ALLEN

Was borne in Staffordshire. Mr. Theod. Haak, a German, R. Soc. Soc. was of Glocester Hall, 1626, and knew this learned worthy old gentleman, whom he takes to have been about ninety-six yeares old when he dyed, which was about 1630. The learned . . . . Reynolds who was turned Catholique by his brother the learned Dr. . . . . Reynolds, President of Corpus Xti Colledge, was of Glocester Hall then too, they were both neer of an age, and they dyed both within 12 moneths one of the other. He was at both their funeralls. Mr. Allen came into the hall to commons, but Mr. Reynolds had his brought to his chamber. He sayes that Mr. Allen was a very cheerfull, facetious man, and that every body loved his company, and every house on their *Gaudie-dayes* were wont to invite him. His picture was drawne at the request of Dr. Ralph Kettle, and hangs in the dining roome of the President of Trin. Coll. Oxon. (of which house he first was, and had his education there) by which it appeares that he was a handsome sanguine man, and of an excellent habit of bodie. There is mention of him in *Leicester's Commonwealth* that Dudley, the great Earle of Leicester made use of him for casting nativities, for he was the best astrologer of his time. He hath written a large and learned Commentary in folio, on the Quadripartite of Ptolemie, which Elias Ashmole hath in MS. fairly written, and I hope will one day be printed. In those darke times astrologer, mathematician, and conjurer, were accounted the same things, and the vulgar did verily believe him to be a conjurer. He had a great many mathematicall instruments and glasses in his chamber, which did also confirme the ignorant in their opinion, and his servitor (to impose on freshmen and simple people) would tell them that sometimes he should meet the spirits comeing up his staires like bees. One* of our parish† was of Glocester Hall about 70 yeares and more since, and told me this from his servitor. Now there is to some men a great lechery in lying, and imposing on the understandings of beleeving people, and he thought it for his credit to serve such a master. He was generally acquainted, and every long vacation, he rode into the countrey to visitt his old acquaintance and patrones, to whom his

* J. Power. † Kington.

great learning, mixt with much sweetness of humour, rendered him very welcome. One time being at Home Lacy, in Herefordshire, at Mr. John Scudamore's (grandfather to the Lord Scudamore) he happened to leave his watch in the chamber windowe—(watches were then rarities.) The maydes came in to make the bed, and hearinge a thing in a case cry *Tick, Tick, Tick,* presently concluded that that was his Devill, and tooke it by the string with the tongues, and threw it out of the windowe into the mote (to drowne the Devill.) It so happened that the string hung on a sprig of an Elder, that grew out of the mote, and this confirmed them that 'twas the Devill. So the good old gentleman gott his watch again. Sir Kenelm Digby loved him much, and bought his excellent library of him, which he gave to the University. I have a Stifelius Arithmetique that was his, which I find he had much perused, and no doubt mastered. He was interred in Trinity College Chapell, (the where, as I take it, the outer Chapell.) George Bathurst, B.D. made his funerall oration in Latin, which was printed. 'Tis pitte there had not been his name on a stone over him.

LAUNCELOT ANDREWES

Was borne in London, went to schoole at Merchant Taylers schoole. Mr. Mulcaster was his schoolemaster, whose picture he hung in his studie. Old Mr. Sutton, a very learned man of those dayes, of Blandford St. Maries, Dorset, was his school fellowe, and sayd that Launcelot Andrewes was a great long boy of 18 yeares old at least before he went to the university.* He was a fellowe of Pembroke-hall, in Cambridge (called Collegium Episcoporum, for that, at one time, in those dayes, there were of the house . . . bishops.) The Puritan faction did begin to increase in those dayes, and especially at Emanuel College. That party had a great mind to drawe in this learned young man, whom (if they could make shew) they knew would be a great honour to them. They carried themselves outwardly with great sanctity and strictnesse, so that 'twas very hard matter to —— as to their lives. They preached up very strict keeping and observing the Lord's day, and made upon the matter, damnation to breake it, and that 'twas lesse sin to kill a man. Yet these hypocrites did bowle in a private garden at an other colledge, every Sun-

* Mr. Sutton came to Ch. Ch. Oxon. at eleaven. He wrote much, but printed nothing but a little 8º against the Papists.

day after sermon, and one of the colledge (a loving friend to Mr. L. Andrewes) to satisfie him one time lent him the key of a private back dore for the bowling green, on a Sunday evening, which, he opening, discovered these zealous preachers, with their gownes off, at earnest play. But they were strangely surprized to see the entry of one that was not of the Brotherhood. There was then at Cambridge a good fatt alderman that was wont to sleep at Church, which the alderman endeavoured to prevent but could not. Well! this was preached against as a signe of *Reprobation.* The good man was exceedingly troubled at it, and went to Andrewes his chamber to be satisfied in point of conscience. Mr. Andrewes told him that [it] was an ill habit of body not of mind, and that it was against his will, advised him on Sundays to make a more sparing meale, and to mend it at supper. The alderman did so, but sleepe comes upon [him] again for all that, and was preached at. [He] comes againe to be resolved with teares in his eies—Andrewes then told him, he would have him make a good hearty meale as he was wont to doe, and presently take out his full sleep;—He did so, came to St Maries Church, where the preacher was prepared with a sermon to damme all who slept at sermon, as a certaine signe of *Reprobation.* The good alderman having taken his full nap before, lookes on the preacher all sermon time, and spoyld the designe. But I should have sayd that Andrewes was most extremely spoken against and preached against for offering to assoile or excuse a sleeper in sermon time. But he had learning and witt enough to defend himselfe. His great learning quickly made him known in the university, and also of King James, who much valued him for it, and advanced him, and at last made him Bp. of Winchester, which bishoprick he ordered with great prudence, as to government of the parsons, preferring of ingeniose persons that were staked to poore livings and did *delitescere*. He made it his enquiry to find out such men. Amongst severall others (whose names have escaped my memorie) Nicholas Fuller, minister of Allington neer Amesbury, in Wilts, was one. The bishop sent for him, and the poor man was afrayd and knew not what hurt he had done. He makes him sitt downe to dinner, and, after the desert, was brought in in a dish his institution and induction, or the donation of a prebend, which was his way. He chose out alwayes able men to his chaplaines, whom he advanced. Among others, ... Wren, of St. John's, in Oxon. was his chaplaine, a good generall scholar and good orator, afterwards deane of Winsore, from whom (by his son in lawe, Dr. W. Holder) I have taken this exact account of that excellent prelate. His Life is before his sermons, and also his epitaph, which see. He dyed at Winchester house, in Southwark, and lies buried in a chapell at St. Mary Overies, where his executors . . . . Salmon M.D. and Mr. John Saintlowe, merchant of London, have erected (but I believe according to his last will, els they would not have layen out 1000*l*.) a sumptuose monument for him. He had not that smooth way of oratory as now. It was a shrewd and severe animadversion of a Scotish lord, who, when K. James asked him how he liked Bp. A.'s sermon, sayd, that he was learned, but he did play with his text, as a Jack-an-apes does, who takes up a thing and tosses and playes with it, and then he takes up another, and playes a little with it—Here's a pretty thing, and there's a pretty thing!

WILLIAM AUBREY, DOCTOR OF LAWES.

(Extracted from a MS. in the hands of Sr. Henry St. George, marked thus . . . .* I guesse it to be the hand-writing of Sr. Daniel Dun, Kt. LL.D. who married Joane, 3d da. of Dr. Wm. Aubrey.)

" William Aubrey, the second son of Thomas
" Aubrey, the 4th son of Hopkin Aubrey, of
" Abercumvrig, in the county of Brecon, Esq. in
" the 66th year of his age or thereabouts, and
" on the 25th of June, in the year of our Lord

* [In the original Manuscript, is the figure of a heart. Editor]

" 1595, departed this life, and was buried in the " Cathedral Church of St. Paul, in London, on " the north side of the Chancel, over against " the tomb of Sr. Jno Mason, Knight, at the " base or foot of a great pillar standing upon " the highest step of certain degrees or stairs " rising into the Quire eastward from the same " pillar towards the tomb of the Right Hon. the " Lord William Earl of Pembroke, and his fu- " nerals were performed the 23rd of July, 1595.

" This gentleman in his tender years learned " the first grounds of grammar in the College of " Brecon, in Brecknock town, and from thence " about his age of fourteen years he was sent by " his parents to the University of Oxford, where, " under the tuition and instruction of one Mr. " Morgan, a great learned man, in a few years he " so much profited in humanity and other recom- " mendable knowledge, especially in Rhetoric and " Histories, as that he was found to be fit for " the study of the Civil Law, and thereupon was " also elected into the Fellowship of All Souls " College, in Oxford, where the same law hath " always much flourished, in which College he " earnestly studied and diligently applied himself " to the lectures and exercise of the House as " that he there attained the degree of a Doctor " of the Law Civil, at his age of 25 years, and " immediately after he had bestowed on him the " Q. Public Lecture of Law in the university, " the which he read with so great a commenda-

" tion, as that his fame for learning and know-
" ledge was spred far abroad, and he also es-
" teemed worthy to be called to action in the
" commonwealth. Wherefor, shortly after, he
" was made a judge marshall of the Queen's
" armies at St. Quintins in France, which warrs
" finished, he returned into England, and deter-
" mining with himselfe, in more peaceable man-
" ner, and according to his former education,
" to passe on the course of his life in the exer-
" cise of law, he became an advocate of the
" Arches, and so rested many yeares, but with
" such fame and credit as well for his rare skill
" and science in the law, as also for his sound
" judgment and good experience therein, as that
" of men of best judgment, he was generally
" accounted peerlesse in that facultie. Where-
" upon, as occasion fell out for implovment of a
" civilian, his service was often used as well
" within the realme as in forrein countries. In
" which imployments, he alwaies used such care
" and diligence and good circumspection, as that
" his valour and vertues dayly more appearing,
" ministred means to his further advancement.
" In soe much that he was preferred to be one
" of the councell of the Marches of Wales, and
" shortly after placed Master of the Chancery,
" and the appointed Judge of the Audience, and
" constituted Vicar Generall to the Lord Arch-
" bishop of . . . . . through the whole province,

" and last, by especiall grace of the Queene's " most excell^{t} ma^{tie} Q. Elizabeth, he was taken " to her highnesse nearer service and made one " of the Masters of Request in ordinarie. All " which titles and offices (the Mastership of " Chancery, which seemed not competible with " the office of Master of Requestes, only ex- " cepted) he by her princely favour possessed " and enjoyed untill the time of his death. Be- " sides the great learning and wisdome that this " gent. was plentifully endowed withall, Nature " had also framed him so courteous of dispo- " sition and affable of speech, so sweet of " conversation and amiable behaviour, that " there was never any in his place better be- " loved all his life, nor he himselfe more especi- " ally favoured of her Majestie and the greatest " personages in the realme in any part of his " life then he was when he drew nearest his " death. He was of stature not taull, nor yet " over low, not grosse in bodie, and yet of good " habit, somewhat inclining to fatnesse of visage; " in his youth round, well favoured, well co- " loured and louely, and albeit in his latter " yeares sicknesse had much impaired his " strength and the freshnesse of his hew, yet " there remained there still to the last in his " countenance, such comely and decent gravity, " as that the change rather added unto them, " then ought diminished his former dignitie.

"He left behind him when he died, by a vertu-"ouse gentlewoman Wilgiford his wife (the first "daughter of Mr. John Williams of Tainton, "in the countie of Oxford) whom he maried "very young, a maiden, and enjoyed to his "death, both having lived together in great love "and kindnesse by the space of 40 yeares, three "sons and six daughters, all of them maried, "and having issue, as followeth:

"His eldest son Edward maried unto Joane "daughter and one of the heires of Wm. Ha-"vard, in the countie of Brecon, Esq.

"His second son Thomas maried Mary the "dau^r^ and heire of Anthony Maunsell of Llan-"trithed, in the com. of Glamorgan, Esq.

"His 3d son John,* being then of the age of "18 yeares (or much thereabouts), was maried "to Rachel, one of ye daughters of Rich. Dan-"vers of Tockenham, in com. Wilts, Esq.

"His eldest daughter Elizabeth, maried to "Thomas Norton of Norwood, in the countie of "Kent, Esq.

"His 2d daughter Mary maried Wm. Her-"bert of Krickhowell, in the countie of Breck-"nock, Esq.

* J. Whitgift, A.B. Cant. was his guardian, and the doctor's great friend. I have heard my grandmother say, that her husband told her that his grace kept a noble house, and that with admirable order and œconomy; and that there was not one woman in the family.

"His 3rd daughter Joane maried with S^r^
"Daniel Dun, Knight, and Doctor of the Civill
"Lawe.

"His 4th daughter Wilgiford maried to Rise
"Kemis of Llanvay, in the county of Monmouth,
"Esq.

"His 5th daughter Lucie maried to Hugh
"Powell, Gent.

"His 6th and youngest daughter Anne, ma-
"ried to Jno. Partridge, Esq. of Wishanger,
"in the countie of Glocester, Esq. Of every of
"the which since his death there hath proceeded
"a plentiful issue."

Additions by Aubrey.

He was one of the delegates (together with Dr. Dale, &c.) for the Tryall of Mary Queen of Scots, and was a great stickler for the saving of her life, which kindnesse was remembered by King James att his coming into England, who asked after him, and probably would have made him Lord Keeper, but he dyed, as appears, a little before that good opportunity happened. His ma^tie^ sent for his eldest sonnes, and knighted the two eldest, and invited them to court, which they modestly and perhaps prudently declined. You may find him mentioned in the History of

Mary Queen of Scots, 8o. written, I think, by J. Hayward, as also in Thuanus's Annales, which be pleased to see* and insert his words here in honour to y[e] D[rs] *Manes*. Dr. Zouch mentions him with respect in his De Jure Feciali, and as I remember, he is quoted by Sir Edw. Coke, Ld. Ch. Justice of the K. Bench, in his Reports, about the Legitimacy of the Earle of Hertford.† Qu. if it was Edw. y[e] father, or els his son Wm. about the mariage with the Ladie Arabella Stuart?

Mem. Old Judge Atkins (the father) told me, that the Portugall Ambassador was tryed for his life for killing Mr. Greenway in the New Exchange, (Oliver's time) upon the precedent of the Bishop of Rosse, by Dr. W. Aubrey's advice. Mem. Dr. Cruzo of Drs. Commons hath the MSS. of this bishop's tryall.

He was a good statesman and Queen Elizabeth loved him, and was wont to call him *her little Doctor*. Sr Joseph Williamson, principall secretary of estate, (first under-secretary) has told me that in the letter office are a great many letters of his to the Queen and councell. He sate many times as Lord Keeper, and gave many

* [It will be remembered that this was addressed to Anthony à Wood. *E.*]

† Mem. Mr. Shuter, the proctor, told me that the Dr. appealed to Rome about the E. of Hertford's suite, temp. R. Elizabethæ.

decrees, which Mr. Shuter, &c. told me they had seen.

The learned John Dee was his great friend and kinsman, as I find by letters between them in the custody of Elias Ashmole, Esq. Jo. Dee wrote a booke, *The Soveraignty of the Sea,* dedic. to Q. Eliz. which was printed in fol Mr. Ashmole hath it, and also the originall copie of J. Dee's hand writing, and annexed to it is a letter of his cosen Dr. Wm. Aubrey,* whose advise he desired, in his writing, on that subject.

* MY GOOD COOSEN,

I HAVE sente unto you again my yonge coosen inclosede in a bagge, as my wyffe cariethe yet one of myne; trustinge in God, that shortly both, in theyr severall kyndes, shall come to lyght and live long, and your's having *genium,* for ever. I knowe not, for lack of sufficiencie of witte and learninge, how to judge of it at all. But in that shadowe of judgemente that I have, truste me beinge vearie farre from meanynge to yelde any thyng, to your owne eares, of yourselfe. The matter dothe so strive with the manner of the handlinge that I am in dowpte whyther I shall preferre the matter for ye substance, weyght, and pythines of the multitude of argumentes and reasones, or the manner for the methode, order, perspicuitie, and elocution, in that height and loftynesse that I did nott beleve our tonge (I meane the Englyshe) to be capable of. Marie, our Brittishe, for the riches of the tonge, in my affectionate opinion, is more copious and more advawntageable to utter any thinge by a skillfull artificer. This navie which you aptlie, accordinge to the nature and meaninge of your platt, call pettie, is so

He purchased Abercunvrig (the ancient seate of the family) of his cosen Aubrey. He built

sette furthe by you, thos principall and royall navies of ye Grecianes and Trojanes described by Homer and Vergill are no more bownde to them, then it is to you.

You argue or rather thoondre so thicke and so strong for the necessitie and commoditie of your navie, that you leade or rather drawe me *obtorto collo* to be of opinion wh you, the benefitte therofe to be suche as it wil be a brydle and restreynte for conspiracies of foreyne nationes, and of owr owne a salfegarde to merchants from infestationes of pyrates; a readie meane to breed and augmente noombers of skillfull marryners, and sowldiers for the sea, a mayntynawnce in proces of tyme for multitudes of woorthie men that otherwise wolde be ydle. Who can denie, as you handle the matter, and as it is in trothe, but that it will be a terror to all princes for attemptinge of any soodeyne invasions, and hable readilie to withstande any attempte foreyne or domesticall by sea? And where this noble realme hath been long defamed for suffringe of pyrates disturbers of the comon traffyke vpon these seas yt will, as you trulye prove utterlie extingwishe the incorrigible, and occupie the reformed in that honourable service.

The indignitie that this realme hath long borne in the fyshinge rownde aboute yt, with the intolerable injuries that owre nation hath indured and doe still, at strangers handes, besides the greatnes of the comoditie that they take owte of our mowthes hath ben, and is suche, that the same almoste alone were cause sufficiente to furnishe ye navie if it may have that successe and consideration that it deserveth, it will be a better wache for the securitie of the state than all the intelligencers or becones that may be devisede: and a stronger wall and bulwarke than either Calleys was, or a

the great house at Brecknock, his studie lookes on the river Uske. He could ride nine miles to-

brase of such townes placed in the most convenient parte of any continente of France, or the Lowe Countrey. As her majestie of right is *totius orbis Britannici Domina, et lex maris*, whiche is given in the reste of the worlde by *Labeo* in our learning to Antoninus the Emperor, so she showlde have the execution and effect therof in our worlde, yf your navie were as well setled as you have plottede it. But what doe I by this bare recitall deface your reasones so eloquentlie garnishede by you wth the furniture of so much and so sundrie lernynge? I will of purpose omitt howe fully and howe substanteally you confute the stronge objections and argumentes that you inforce and presse againste y[r] selfe. I wolde God all men wolde as willinglie beare y[e] light burdynes that you lay upon them for the supportation of the chardges as you have wiselie and reasonablie devisede the same. And so the dearthe and scarsitie that curiouse or covetouse men may pretende to feare, you so sowndlie satisfie, that it is harde with any probabilitie to replie. As for the sincere handlinge and govermete it is not to be disperede yf the charge shall be wth good ordinawnces and instructiones placed carefullie in chosen persones of good credite and integritie. See howe boldlie upon one soodeyne readinge I powre my opinion to your bosome of this notable and strange discowrse. And yet I will make bold to censure it also as he dyd in the poore slipper when he was nott able to fynd any faulte in any one parte of the workemanship of the noble picture of that goddes. I pray you, Sir, seyinge you meane that your navie shall contynewe in time of peace furnished with y[e] noombre of men, what provision or ordre make you, howe they shall occupie and exercise themselves all the while? Assure your selfe these whelpes of yours neyther can nor will

gether in his owne land in Breconshire. In Wales and England he left 2500lib. per ann.

be ydle, and excepte it may please you to prescribe unto them some good occupation and exercise, they will occupie themselves in occupationes of their owne choice, wherof few shall be to your lykinge or meanynge. Peradventure you meane of purpose to reserve that to the consideration of ye state. And where you in vearie good proportion, lawierlike, share goodes taken by pyrates amonge sundrie persones of your navie, and some portion to itselfe, reservinge the moytie to the prince, you are to remembre that the same are challenged holly to belong to her highnesse by prerogative. Let me be also bold to offer to your consideration whether it be expedient for you so freely to deale w[h] the carryinge of ordinawnces out of the realme beinge a matter lately pecuted* by the knowledge *et convenientia* of, &c. You doe, to veary great purpose inserte the two orationes of Georgius Gemistus Pletho, the one to Emanuel by fragments, and the other to his sonne Theodore *ad verbum*, for the worthynes and varietye of many wise and sownd advises given by him to those princes in a hard tyme, when they were in feare of that Turkish conquest, that did after followe to the ruine of that empire of Constantinople. However well doeth he handle the differences and rates of customes and tributes; the moderate and sober use of apparell *in ipsis principibus!* How wisely doethe he condemne the takeinge up of all the newe attires and apparell of strange nations, as though he had written to us at this tyme, who offend as deeply therein as the Greeks then dyd! How franke is he to his prince in useinge the comparisone between the Eagle that hath no varietie of colours of feathers, and yet of a princelie nature

* [Sic.]

whereof there is now none left in the family. He made one Hugh George (his chiefe clark) his executor, who ran away into Ireland and cosened all the legatees, and among others my grandfather (his youngest son) for the addition of whose estate he had contracted with ..... for Pembridge castle in the com. of Hereford, w[ch] appeares by his will, and for which his executor was to have payd. He made a deed of entaile (36 Eliz.) w[ch] is also mentioned in his will,

and estimation, and the Peacock, a bird of no regall propertie nor credit yet glisteringe angelically with varietie of feathers of all lively colours. There is one sentence in the later oration which I have thought to note because in apparence it dothe oppugne in maner your treatise. The wordes are these, *Præstat longè terrestribus copiis ac militum et ducum virtute, quàm nautarum et similium hominum vilium arte fiduciam ponere.*

Good coosen, pardon my boldnes. I doe this bicause you may understande that I have roone over it. And yet was I abrode all the fowle day yesterday. I pray you pardon me agayne for nott sendinge of it to you accordinge to promisse. And for that your man is come, and for that I have spente all my paper, I will no longer trowble you at this tyme, savinge w[h] my right hartie commendations to your selfe and to my coosen your good mother from me and from my woman. From Kewe this Soonday in the morninge, the 28 of July.

Yo[rs] assuredlie at comawndment,

W. Aubrey.

To his verie lovinge coosin and assured freende Mr. John Dee, at Mortelake.

whereby he entailes the Brecon estate on the issue male of his eldest son, and in defailer, to skip the 2d son (for whom he had well provided, and had married a great fortune) and to come to the third. Edward the eldest had seaven sonnes, his eldest son, Sir Will. had also seaven sonnes, and so I am heere the 18th man in remainder, w[ch] putts me in mind of Dr. Donne,

For what doeth it availe
To be the twentieth man in an entaile?

Old Judge Atkins remembered Dr. A. when he was a boy, he lay at his father's house in Glocestershire: he kept his coach, w[ch] was rare in those dayes. The Judge told me they then (vulgarly) call'd it a *Quitch*. I have his originall picture. He had a delicate, quick, lively and piercing black eie, a severe eie browe, and a fresh complexion. The figure in his monument at St. Paules is not like him, it is too big. He engrossed all the witt of the family, so that none descended from him can pretend to any. 'Twas pitty that Dr. Fuller had not mentioned him amongst his Worthys in that countie.

When he lay dyeing, he desired them to send for a *good man*, they thought he meant Dr. Goodman, deane of St. Paules, but he meant a priest, as I have heard my cos. Jo. Madock say. Capt. Pugh was wont to say, that civilians (as most learned and gent.) naturally incline to the church of Rome; and the common lawyers, as more ignorant and clownish, to the church of Geneva.

Wilgiford, his relict, maried . . . . Browne, of Willey, in com. Surrey.

The inscription on his monument in St. Paul's church: Gulielmo Aubræo clara familia in Bre-
" conia orto, LL. in Oxonia Doctori, ac Regio
" Professori, Archiepiscopi Cantuariensis causa-
" rum Auditori et Vicario in spiritualibus Genera-
" li, Exercitus Regii ad St. Quentin Supremo Ju-
" ridico, in Limitaneum Walliæ consilium adscito,
" Cancellariæ Magistro, et Reginæ Elizabethæ a
" supplicum libellis: Viro exquisita eruditione,
" singulari prudentia, et moribus suavissimis
" (qui tribus filiis, et sex filiabus e Wilgiforda
" uxore susceptis), æternam in Christo vitam ex-
" pectans, animam Deo xxiij Julii 1595, ætatis
" suæ 66, placidè reddidit;

" Optimo Patri Edvardus et Thomas, milites,
" ac Johannes, armiger, filii, mœtissimi po-
" suerunt."

This Dr. W. Aubrey was related to the first W. E. of Pembroke, two wayes, (as appeares by comparing the old pedegre at Wilton with that of the Aubreys,) by Melin and Philip ap Elidex (the Welsh men are all kinne) and it is exceeding probable that the Earle was instrumentall in his rise. When the E. of Pemb. was generall at St.

Quintins in France, Dr. Aubrey was his judge advocat. In the Doctor's will is mention of a great piece of silver plate, the bequest of the Right Honble the Earle of Pembroke.

. . . . Stephens, the clarke of St. Benets, Paules Wharfe, tells me that Dr. W. Aubrey gave xx*s.* per annum for ever to that parish.

SIR FRANCIS BACON, KT.

BARON OF VERULAM, VISCOUNT OF ST. ALBAN's, AND LORD HIGH CHANCELLOR OF ENGLAND.

In his Lordship's prosperity Sr Fulke Grevil, Lord Brooke, was his great friend and acquaintance, but when he was in disgrace and want, he was so unworthy as to forbid his butler to let him have any more small beer, which he had often sent for, his stomack being nice, and the small beere of Grayes Inne not liking his pallet. This has donne his memorie more dishonour then S^r^ Ph. Sydney's friendship engraven on his monument hath donne him honour.

Richard Earle of Dorset was a great admirer and friend of the L^d^ Ch. Bacon, and was wont to have Sr Tho. Billingsley* along with him, to

* He was the best horseman in England, and out of England no man exceeded him. He taught this Earle, and his 30 gentlemen to ride the great horse. He taught the

remember and to putt down in writing my Lord's sayinges at table. Mr. Ben Jonson was one of his friends and acquaintance, as doeth appeare by his excellent verses on his Lo$^{p's}$ birth day, in his 2d vol. and in his *Vnderwoods,* where he gives him a character, and concludes, That about his time, and within his view, were borne all the witts that could honour a nation or help studie. He came often to Sr John Danvers at Chelsey. Sir John told me that when his Lo^{p} had wrote the *Hist. of Hen.* 7, he sent the manuscript copie to him to desire his opinion of it before 'twas printed. Qd. Sir John, Your Lordship knowes that I am no scholar. 'Tis no matter, said my Lord, I know what a schollar can say; I would know what *you* can say. Sir John read it, and gave his opinion what he misliked (wch I am sorry I have forgott) wch my L^{d} acknowledged to be true, and mended it. "Why," said he, "a schollar would never have told me this."

Mr. Tho. Hobbes (Malmesburiensis) was beloved by his Lo^{p} who was wont to have him walke with him in his delicate groves, when he did meditate: and when a notion darted into his mind, Mr. Hobbes was presently to write it downe, and his Lo^{p} was wont to say that he did

Prince Elector Palatine of the Rhine and his brothers. He ended his dayes at the Countesse of Thanet's (da. and coheire of Rich. Earl of Dorset) .... 167.. He dyed praying on his knees.

it better than any one els about him; for that many times, when he read their notes he scarce understood what they writt, because they understood it not clearly themselves. In short, all that were *great and good* loved & honoured him. Sir Edward Coke, Ld. Chiefe Justice, alwayes envyed him, and would be undervalueing his lawe. I knew old lawyers that remembred it.

He was Lord Protector during King James's progresse into Scotland, and gave audience in great state to Ambassadors in the banquetting house at Whitehall. His Lo^p would many times have musique in the next roome where he meditated. The Aviary at Yorke house was built by his Lo^p; it did cost 300lib. Every meale, according to the season of the yeare, he had his table strewed with sweet herbes and flowers, which he sayd did refresh his spirits and memorie. When his Lo^p was at his country house at Gorhambery, St. Alban's seemed as if the court had been there, so nobly did he live. His servants had liveries with his crest;* his watermen were more imployed by gentlemen than even the kings.

King James sent a buck to him, and he gave the keeper fifty pounds.

He was wont to say to his servant, *Hunt,* (who was a notable thrifty man, and loved this world,

* A boare.

and the only servant he had that he could never gett to become bound for him) "The world was made for man (Hunt), and not man for the world." Hunt left an estate of 1000lib. *per ann.* in Somerset.

None of his servants durst appeare before him without Spanish leather bootes: for he would smell the neates leather, which offended him.

The East India merchants presented his Lo^p^ with a cabinet of jewells, which his page, Mr. Cockaine, received, and deceived his Lord.

His Lordship was a good Poet, but conceal'd, as appeares by his Letters. See excellent verses of his Lo^p's^ which Mr. Farnaby translated into Greeke, and printed both in his Ανθολογια, sc.

The world's a bubble, and the life of man,
Less than a span, &c.

Apothegmata.

His Lordship being in Yorke house garden looking on Fishers, as they were throwing their nett, asked them what they would take for their draught; they answered *so much:* his Lo^p^ would offer them no more but *so much.* They drew up their nett, and it were only 2 or 3 little fishes, his Lo^p^ then told them, it had been better for them to have taken his offer. They replied, they hoped to have had a better draught;

but, said his Lo^p "*Hope is a good breakfast, but an ill supper.*"

When his Lo^p was in disfavour, his neighbours hearing how much he was indebted, came to him with a motion to buy Oake-wood of him. His Lo^p. told them, "*He would not sell his Feathers.*'

The Earle of Manchester being removed from his place of Lord Chiefe Justice of the Co̅mon Pleas, to be Lord President of the Councell, told my Lord (upon his fall) that he was sorry to see him made such an example. Lord Bacon replied, It did not trouble him, since *he* was made *a President.*

The Bishop of London did cutt downe a noble clowd of trees at Fulham. The Lord Chancellor told him that he was *a good expounder of darke places.*

Upon his being in disfavour, his servants suddenly went away, he compared them to the flying of the vermin when the house was falling.

One told his Lordship it was now time to look about him. He replyed, "I doe not looke *about* me, I looke *above* me.

Sir Julius Cæsar (Master of the Rolles) sent to his Lo^p in his necessity a hundred pounds for a present.* His Lordship would often drinke a

* Most of these informations I have from Sr John Danvers.

good draught of strong beer (March beer) to-bed-wards, to lay his working fancy asleep: which otherwise would keepe him from sleeping great part of the night. I remember Sir John Danvers told me, that his Lo? much delighted in his curious garden at Chelsey, and as he was walking there one time, he fell downe in a sowne. My Lady Danvers rubbed his face, temples, &c. and gave him cordiall water: as soon as he came to himselfe, sayd he, "Madam, I am no good *footman.*"

Three of his Lordship's servants* kept their coaches, and some kept race-horses.

. . . . . His Favourites tooke bribes, but his Lo? alwayes gave judgement *secundum æquum et bonum.* His Decrees in Chancery stand firme, there are fewer of his decrees reverst, then of any other Chancellor.

His daughter maried her Gentleman Usher, Sir Thomas† Vnderhill, whom she made deafe and blind, with too much of Venus. She was living since the beheading of the late King.

He had a delicate, lively hazel eie; Dr. Harvey told me it was like the eie of a viper.

I have now forgott what Mr. Bushell sayd, whether his Lordship enjoyed his Muse best at night, or in the morning.

* Sir Tho. Meautys, Mr. . . . Bushell, Mr. . . . Idney.

† I thinke.

Mr. Hobbes told me that the cause of his Lp's death was trying an experiment. As he was taking the aire in a coach with Dr. Witherborne (a Scotchman, Physician to the King) towards Highgate, snow lay on the ground, and it came into my Lord's thoughts, why flesh might not be preserved in snow as in salt. They were resolved they would try the experiment presently. They alighted out of the coach, and went into a poore woman's house at the bottome of Highgate hill, and bought a hen, and made the woman exenterate it, and then stuffed the bodie with snow, and my Lord did help to doe it himselfe. The snow so chilled him, that he immediately fell so extremely ill, that he could not returne to his lodgings, (I suppose then at Graye's Inne,) but went to the Earl of Arundell's house, at Highgate, where they putt him into a good bed warmed with a panne, but it was a damp bed that had not been layn in about a yeare before, which gave him such a cold that in 2 or 3 dayes, as I remember he [Mr. Hobbes] told me, he dyed of suffocation.

He had a uterine* brother, ANTHONY BACON, who was a very great statesman, and much beyond his brother Francis for the Politiques. A lame man; he was a pensioner to, and lived with, . . . Earle of Essex, and to him he [Francis]

* His mother was .... Cooke, sister of .... Cooke of Giddy-hall, in Essex, 2d wife to Sir Nicholas Bacon.

dedicates the first edition of his Essayes, a little booke no bigger then a Primer, which I have seen in the Bodleian Library.

His sisters were ingeniose and well-bred; they well understood the use of the Globes, as you may find in the preface of Mr. Blundeville of the Sphere: see if it is not dedicated to them. One of them was maried to S[r] John Cunstable of Yorkshire. To this bro. in lawe he dedicates his second edition of his Essayes in 8vo. his last in 4to. to the D. of Bucks.

I will now say something of VERULAM, and his house at Gorhambery. At Verulam is to be seen in some few places, some remains of the wall of this Citie; which was in compass about —— miles. This magnanimous Lord Chancellor had a great mind to have made it a citie again: and he had designed it, to be built with great uniformity: but Fortune denyed it him, though she proved kinder to the great Cardinal Richelieu, who lived both to designe, and finish that specious towne of Richelieu, where he was borne; before an obscure and small village.

Within the bounds of the walls of this old citie of Verulam (his Lordship's Barony) was Verulam house, about ½ a mile from St. Alban's; which his Lordship built, the most ingeniosely contrived little pile,* that ever I saw. No question but his Lordship was the chiefest Architect, but he had for his assistant, a favourite of his (a St. Alban's man) Mr. .... Dobson (who was his Lordship's right hand) a very ingeniose person (Master of the Alienation Office) but he spending his estate upon woemen (luxuriously) necessity forced his son Will. Dobson to be the most excellent painter, that England hath yet bred.

This house did cost nine or ten thousand the building, and was sold about 1665 or 1666 by Sir Harbottle Grimston, Baronet, (now Master of the Rolls) to two carpenters for fower hundred poundes; of which they made eight hundred poundes. Mem. There were good chimney-pieces, the roomes very loftie and were very well wainscotted. There were two bathing-roomes or stuffes, whither his Lordship retired afternoons as he saw cause. The tunnells of the chimneys were carried into the middle of the house, and round about them were seates. The top of the house was well leaded. From the leads was a lovely prospect to the ponds, which were opposite to the east side of the house, and were on the other side of the stately walke of trees, that leads to Gorhambery-howse: and also, over that long

* I am sorry I measured not the front and breadth: but I little suspected it would be pulled downe for the sale of the materialls,

walke of trees, whose topps afford a most pleasant variegated verdure, resembling the works in Irish stitch. The kitchen, larder, cellar, &c. are under ground. In the middle of this house was a delicate staire-case of wood, which was curiously carved, and on the posts of every interstice was some prettie figure, as of a grave divine with his booke and spectacles; a mendicant friar, &c. (not one thing twice.) Mem. On the dores of the upper storie on the outside (which were painted darke umber) were figures of the gods of the Gentiles: viz. on the south dore, 2d storie, was Apollo; on another Jupiter with his thunder-bolt, &c. bigger than the life, and donne by an excellent hand, the heightnings were of hatchings of gold, w[ch] when the sun shone on them made a most glorious shew.

Mem. The upper part of the uppermost dore, on the east side, had inserted into it a large looking-glasse, with w[ch] the stranger was very gratefully deceived, for after he had been entertained a pretty while, with the prospects of the ponds, walks, and country, w[ch] this dore faced: when you were about to returne into the room, one would have sworn *primo intuitu*, that he had beheld another prospect through the house: for as soon as the stranger was landed on the balconie the concierge* that shewed the house would shutt

* [Fr. the keeper of a palace, or nobleman's house. *E.*]

the dore to putt this fallacy on him with the looking-glasse. This was his Lordship's summer-house: for he sayes* one should have seates for summer and winter as well as cloathes.

From hence to Gorhambery is about a little mile, the way easily ascending, hardly so acclive as a desk: from hence to Gorambery in a straite line leade three parallell walkes: in the middle-most three coaches may passe abreast: in the wing-walkes two. They consist of severall stately trees of the like groweth and height, viz. elme, chesnut, beach, hornebeame, Spanish ash, cervice tree, &c. whose topps (as aforesaid) doe afford from the walke on the house the finest shew that I have seen, and I sawe it about Michaelmas, at which time of the yeare the colours of leaves are most varied.

The figures of the ponds were thus: they were pitched at the bottomes with pebbles of severall colours, which were work't into severall figures, as of fishes, &c. which in his Lordship's time were plainly to be seen through the cleare water, now over-grown with flagges and rushes. If a poor bodie had brought his Lordship halfe a dozen pebbles of a curious colour, he would give them a shilling, so curious was he in perfecting his fish-ponds, which I guesse doe containe four

* In his Essayes.

acres. In the middle of the middlemost pond, in the island, is a curious banquetting-house of Roman architecture, paved with black and white marble; covered with Cornish slate, and neatly wainscotted.

Mem. About the mid-way from Verulam-house to Gorambery, on the right hand, on the side of a hill which faces the passer-by, are sett in artificial manner the afore-named trees, whose diversity of greens on the side of the hill are exceeding pleasant. These delicate walks and prospects entertain the eie to Gorambery-howse, which is a large, well-built Gothique howse, built (I thinke) by Sir Nicholas Bacon, Lord Keeper, father to this Lord Chancellor, to whom it descended by the death of Anthony Bacon, his middle brother, who died sans issue. The Lord Chancellor made an addition of a noble portico, which fronts the garden to the south: opposite to every arch of this portico, and as big as the arch, are drawn, by an excellent hand (but the mischief of it is, in water colours) curious pictures, all emblematicall with mottos under each: for example, one I remember, a ship tossed in a storme, the motto, *Alter erit tum Tiphys.*

Over this portico is a stately gallerie, whose glasse windowes are all painted; and every pane with severall figures of beast, bird, or flower, perhaps his Lordship might use them as topiques for locall memory. The windowes looke into the garden, the side opposite to them no window, but is hung all with pictures at length, as of King James, his Lordship, and severall illustrious persons of his time. At the end you enter is no window, but there is a very large picture:—in the middle on a rock in the sea stands King James in armour, with his regall ornaments, on his right hand stands, (but whether or no on a rock I have forgott) King Hen. 4, of France, in armour, and on his left hand, the King of Spain in like manner. These figures are (at least) as big as the life: they are donne only with umbre and shell gold: and the shadowed umbre, as in the pictures of the gods on the dores of Verulam-house. The roofe of this gallerie is semi-cylindrique, and painted by the same hand and same manner, with heads and busts of Greek and Roman Emperors and Heroes.

In the Hall (which is of the auncient building) is a large storie very well painted of the feasts of the gods, where Mars is caught in a net by Vulcan. On the wall, over the chimney, is painted an oake with akornes falling from it, the word, *Nisi quid potius*. And on the wall over the table is painted Ceres teaching the soweing of corne, the word, *Moniti meliora*. The garden is large which was (no doubt) rarely planted and kept in his Lordship's time. Here is a handsome dore, which opens into Oake-wood; over this dore in golden letters on blew are six verses. The oakes of this wood are very great and shadie. His Lordship much delighted himselfe here: under every tree he planted some fine flower, or flowers, some whereof are there still, (1656) viz. Pæonies, tulips. From this wood a dore opens into ..... a place as big as an ordinary parke, the west part wherof is coppice wood, where are walks cutt out as straight as a line, and broade enough for a coach, a quarter of a mile long or better. Here his Lordship much meditated, his servant Mr. Bushell attending him with his pen and inke-horne to sett downe his present notions. Mr. Tho Hobbes told me, that his Lordship would employ him often in this service whilst he was there, and was better pleased with his *minutes*, or notes, sett downe by him, than by others who did not well understand his Lordship. He told me that he was employed in translating part of the Essayes, viz. three of them, one whereof was that of the Greatnesse of Cities, the other two I have now forgott. The east of this parquet, (which extends to Verulam-howse) was heretofore, in his Lordship's prosperitie, a paradise, now is a large ploughed field. This eastern division consisted of severall parts; some thicketts of plumme-trees with delicate walkes; some of rasberies. Here was all manner of fruit-trees, that would grow in England; and a great number of choice forest trees; as the whitti-tree, sorbe, cervice, &c. The walkes both in the coppices and other boscages were most ingeniosely designed: at several good (Belvidere) viewes, were erected elegant summer-howses well built of Roman architecture, well wainscotted and ceiled, yet standing, but defaced, so that one would have thought the Barbarians had made a conquest here. This place in his Lordship's time was a sanctuary for phesants, partridges, &c. birds of several kinds and countries, as white, speckled, &c. partridges. In April, and the Spring time, his Lordship would, when it rayned, take his coach (open) to receive the benefit of irrigation, which he was wont to say was very wholsome, because of the nitre in the aire, and the *universal spirit of the world.* His Lordship was wont to say, *I will lay my mannor of Gorambery on't,* to which Judge ..... made a spightfull reply, saying he would not hold a wager against that, but against any other mannor of his Lordship's he would. Now this illustrious Lord Chancellor had only this Mannor of Gorambery.

JOANNES BARCLAIUS, SCOTO-BRITANNUS,

(From Sam. Butler.)

Was in England some time tempore R. Jacobi. He was then an old man, white beard, and wore a hatt and a feather, which gave some severe people offence. Dr. J. Pett tells me, that his last employment was Library-Keeper of the Vatican, and that he was there poysoned.

Mem. This Jo. Barclay has a sonne, now (1688) an old man, and a learned quaker, who wrote a Systeme of the Quakers' Doctrine in Latine, dedicated to K. James II. now translated by him into English in ..... The Quakers mightily value him. The book is common.

MR. FRANCIS BEAUMONT

Was the son of Judge Beaumont. There was a wonderfull consimility of phansy between him and Mr. Jo. Fletcher,* which caused that dearnesse of frendship between them. I thinke they were both of Queene's coll. in Cambridge. I

* —— utrumque vestrum incredibili modo
Consentit astrum.

Horat. *Lib.* 2, *Od.* 7.

have heard Dr. Jo. Earle, (since Bp. of Sarum)* say, who knew them, that his maine businesse was to correct the overflowings of Mr. Fletcher's witt. They lived together on the Banke side, not far from the Play-house, both batchelors lay together,† had one wench in the house between them, which they did so admire; the same cloaths and cloake, &c. between them. He writt (amongst many other) an admirable Elegie on the Countesse of Rutland, which is printed with verses before Sir Thomas Overburie's characters. Jo. Earle, in his verses on him, speaking of them,

" A monument that will then lasting bee,
When all her marble is more dust than shee."

He was buryed at the entrance of St. Benedict's chapell, in Westminster Abbey, March 9, 1615-6.‡ I searched severall yeares since in the Register Booke of St. Mary Overies, for the obijt of Mr. John Fletcher, which I sent to Mr. Anthony à Wood.

He hath a very good prefaratory letter before

* [See vol. i. page 141. Edit.]

† From Sr James Hales.

‡ Mem. Isaac Casaubon was buryed at the entrance of the same chapell. He dyed July 8, 1614.

before Mr. Speght's edition of Sir Geofrey Chaucer's Works, printed by Adam Islip, 1602, London, where he hath judicious observations of his writings.

SR. JOHN BIRKENHEAD, KT.

Was borne at Nantwych,* in Cheshire. His father was a sadler there, and he had a brother a sadler, a trooper in S[r] Tho. Ashton's regiment, who was quartered at my father's, who told me so. He went to Oxford university at .... old, and was first a servitor of Oriall colledge. Mr. Gwin, minister of Wilton, was his contemporary there, who told me he wrote an excellent hand, and, in 1631 or 8, when Wm. Laud, A. B. C.† was last there, he had occasion to have some things well transcribed, and this Birkenhead was recommended to him, who performed his businesse so well, that the A. B[p] recommended him to All Soule's coll. to be a fellow, and he was accordingly elected. He was scholar enough, and a poet. After Edgehill fight, when King

* Northwich. [In the hand-writing of Anthony à Wood. Edit.]

† [A[rch] B[ishop of] C[anterbury. Edit.]

Cha. I. first had his court at Oxford, he was pitched upon as one fitt to write the newes, which Oxford newes was called *Mercurius Aulicus,* which he writt wittily enough, till the surrender of the towne (which was June 24, 1646.) He left a collection of all his *Merc. Aulicus's* and all his other pamphletts, which his executors* were ordered by the king to give to the A. B[p]. of Canterbury's library. After the surrender of Oxford, he was putt out of his Fellowship by the Visitors, and was faine to shifte for himselfe as well as he could. Most part of his time he spent at London, where he mett with severall persons of quality that loved his company, and made much of him. He went over into France where he stayed some time. I thinke not long. He received grace there from the Dutchess of Newcastle, I remember he tolde me. He gott many a fourty shillings (I believe) by Pamphletts, such as that of "Col. Pride," and "The Last Will and Testament of Philip Earl of Pembroke," &c.

At the restauration of his Ma[tie] he was made Master of the Facultees, and afterwards one of the Masters of Requests. He was exceedingly confident, witty, not very gratefull to his benefactors, would lye damnably. He was of middling stature, great goggle eies, not of a sweet aspect.

He was chosen burghes of Parliament at

* Sir Rich. Mason and S[r] Muddiford Bramston.

Wilton, in Wiltshire, A^o. D^{ni.} 166...* A^o. 167.. upon the choosing of this Parliament, he went downe to be elected, and at Salisbury heard how he was scorned and mocked at Wilton (whither he was going) and called *Pensioner*, &c. he went not to the borough where he intended to stand, but returned to London, and tooke it so to heart, that he insensibly decayed and pined away, and so Decemb. 1679, dyed at his lodgings in Whitehall, and was buried Decemb. 6. in St. Martyn's church-yard† (in the Fields) neer the church, according to his will and testament. His executors intend to sett up an inscription for him against the wall.

He had the art of locall memory and his topiques were the chambers, &c. in All Soules colledge about 100, so that for 100 errands, &c. he would easily remember.

He was created Dr. of LL.

His Library sold to Sr Robert Atkins for 200lib. His MSS. (chiefly copies of Records) for 900lib.

* Of the King's Long Parliament.

† His reason was because he sayd they removed the bodies out of the church.

ADMIRALL BLAKE

Was borne at .... in com. Somerset, was of Albon-hall, in Oxford. He was there a young man of strong body, and good parts. He was an early riser and studyed well, but also tooke his robust pleasures of Fishing, Fowling, &c. He would steale swannes.*

He served in the House of Comons for ....

A°. Dn̄i. .... he was made admirall He did the greatest actions at sea that ever were done.

He died A°. Dn̄i ..... and was buried in K. H. 7th's chapell; but upon the returne of the Kinge, his body was taken up again and removed by Mr. Wells' occasion, and where it is now, I know not. Qu. Mr. Wells of Bridgewater?

SIR HENRY BLOUNT, KNIGHT.

He was borne (I presume) at Tittinghanger, in the countie of Hertford. It was heretofore the summer seate of the Lord Abbot of St. Alban's. He was of Trinity College, in Oxford, where was a great acquaintance between him and Mr. Francis Potter. He stayed there about .... yeares, from thence he went to Grayes Inne,

* From H. Norbone, B.D. his contemporary there.

where he stayd .... and then sold his chamber there to Mr. Thomas Bonham (the poet) and [made a] voyage into the Levant.* He returned ..... He was pretty wild when young, especially addicted to comon wenches. He was a 2d brother. He was a gentleman pensioner to King Charles I. on whom he wayted (as it was his turne) to Yorke (when the King deserted y[e] Parliament), was with him at Edge-hill fight, came with him to Oxford, and so returned to London; walkt into Westminster hall with his sword by his side; the Parliamentarians all stared upon him as a *Cavaleer*, knowing that he had been with the King: was called before the House of Co̅mons, where he remonstrated to them, he did but his duty, and so they acquitted him. In these dayes he dined most commonly at the Heycock's ordinary, neer the Pallsgrave-head taverne, in the Strand, which was much frequented by Parliament-men and gallants. One time Col. Betridge being there (one of the handsomest men about the towne) bragged much how the woemen loved him; S[r] H. Blount did lay a wager of .... with him, that let them two goe together to a *Bordello*, he only, without money, with his handsome person, and S[r] Henry with a xx[s] piece on his bald crowne, that the wenches should

* May 7, 1634, he embarqued at Venice for Constantinople.

choose Sr. Henry before Betridge; and Sr. H. won the wager. E. W. Esq. was one of the witnesses.

Memorandum. There was about 164.. a pamphlet (writt by Hen. Nevill, Esq. ἀνονυμῶς) called *The Parliament of Ladies*, 3 or 4 sheets in 4to. wherein Sr. Henry Blount was first to be called to the barre for spreading abroad that abominable and dangerous doctrine, that it was far cheaper and safer to lye with common wenches then with ladies of quality. His estate left him by his father was 500lib. pr. annum wch he sold to .... for an annuitie of 1000lib. pr. annm. in Anno Dni. 16.. and since his elder brother dyed: Ao. Dni. 165.. he was made one of the comittee for regulating the Lawes. He was severe against tythes, and for the abolishing them, and that every minister should have 100lib. pr. an. and no more. Since he was .... year old he dranke nothing but water or coffee. 1647 or thereabout, he maryed to Mris. Hestr. Wase, daugh. of Sr. Christop. Wase, who dyed 1679, by whom he hath two sonnes, ingeniose young gentlemen. Charles Blount (his second son) hath writt *Anima Mundi*, 8o. 167.. burnt by order of the Bp. of London, and *of Sacrifices*, 8o.

I remember twenty yeares since he inveighed much against sending youths to the universities, because they learnt there to be debaucht; and that the learning that they learned there they were to unlearne againe, as a man that is buttoned or laced too hard, must unbutton before he can be at his ease. Drunkennesse he much exclaimed against, but wenching he allowed. When coffee first came in he was a great upholder of it, and hath ever since been a constant frequenter of coffee houses, especially Mr. Farres at the Rainbowe, by Inner Temple Gate, and lately John's coffee house, in Fuller's Rents. The first coffee house in London was in St. Michael's Alley, in Cornhill, opposite to the Church, which was sett up by one ..... Bowman (coachman to Mr. Hodges, a Turkey merchant, who putt him upon it) in or about the yeare 1652. 'Twas about 4 yeares before any other was sett up, and that was by Mr. Far. Jonathan Paynter, o:* to St. Michael's Church, was the first apprentice to the trade, viz. to Bowman. Mem. The Bagneo, in Newgate Street, was built and first opened in Decemb. 1679: built by .... Turkish merchants.

He is a gentleman of a very clear judgment, great experience, much contemplation, not of very much reading, of great foresight into Government. His conversation is admirable. When he was young, he was a great collector of bookes, as his sonne is now. He was heretofore a great *Shammer*, (i. e.) one that tells falsities not to doe

* [Sic. Perhaps over-against or opposite. Edit.]

any body any injury, but to impose on their understanding:—e.g. at Mr. Farres; That at an inne (nameing the signe) in St. Alban's, the inkeeper had made a hogs-trough of a free-stone coffin, but the pigges after that grew leane, dancing and skipping, and would run up on the topps of the houses like goates. Two young gent. that heard Sr H. tell this *sham* so gravely, rode the next day to St. Alban's to enquire: comeing there, nobody had heard of any such thing, 'twas altogether false. The next night as soon as they allighted, they came to ye Rainbowe and found Sr H. looked learingly on him, and told him they wondered he was not ashamed to tell such storys as, &c. "Why, Gentlemen," (sayd Sir H.) "have you been there to make enquiry?" "Yea," sayd they. "Why truly, Gentlemen," sayd Sr H. "I heard you tell strange things that I knew to be false. I would not have gonne over the threshold of the dore to have found you in a lye:" at wch all the company laught at the 2 young gent. He was wont to say that he did not care to have his servants goe to church for there servants infected one another to goe to the alehouse and learne debauchery; but he did bid them goe to see the executions at Tyburne, wch works more upon them then all the oratorye in the sermons. His Motto over his printed picture is that wch I have many yeares ago heard him speake of, viz. *Loquendum est cum vulgo, sentiendum cum sapien-*

tibus. He is now (1680) neer or altogether 80 yeares, his intellectualls good still, and body pretty strong.

This last weeke* of Sept. 1682, he was taken very ill at London, and his feet swelled; and [he was] removed to Tittinghanger.

JAMES BOVEY, ESQ.

Was the youngest son of Andrew Bovey, master cash-keeper to Sr Peter Vanore, in London. He was borne in the middle of Mincing Lane, in the parish of Saint Dunstan's in the East, London, A^o^ 1622, May 7, at six a clock in the morning. Went to schoole at Mercers Chapell, under Mr. Augur. At 9 sent into ye Lowe Countreys, then returned, and perfected himselfe in the Latin and Greeke. 14 travelled into France and Italie, Switzerland, Germany, and the Lowe Countreys. Returned into England at 19; then lived with one Hoste, a banquier, 8 yeares, was his cashier 8 or 9 yeares. Then traded for himselfe (27) till he was 31, then maried the only daughter of William de Vischer, a merchant, lived 18 yeares with her, then continued single. Left off trade

* [This last sentence was evidently written long after the former account. EDIT.]

at 32, and retired to a countrey life, by reason of his indisposition, the ayre of the citie not agreing with him. Then in these retirements he wrote *Active Philosophy*, (a thing not done before) wherein are enumerated the Arts and Tricks practised in Negotiation, and how they were to be ballanced by prudentiall rules. Whilest he lived with Mr. Hoste, he kept the cash of ambassadors of Spaine, and of the farmers* that did furnish the Spanish and Imperiall armies of the Lowe Countreys and Germany, and also many other great cashes, as of Sr. Theo. Mayern, &c. by which meanes he became acquainted with the ministers of state both here and abroad. When he was abroad, his chiefe employment was to observe the affaires of state and their judicatures, and to take the politique surveys in the countreys he travelled through, more especially in relation to trade. He speakes the Lowe Dutch, High Dutch, French, Italian, Spanish and Lingua Franco, and Latin, besides his owne. When he retired from business he studied the Lawe-Merchant, and admitted himselfe of the Inner Temple, London, about 1660. His judgment has been taken in most of the great causes of his time in points concerning the Lawe-Merchant. As to his person he is about about 5 foot high, slender

* Called by them Assentistes.

body, straight, haire exceeding black and curling at the end, a dark hazell eie, of a midling size, but the most sprightly that I have beheld. Browes and beard of the [same] colour as his haire. A person of great temperance, and deepe thoughts, and a working head never idle. From 14 he had a candle burning by him all night, with pen, inke, and paper, to write downe thoughts as they came into his head; that so he might not loose a thought. Was ever a great lover of Naturall Philosophie. His whole life has been perplex'd in lawe-suites, which have made him expert in humane affaires, in which he alwaies over-came. He had many lawe-suites with powerfull adversaries; one lasted 18 yeares. In all his travells he was never robbed.

He has one son, and one daughter who resembles him.

From 14 he began to take notice of all prudentiall rules as came in his way, and wrote them downe, and so continued till this day, Sept. 28, 1680, being now in his 59th yeare.

For his health he never had it very well, but indifferently, alwaies a weake stomach, which proceeded from the agitation of the braine. His diet was alwayes fine diet: much chicken.

He wrote a "Table of all the Exchanges in Europe."

He hath writt (which is in his custodie, and

which I have seen, and many of them read) these treatises, viz.

1. The Characters, or Index Rerum. In 4 Tomes.
2. The Introduction to Active Philosophie.
3. The Art of Building a Man: or Education.
4. The Art of Conversation.
5. The Art of Complyance.
6. The Art of Governing the Tongue.
7. The Art of Governing the Penne.
8. The Government of Action.
9. The Government of Resolution.
10. The Government of Reputation.
11. The Government of Power. In 2 Tomes.
12. The Government of Servients.
13. The Government of Subserviency.
14. The Government of Friendship.
15. The Government of Enmities.
16. The Government of Lawe-suites.
17. The Art of Gaining Wealth.
18. The Art of Preserving Wealth.
19. The Art of Buying and Selling.
20. The Art of Expending Wealth.
21. The Government of Secrecie.
22. The Government of Amor Conjugalis. In 2 Tomes.
23. Of Amor Concupiscentiæ.
24. The Government of Felicitie.
25. The Lives of Atticus, Sejanus, Augustus.
26. The Causes of the Diseases of the Mind.

27. The Cures of the Mind, viz. Passions, Diseases, Errors, Defects.

28. The Art of Discerning Men.

29. The Art of Discerning Man's selfe.

30. Religion from Reason. In 3 Tomes.

31. The Life of Cum-fu-zu, so farr wrote by J. B.

32. The Life of Mahomett, wrote by S[r] Walter Raleigh's papers, with some small addition for methodizing the same.*

He made it his businesse to advance the trade of England, and many men have printed his conceptions.

RICHARD BOYLE, FIRST EARL OF CORKE,

AND

HIS 7th DAUGHTER,

MARY COUNTESS OF WARWICK.

"The Virtuous Woman found: Being a Sermon preached at Felsted, in Essex, at the Funerall of the most excellent and religious lady, the Right-honourable MARY Countesse Dowager of Warwick. By Anthony Walker, D.D. rector of Fyfield, in the sayd countie. The 2d Edition

* I have desired him to give these MSS. to the library of the R. Soc.

corrected. Printed at London, for Nath. Ranew, at the King's Arms, in St. Paul's Church-yard, 1680." (The Epistle dedicatory is dated, May 27, 1678.)

Pag. 44. She was truly excellent and great in all respects: great in the honour of her birth, being born a lady and a virtuosa both; seventh daughter of that eminently Honourable Richard, the first Earle of Cork, who being born a private gentleman, and younger brother of a younger brother, to no other heritage than is expressed in the device and motto, which his humble gratitude inscribed on all the pallaces he built,

God's Providence, mine Inheritance.

By that Providence, and his diligent and wise industry, raised such an honour and estate, and left such a familie as never any subject of these three kingdomes did, and that with so unspotted a reputation of integrity, that the most invidious scrutiny could find no blott, though it winnowed all the methods of his rising most severely, which our good Lady hath often told me with great content and satisfaction.

This noble Lord by his prudent and pious consort, no lesse an ornament and honour to their descendants than himself, was blessed with five sonnes, of which he lived to see four Lords and Peeres of the kingdome of Ireland.

And a fifth, more than these titles speak, a Soveraigne and Peerlesse, in a larger province,—that of universall nature, subdued and made obsequious to his inquisitive mind.

And eight daughters.

And that you may remark how all things were extraordinary in this great personage, it will, I hope, be neither unpleasant nor impertinent to add a short story I had from our Lady's own mouth.

Master Boyl, after Earle of Cork (who was then a widdower), came one morning to waite on S[r] Jeoffry Fenton, at that time a great officer* of state in that kingdome of Ireland, who being ingaged in business, and not knowing who it was who desired to speake with him, a while delayed him access; which time he spent pleasantly with his young daughter in her nurse's arms. But when S[r] Jeoffry came, and saw whom he had made stay somewhat too long, he civilly excused it. But master Boyl replied, he had been very well entertayned; and spent his time much to his satisfaction, in courting his daughter, if he might obtaine the honour to be accepted for his son-in-lawe. At which S[r] Jeoffry, smiling (to hear one who had been formerly married, move for a wife carried in arms, and under two years old,) asked him if he would stay for her? To which he

* Secretary of Estate.

frankly answered him he would, and S[r] Jeoffry as generously promised him, he should then have his consent. And they both kept their words honourably. And by this virtuous lady he had thirteen children, ten of which he lived to see honourably married, and died a grandfather by the youngest of them.

Nor did she derive less honour from the collateral, than the descending line, being sister by soul and genius as well as bloud to these great personages, whose illustrious, unspotted, and resplendent honour and virtue, and whose usefull learning and accurate pens, may attone and expiate, as well as shame, the scandalous blemishes of a debauched, and the many impertinencies of a scribling, age.

1. Richard, the truly Right Honourable, Loyal, Wise, and Vertuous, Earl of Burlington and Cork, whose Life is his fairest and most laudable character.

2. The Right Honourable Roger Earle of Orrery, that great Poet, great Statesman, great Soldier, and great Every-thing, which merits the name of Great or Good.

3. Francis Lord Shannon, whose *Pocket-Pistol,* as he stiles his book, may make as wide breaches in the walls of the Capitol, as many canons.

4. And that honourable and well known name

R. Boyl, Esquier, that profound Philosopher, accomplished Humanist, and excellent Divine, I had almost sayd Lay-Bishop, as one hath stiled Sr H. Savil, whose works alone may make a librarie.*

The Female branches also (if it be lawfull so to call them whose virtues were so masculine, souls knowing no difference of sex) by their Honours and Graces (by mutuall reflections) gave, and received lustre, to, and from, her.

The eldest of which, the Lady Alice, was married to the Lord Baramore.

The second, the Lady Sarah, to the Lord Digby, of Ireland.

The third, the Lady Lætitia, to the eldest son of the Lord Goring, who died Earle of Norwich.

The fourth, the Lady Joan, to the Earle of Kildare, not only primier Earle of Ireland, but the *ancientest house* in Christendome of that degree, the present earle being the six and twentieth, or the seven and twentieth of lineal descent. And, as I have heard, it was that great antiquary, King Charles the First, his observation, that the three ancientest families of Europe for nobility, were the *Veres* in England, Earls of Oxford, and the *Fitz-Geralds* in Ireland, Earls of Kildare,

* Why does he not mention — Lord Killimeke, who was slain at the great battell of Liskarrill, in Ireland?

and *Momorancy* in France. 'Tis observable, that the present Earle of Kildare is a mixture of blood of Fitz-Geralds and Veres.

The fifth, the Lady Katharine, who was married to the Lord Viscount Ranelaugh,* and mother to the present generous Earle of Ranelaugh, of which family I could have added an eminent remark, I meet with in Fuller's "Worthies."

This Lady's character is so signalized by her known merit among all persons of honour, that as I need not, so I dare not attempt beyond this one word—she was our Lady's *Friend-Sister*.

The sixth, the Lady Dorothy Loftus.

The seaventh, (the number of perfection) which shutt-up and crown'd this noble train (for the eighth, the Lady Margaret, died unmarried), was our excellent Lady Mary, married to Charles Earle of Warwick; of whom, if I should use the language of my text, I should neither despair their pardon, nor fear the reproach of rudeness. *Many daughters*, all his daughters, *did virtuously but thou*— PROV. 31; 29, 30, 31.

———— But shee† needed neither borrowed shades, nor reflexious lights, to set her off, being personally great in all naturall endowments and accomplishments of soul and body, wisdome, beautie, favour, and virtue.

Great by her tongue, for never woman used

* Jones. † Ma. Countess of Warwick.

one better, speaking so gracefully, promptly, discreetly, pertinently, holily, that I have often admired the edifying words that proceeded from her mouth.

Great by her pen, as you may *(ex pede Herculem)* discover by that little* tast of it, the world hath been happy in, the hasty fruit of one or two interrupted houres after supper, which she professed to me, with a little regret, when she was surprised with its sliding into the world without her knowledge, or allowance, and wholly beside her expectation.

Great by being the greatest mistresse and promotress, not to say the Foundress and Inventress of a new science—the art of obliging; in which she attain'd that sovereign perfection, that she reigned over all their hearts with whom she did converse.

Great in her nobleness of living and hospitality.

Great in the unparalleled sincerity of constant, faithfull, condescending friendship, and for that law of kindness which dwelt in her lips and heart.

Great in her dexterity of management.

Great in her quick apprehension of the difficulties of her affaires, and where the stress and pinch lay, to untie the knot, and loose and ease them.

Great in the conquest of herselfe.

* Her Ladyship's *Pious Meditations.*

Great in a thousand things beside, which the world admires as such: but she despised them all, and counted them but loss and dung in comparison of the feare of God, and the excellency of the knowledge of Chr. Jesus.

THE HON. ROBERT BOYLE, ESQ.

The . . . son of Richard Boyle, first Earle of Corke, was borne at Lismor, in the county of Corke, the . . . day of . . . . A°. . . . . He was nursed by an Irish nurse, after the Irish manner, wher they putt the child into a pendulous satchell instead of a cradle, with a slitt for the child's head to peepe out. He learn't his Latin . . . . went to the university of Leyden. Travelled to France, Italy, Switzerland. I have often heard him say that after he had seen the antiquities and architecture of Rome, he esteemed none any where els. He speakes Latin very well, and very readily as most men I have mett with. I have heard him say that when he was young, he read over "Cowper's Dictionary," wherein I thinke he did very well, and I beleeve he is much beholden to him for his mastership of that language. His father in his will, when he comes to the settlement and provision for his son Robert, thus. *Item, to my son Robert, whom I beseech God to blesse with a particular blessing, I bequeath, &c.* Mr. R. H. who has seen the rentall sayes it was 3000lib. p^r^ ann^m^. The greatest part is in Ireland. His father left him the mannor of Stalbridge, in com. Dorset, where is a great free-stone house; it was forfeited by the Earle of Castlehaven. He is very tall (about six foot high) and streight, very temperate, and vertuouse, and frugall: a batcheler, keepes a coach, sojournes att his sister's, the Lady Ranalagh. His greatest delight is Chymistrey. He has at his sister's a noble laboratory, and severall servants (prentices to him) to looke to it. He is charitable to ingeniouse men that are in want, and foreigne chymists have had large proofe of his bountie, for he will not spare for cost to gett any rare secret. At his owne costs and chardges he gott translated and printed the *New Testament* in Arabique, to send into the Mahumetan countreys. He has not only a high renowne in England, but abroad, and when foreigners come hither, 'tis one of their curiosities to make him a visit.

WILLIAM LORD BRERETON.

This vertuous and learned lord (who was my most honoured and obligeing friend) was educated at Breda, by Jo. Pell, D.D. then Math. Professor there of the Prince of Orange's illustrious schoole. S[r] Geo. Goring, E. of Norwich (who was my Lord's grandfather) did send for him over, where he (then Mr. J. Pell) tooke great care of him, and made him a very good Algebrist.

He hath wrote a poem called *Origenes Moriens*, a MS.

Obijt March 17, 1679, London, and is buried at S[t] Martin's Church in the fields.

He was an excellent musitian, and also a good composer.

WILLIAM LORD VISCOUNT BROUNCKOR, OF LIONS, IN IRELAND.

He lived in Oxford when 'twas a garrison for the King: but he was of no university, he told me. He addicted himselfe only to the study of the mathematicks, and was a very great artist in that learning. His mother was an extraordinary great gamester, and playd all gold play; she kept the box herselfe. Mr. . . . Arundell (brother of the Lord Wardour) made a song in characters of the nobility. Among others, I remember this,

> Here's a health to my lady Brounckor and the best card in her hand,
> And a health to my lord her husband, with ne're a foot of land.

He was president of the Royall Society about 15 yeares.

He was . . . . . . of the Navy office.

He dyed April the 5th, 1684, bureed the 14th following in the vault which he caused to be made (8 foot long, 4 foot broad, and about 4 foot high) in the middle of the quire of Saint Katharine's, neer the tower, of which convent he was governour. He gave a fine organ to this church a little before his death, and whereas it was a noble and large choire, he divided it in the middle with a good skreen (at his owne chardge) which has spoiled ——

MR. BUSHELL

Was the greatest arts-master to runne in debt, perhaps in the world. He died one hundred and twenty thousand pounds in debt. He had so delicate a way of making his projects alluring, feasible, and profitable, that he drewe to his baites, not only rich men of no designe, but also the craftiest knaves in the countrey, such who had cosened and undon others: *e. g.* Mr. Goodyeere, who undid M[r] Nich. Mees's father, &c.

Mr. E. W. sayes, that he tap't the mountaine of Snowdon, in Wales, wch was like to have drowned all the countrey, and they were like to knock him and his men in the head.

[He] lay some time at Capt. Norton's, in the gate at Scotland-yard, where he dyed seven yeares since (now 1684), about 80 ætat. Buried in the little cloysters at Westminster Abbey. Somebody putt B. B. upon the stone, (now, 1687, gon, all new paved.)*

Qu. his servant John Sydenham, for the collection of Remarques of severall parts of England, by the said Mr. Bushell.

MR. SAMUEL BUTLER

Was borne at Pershore, in Worcestershire, as we suppose;† his brother lives there: went to schoole at Worcester. His father a man but of slender fortune, and to breed him at schoole was as much education as he was able to reach to. When but a boy he would make observations and reflections on every thing one sayd or did, and censure it to be either well or ill. He never was at the university for the reason alledged. He came when a young man to be a servant to the Countesse of Kent,‡ whom he served severall

* From Mr. Beech ye Quaker.

† He was born in Worcestershire, hard by Barton-bridge, ½ a mile from Worcester, in the parish of St. John, Mr. Hill thinkes, who went to schoole with him.

‡ Mr. Saunders (ye Countesse of Kent's kinsman) sayd

yeares. Here, besides his study, he employed his time much in painting* and drawing, and also in musique. He was thinking once to have made painting his profession.† His love to and skill in painting made a great friendship between him and Mr. Samuel Cowper (the prince of limners of this age). He then studyed the common lawes of England, but did not practise. He maried a good jointuresse, the relict of ..... Morgan, by which meanes he lives comfortably. After the restauration of his ma[tie] when the court at Ludlowe was againe sett up, he was then the king's steward at the castle there. He printed a witty Poeme called *Hudibras*, the first part A[o] 166. . which tooke extremely, so that the king and Lord Chanc. Hyde would have him sent for, and accordingly he was sent for. (The L[d] Ch. Hyde hath his picture in his library over the chimney.) They both promised him great mat-

that Mr. J. Selden much esteemed him for his partes, and would sometimes employ him to write letters for him beyond sea, and to translate for him. He was secretarie to the D. of Bucks, when he was Chancellor of Cambridge. He might have had preferments at first; but he would not accept any but very good, so at last he had none at all, and dyed in want.

* He painted well, and made it (sometime) his profession. He wayted some yeares on the Countess of Kent. She gave her gent. 20lib. p[r] an. a-piece.

† From Dr. Duke.

ters, but to this day he has got no employment, only the king gave him . . . . . . lib.

He is of a middle stature, strong sett, high coloured, a head of sorrell haire, a severe and sound judgement: a good fellowe. He hath often sayd that way (*e. g.* Mr. Edm. Waller's) of quibling with sence will hereafter growe as much out of fashion and be as ridicule* as quibling with words. Q[d] N.B. He hath been much troubled with the gowt, and particularly 1679, he stirred not out of his chamber from October till Easter.

He† dyed of a consumption Septemb. 25. (Anno D[ni] 1680, 70 circiter), and buried 27, according to his owne appointment in the church-yard of Covent Garden; sc. in the north part next the church at the East end. His feet touch the wall. His grave, 2 yards distant from the pillaster of the dore, (by his desire) 6 foot deepe.

About 25 of his old acquaintance at his funerall: I myself being one.

Hudibras unprinted.

No Jesuite ever took in hand,
To plant a church in barren land;
Or ever thought it worth his while
A Swede or Russe to reconcile.

* [Sic. Edit.]

† [Evidently written some time after the former part. *E.*]

For where there is not store of wealth,
Souls are not worth the chardge of health.
Spaine and America had designes
To sell their Ghospell for their Wines,
For had the Mexicans been poore,
No Spaniard twice had landed on their shore.
'Twas Gold the Catholick Religion planted,
Which, had they wanted Gold, they still had
wanted.

He had made very sharp reflexions upon the court in his last part.

Writt my Lord (John*) Rosse's Answer to the Marquesse of Dorchester.

Memorandum. Satyricall witts disoblige whom they converse with, &c. consequently make to themselves many enemies and few frends, and this was his manner and case. He was of a leonine-colored haire, sanguine, cholerique, middle sized, strong.

* [In the hand-writing of Anthony à Wood. Edit.]

WILLIAM BUTLER, PHYSITIAN.

He was of Clare-hall, in Cambridge; never took the degree of Doctor, though he was the greatest Physitian of his time. The occasion of his first being taken notice of was thus:* About the comeing in of K. James, there was a minister of . . . . . . (a few miles from Cambridge,) that was to preach before his ma[tie] at New-market. The parson heard that the K. was a great scholar, and studyed so excessively that he could not sleep, so somebody gave him some opium, w[ch] had made him sleep his last had not this physitian (Dr. Butler) used this following remedy. He was sent for by the parson's wife; when he came and sawe the parson, and asked what they had donne, he told her that she was in danger to be hanged for killing her husband, and so in great choler left her; it was at that time when the cowes came into the backside to be milkt; he turnes back, and asked whose cowes these were, she sayd her husband's. Sayd he, "Will you give one of these cowes to fetch your husband to life again?" That she would with all her heart. He then causes one presently to be killed and opened, and the parson to be taken out of his bed and putt into the cowes warme belly,† which

* From Edm. Waller, Esq.

† Mem. There is a parallell storie to this in Machiavell's

after some time brought him to life, or els he had infallibly dyed. He was a man of great moodes. One time K. James sent for him to New-market, and when he was gon halfe way [he] left the messenger and turned back ; so then the messenger made him ride before him. I thinke he was never married. He lived in an apothecary's shop, in Cambridge, . . . Crane, to whom he left his estate ; and he in gratitude erected the monument for him, at his owne chardge, in the fashion he used. He was not greedy of money, except choice pieces of gold or rarities. He would many times (I have heard say) sitt among the boyes at St. Maries church in Cambridge, and just so would the famous attorney-generall Noy, in Lincoln's Inne, who had many such froliques and humours. I remember Mr. Wadenish, of K. coll. told me, that being sent for to . . . . . . he told him that his disease was not to be found in Galen or Hippocrates, but in Tullie's Epistles, *Cum non sis ubi fueris, non est cur velis vivere.* * * * He gave to the chapell of Clare-hall, a bowle for the communion, of gold (cost, I thinke, 2 or 300lib.), on w[ch] is engraved a Pelican feeding her young with the bloud from her breast (an embleme of the passion of Christ), no motto, for the embleme explained itselfe. He lies buried in the

Florentine History, where 'tis sayd that one of the Cosmos being poysoned was putt into a mule's belly, sowed up with a place only for his head to come out.

south side of St. Maries chancell, in Cambridge, wherein is a decent monument with his body halfe way, and an inscription, w^cli gett. He was much addicted to his humours, and would suffer persons of quality to wayte sometimes some houres at his dore, with coaches, before he would receive them. Once, on the rode from Cambridge to London, he tooke a fancy to a chamberlayn or tapster in his inne, and tooke him with him, and made him his favourite, by whom only accession was to be had to him, and thus enriched him. Dr. Gale, of St. Paul's schoole, assures me, that a French man came one time from London to Cambridge, purposely to see him, whom he made stay two houres for him in his gallery, and then he came out to him in an old blew gowne. The French gentleman makes him 2 or 3 very lowe bowes downe to the ground; Dr. Butler whippes his legge over his head, and away goes into his chamber, and did not speake with him. He kept an old mayd whose name was Nell. Dr. Butler would many times goe to the taverne, but drinke by himselfe: about 9 or 10 at night old Nell comes for him with a candle and lanthorne, and sayes, "Come home you drunken beast." By and by Nell would stumble, then her master calls her "drunken beast," and so they did *drunken beast* one another all the way till they came home.

A serving man brought his master's water to Dr. Butler, being then in his studie, (with turned barres) but would not be spoken with. After much fruitlesse importunity, the man told ye Dr. he was resolved he should see his master's water ; he would not be turned away—[and so] threw it on the Dr's head. This humour pleased the Dr. and he went to the gent. and cured him.*

A gent. lying a dyeing, sent his servant with a horse for ye Dr., the horse being exceeding dry, ducks downe his head strongly into ye water, and plucks downe the Dr. over his head, who was plunged in the water over head and eares. The Dr. was madded, and would returne home. The man swore he should not ; drew his sword, and gave him ever and anon (when he would returne) a little prick, and so drove him before him.†

Some instances of Dr. Butler's cures.

(From Mr. James Bovey.)

The Dr. lyeing at the Savoy in London, next the water side, where was a balcony look't into the Thames, a patient came to him that was grievously tormented with an ague. The Dr. orders a boate to be in readinesse under his windowe, and discoursed with the patient (a gent.) in the balcony, when on a signall given, 2 or 3 lusty fellowes came behind the gent. and threw

* Mr. R. Hooke. † Mr. . . . . Godfrey.

him a matter of 20 feete into the Thames. This surprize absolutely cured him.

A gent. with a red, ugly, pumpled* face came to him for a cure. Said the Dr., "*I must hang you.*" So presently he had a device made ready to hang him from a beame in the roome; and when he was een almost dead, he cutts the veines that fed these pumples,* and lett out the black ugly bloud, and cured him.

*   *   *

Inscription on his monument:

Nunc positis novus exuviis.

Gulielmus Butlerus, Clarensis Aulæ quondam Socius, Medicorum omnium quos præsens ætas vidit facile princeps, hoc sub marmore secundum Christi adventum expectat, et monumentum hoc privata pietas statuit, quod debuit publica. Abi, viator, et ad tuos reversus, narra te vidisse locum in quo salus jacet.

Nil proh! marmor agis, Butlerum du~ tegis, ullu
Si splendore tuo nomen habere putas.
Ille tibi monumentum est, tu diceris ab illo,
Butleri vivis munere marmor iners.
Sic homines vivus, mira sic mortuus arte,
Phœbo chare senex, vivere saxa facis.

* [Sic. Edit.]

Butlero Herôum hoc posuere dolorque fidesque
Hei ! quid agam, exclamas et palles, Lector ? At unum
Quod miseris superesse potest, locus hic monet : ora.
Obiit CIƆIƆCXVII. Janua. XXIX. Æta. suæ LXXXIII.

This ins. was sent to me by my learned and honoured friend Dr Henry More, of Cambridge.

A scholar made this drolling Epitaph :—
Here lies Mr. Butler, who never was doctor,
Who dyed in the yeare that the Devill was proctor.

Mem. There is now in use in London a sort of ale called Dr Butler's ale.

MR. WILLIAM CAMDEN, CLAREN[x].

Mr. Edward Bagshawe (who had been second schoolemaster of Westminster schoole) has told me that Mr. Camden had first his place and his lodgings, (which is the gatehouse by the queen's schollars' chamber in Deanes-yard,) and was after made the head schoolemaster of that schoole, where he writt and taught *Institutio Græcæ Grammatices Compendiaria. In usum Regiæ Scholæ Westmonasteriensis,* wch is now the com̄on Greeke gram̄ar of England, but his name is not sett to it. Before they learned the prolix Greeke Gramar of Cleonard.

He writt his *Britannia* first in a large 8º.

Annales R. Elizabethæ.

There is a little booke in 16º. of his printed, viz. A Collection of all the Inscriptions then on the Tombes in Westminster Abbey.

'Tis reported, that he had bad eies (I guesse lippitude) wch was a great inconvenience to an antiquary.

Mr. N. Mercator has Stadius's *Ephemerides*, which had been one of Mr. Camden's; his name is there (I knowe his hand) and there are some notes by which I find he was astrologically given.*

My honrd and learned friend, Tho. Fludd, esq. (75, 1680) a Kentish gentleman, was neighbour and an acquaintance to Sr. Robert Filmore, in Kent, who was very intimately acquainted with Mr. Camden, who told Sr. Robert, that he was not suffered to print many things in his "Elizabetha" which he sent over to his acquaintance and correspondent Thuanus, who printed it all

* In his "Britannia" he hath a remarkable astrologicall observation, that when ♄ is in ♑ a great plague is certainly in London. He had observed it all his time, and setts downe the like made by others before his time. ♄ was so posited in the great plague 1625, and also in the last great plague 1665. He likewise delivers that when an eclipse happens in . . . . . . that 'tis fatall to the towne of Shrewsbury.

faithfully in his "Annalls" without altering a word.

He lies buried in the South cross-isle of Westminster Abbey, his effigies ½ on an altar; in his hande a booke, on the leaves whereof is writt BRITANNIA.

Mr. Camden much studied the Welsh language, and kept a Welsh servant to improve him in that language, for the better understanding of our antiquities.*

S[r] William Dugdale tells me that he hath Minutes of King James's life to a moneth and a day, written by Mr. Wm. Camden, as also his owne life, according to yeares and days, which is very briefe, but 2 sheetes; Mr. Camden's owne hand writing. Sr William Dugdale had it from . . . . . Hacket, bishop of Coventry and Lichfield, who did filch it from Mr. Camden as he lay a dyeing.†

* From Mr. Sam. Butler.

† Quære Mr. Ashmole to retrieve and looke out Mr. Camden's minutes (memorandums) of King James I. from his entrance into England, which Dr. Thorndyke filched from him as he lay a dyeing. 'Tis not above 6 or 8 sheetes of paper, as I remember. Dr. Thorndyke told S[r]. Wm. Dugdale so, who told me of it. Those memoires were continued within a fortnight of his death.

SIR CHARLES CAVENDISH*

Was borne at . . . . the younger brother to William Duke of Newcastle. He was a little, weake, crooked man, and nature having not adapted him for the court nor campe, he betooke himselfe to the study of the mathematiques, wherein he became a great master. His father left him a good estate, the revenue whereof he expended on bookes and on learned men. He had collected in Italie, France, &c. with no small chardge, as many manuscript mathematicall bookes as filled a hoggeshead, which he intended to have printed, which if he had lived to have donne, the growth of mathematicall learning had been 30 yeares or more forwarder than 'tis. But he died of the scurvey, contracted by hard study about 1652, and left one Mr. . . . . an attorney of Clifford's Inne, his executor, who shortly after died, and left his wife executrix, who sold this incomparable collection aforesayd by weight, to the past-board maker for waste paper. A good caution for those that have good MSS. to take care to see them printed in their life-times. He dyed . . . . and was buried in the vault of the family of the Duke of Newcastle, at Bolsover, in the countie of . . . . . . He is mentioned by Mersennus. Dr. John Pell (who knew him, and

* From Mr. Jo. Collins, mathematician.

made him one of his XII jurymen contra Longomontanum) tells me that he writt severall things in mathematiques for his owne pleasure.

COLONEL CHARLES CAVENDISH

Was 2d son to the right honb[le] . . . . . Earle of Devonshire, brother to this present Earle William. He was borne at . . . . . A°. . . . He was well educated, and then travelled into France, Italie, &c. but was so extremely delighted in travelling, that he went into Greece, all over, and that would not serve his turne but he would goe to Babylon, and then his governour would not adventure to goe any further with him; but to see Babylon he was to march in the Turkes armie. This account I had many yeares since, sc. 1642, from my cosen Edmund Lyte, who was then gentleman usher to his mother the countesse dowager. Mr. Th. Hobbes told me that this Mr. Cavendish told him that the Greekes doe sing their Greeke. In Herefordshire they have a touch of this singing, our old divines had. Our old vicar of Kington St. Michael, Mr. Hynd, did sing his sermons rather than reade them. You may find in Erasmus that the monkes used this fashion, who mocks them, that sometimes they would be very lowe, and by and by they would be mighty high, *quando nihil opus est.* Aº. 1660 comeing one morn. to Mr. Hobbes, his Greeke Xenophon lay open on the boarde: sayd he, Had you come but a little sooner you had found a Greeke here, that came to see me, who understands the old Greeke. I spake to him to read here in this booke, and he sang it, wch putt me in mind of what Mr. Ch. Cavendish told me (as before). The first word is Ἔννοια, he pronounced it *ennia.* The better way to explaine is by prick-song,

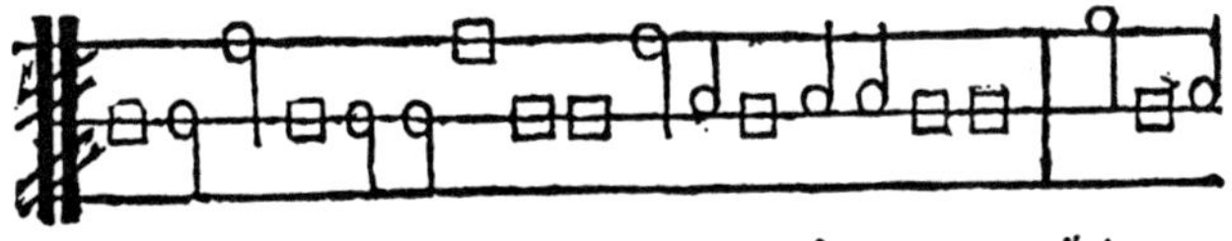

Μῆνιν ἄειδε θεὰ Πηληϊάδεω Ἀχιλῆος· ἄνθρωπος

Upon his returne into England the civill warres broke out, and he tooke a commission of a colonel in his ma^{ties} cause, wherein he did his majestie great service, and gave signall proofes of his valour ;—e. g. Grantham, in Lincolnshire, taken by Col. Cavendish for the king, 23 March, 1642-3, and after demolished.—Young Hotham routed at Ancaster by Col. Cavendish, 11 Apr. 1643.—Parliament forces routed or defeated at Dunnington by Col. Cavendish, 13 June, 1643. Mercurius Aulicus, Tuesday, Aug. 1. 1643; It was advertised from Newarke that his majesties forces having planted themselves at the siege of Gainsborough, in com. Linc. were sett upon by the united powers of Cromwell, Nottingham, and

Lincolne, the garrisons of these townes being almost totally drawn out to make up this army, which consisted of 24 troupes of horse and dragoons. Against this force, Col. Cavendish having the command of 30 troupes of horse and dragoons, drawes out 16 only, and leaving all the rest for a reserve, advanced towards them, and engaged himselfe with this small partie against all their strength, which being observed by the rebells, they gott between him and his reserve, routed his 16 troupes, being fore-spent with often watches, killed Lieutenant-colonel Markham, most valiantly fighting in defence of his king and countrey. The most noble and gallant colonel himselfe, whilest he omitted no part of a brave commander, being cutt most dangerously in the head, was struck off his horse, and so unfortunately shott with a brace of bulletts after he was on the ground, whose life was most pretious to all noble and valiant gentlemen. Whereupon the reserve coming, routed and cutt downe the partie. This was donne either the 28 or 29 of July, 1643, for upon this terrible rout, ye Lord Willoughby of Parham forthwith yealded Gainsborough to the king's pàrtie, July 30. The Earle of Newcastle being then generall of that partie. His body was first buried at .... *

* Qu. if at Gainsborough or Newarke, as I remember at Newarke.

but by order of his mother's will, when she was buried at Darby (where she had erected a noble monument for herselfe and lord) she ordered her sonnes body to be removed, and both to be layd in the vault there together, w[ch] was Febr. 18. 1674.

*"He was the souldiers mignion, and his ma[ties] darling, designed by him generall of the Northern horse (and his commission was given him), a great marke of honour for one of about five and twenty. Thus shall it be donne to the man whom the king delights to honour. Col. Cavendish was a princely person, and all his actions were agreeable to that character, he had in an eminent degree that which the Greekes call εἶδος ἄξιον τυραννίδος, the semblance and appearance of a man made to governe. Methinkes he gave cleare this indication, the king's cause lived with him, the king's cause died with him; when Cromwell heard that he was slaine, he cried upon it, *We have done our businesse.* And yet two things (I must confess) this commander knew not, pardon his ignorance,—he knew not to flee away—he knew not how to aske quarter.† If Cato thought

* Funerall Sermon, by Will. Naylour, her Chaplain, preached at Darby, Feb. 18, 1674. Lond. for Henry Broome. Text, 2 Sam. iii. 38th verse.

† This youthfull commander knew not to fly away, though an older did, I meane Henderson; for when this bold person

it usurpation in Cæsar to give him his life, Cavendish thought it a greater for traytors and rebells of a common size to give him his. This brave hero might be opprest, (as he was at last by numbers) but he could not be conquered; the dying words of Epaminondas will fitt him, *Satis vixi, invictus etiam morior.*

"What wonders might have been expected from a commander so vigilant, so loyall, so constant, had he not dropt downe in his blooming age? But though he fell in his green years, he fell a prince, and a great one too, in this respect greater than Abner; for Abner, that son of Mars, deserved his father's epithete, ἀλλοπρόσαλλος, *one of both sides*, first he setts up Ishbosheth, and then deserts him. Whereas Cavendish merited such a statue as the Roman senate decreed L. Vitellius, and the same inscription, *Pietatis immobilis erga Principem*, one whose loyaltie to his great master nothing could shake.

"Secondly, consider the noble Charles Cavendish in his extraction, and so he is a branch of that family, of which some descended that are Kings of Scotland, this the word *Fuimus* joyned to his maternall* coate does plainly point at. Not to

entred Grantham on the one side, that wary gentleman, who should have attaqued it, fled away on the other.

* His mother was daughter to the Lord Bruce, whose ancestors had been Kings of Scotland.

urge at this time his descent by the father's side from one of the noblest families in England. An high extraction to some persons is like the dropsie, the greatnesse of the man is his disease, and renders him unwieldie; but here is a person of great extract free from the swelling of greatnesse, as brisk and active as the lightest horseman that fought under him. In some parts of India, they tell us, that a nobleman accounts himselfe polluted if a plebeian touch him; but here is a person of that rank who used the same familiaritie* and frankness amongst the meanest of his souldiers, the poorest miner, and amongst his equalls; and by stooping so low, he rose the higher in the common account, and was valued accordingly as a prince, and a great one; thus Abner and Cavendish run parallell in their titles and appellations.

"Consider Abner in the manner of his fall, that was by a treacherous hand, and so fell Cavendish. 'And when Abner was returned to Hebron, Joab tooke him aside in the gate to speake

* S[r] Rob. Harley (son), an ingeniose gent. and expert soldier, has often sayd, that (generally) the comanders of the King's army would never be acquainted with their soldiers, w[ch] was an extraordinary prejudice to the king's cause. A captaines good looke, or good word (some times) does infinitely winne them, and oblige them; and he would say 'twas an admiration how souldiers will venture their lives for an obligeing officer.

with him quietly, and smote him there under the fifth rib, that he died, for the bloud of Asahel his brother.' Thus fell Abner; and thus Cavendish,—the Colonells horse being mired in a bog at the fight before Gainsborough, 1643. the rebels surround him, and take him prisoner, and after he was so, a base raskall comes behind him, and runs him through; thus fell two great men by treacherous hands.

"Thirdly and lastly, the place of his fall, that was in Israel. Here Abner fell in his, and Cavendish fell in our Israel—the Church of England.

"In this Church brave Cavendish fell, and what is more then that, in his Churches quarrel.

"Thus I have compared Colonel Cavendish with Abner, a fighting and a famous man in Israel, you see how he does equal, how he does exceed him."

CECIL, LORD BURLEIGH.

Memorand. The true name is *Sitsilt,* an ancient Monmouthshire family, but now come to be about the degree of yeomanry. In the church at Monmouth, I remember in a South windowe an ancient scutcheon of the family, the same that this family beares. 'Tis strange that they should be so vaine to leave off an old British name for a Roman one, which I beleeve Mr. Verstegan did putt into their heads, telling his Lo^{p} in his booke, that they were derived from the ancient Roman *Cecilij*. The first Ld Burleigh (who was secretary of estate) was at first but a country-schoole-master, and (I thinke Dr. Tho. Fuller sayes, v. "Holy State") borne in Wales. I remember (when I was a schoolboy at Blandford) Mr. Basket, a reverend divine, who was wont to beg us play-dayes, would alwayes be uncovered, and sayd, that 'twas the Ld. Burleigh's custome, for said he, "Here is my Lord Chanceller, my Lord Treasurer, my Lord Ch. Justice, &c. predestinated."

He made Cicero's Epistles his glasse, his rule, his oracle, and ordinarie pocket-booke.*

THOMAS CHALONER, ESQ.

Was the son of Dr Chaloner, who was tutor (*i. e.* informator) to Prince Henry, or Prince Charles.† He was a well-bred gentleman, and of very good naturall parts, and of an agreeable humour. He had the accomplishments of studies at home,‡ and travells in France, Italie, and

* Dr. J. Web in preface of his translation of Cicero's Familiar Epistles.

† V. Bp. Hall's Letters de hoc.

‡ Bred up in Oxon. [In Anthony à Wood's hand-writing. Edit.]

Germanie. About A°. . . . . riding a hunting in Yorkshire (where the allum workes now are) on a common, he tooke notice of the soyle and herbage, and tasted the water, and found it to be like that where he had seen the allum workes in Germanie. Wherupon he gott a patent of the king (Cha. I.) for an allum worke (which was the first that ever was in England), which was worth to him two thousand pounds per annum, or better: but tempore Car. 1^mi^ some courtiers did think the profitt too much for him, and prevailed so with the king, that notwithstanding the patent aforesayd, he graunted a moietie, or more, to another (a courtier), which was the reason that made Mr. Chaloner so interest himselfe for the Parliament cause, and, in revenge, to be one of the king's judges. He was as far from a puritan as the East from the West. He was of the naturall religion, and of Hen. Martyn's gang, and one who loved to enjoy the pleasures of this life. He was (they say) a good scholar, but he wrote nothing that I heare of, onely an anonymous pamphlett 8°. *An Account of the Discovery of Moyses's Tombe*; which was written very wittily. It was about 1652. It did sett the witts of all the Rabbis of the assembly then to worke, and 'twas a pretty while before the shamme was detected, which was by ———

He had a trick sometimes to goe into Westminster hall in a morn. in terme time, and tell some strange, false story (sham), and would come thither again about 11 or 12 to have the pleasure to heare how it spred; and sometimes it would be [so] altered, with additions, he could scarce knowe it to be his owne. He was neither proud nor covetous, nor a hypocrite: not apt to doe injustice, but apt to revenge.

After the restauration of King Charles the Second, he kept the castle at the Isle of Man,* where he had a prettie wench that was his concubine. When the newes was brought him that there were some come to the castle to demaund it for his majestie, he spake to his girle to make him a posset, into which he putt, out of a paper he had, some poyson, which did, in a very short time, make him fall a vomiting exceedingly; and after some time vomited nothing but bloud. His retchings were so violent that the standers by were much grieved to behold it. Within three hours he dyed. The demandants of the castle came and sawe him dead; he was swollen so extremely that they could not see any eie he had, and no more of his nose then the tip of it, which

* This is a mistake. E. W. Esq. assures me that twas James Chaloner that dyed in the Isle of Man: and that Tho. Chaloner dyed or went beyond the sea; but which of them was the eldest brother he knowes not, but he ghesses James to be the elder, because he had 1500lib. per an. (circiter), which Thomas had not.

shewed like a wart. This account I had from Geo. Estcourt, D.D. whose brother-in-lawe, Nathan, was one of those that sawe him.

SIR GEOFFREY CHAUCER.

Memorand. Sr Hamond L'Estrange, of ..... had his Workes in MS. a most curious piece, most rarely writt and illumined, wch he valued at 100lib. His grandson and heire still hath it.*

He taught his sonne the use of [the] astrolabe at 10.

Dunnington Castle, neer Newbury, was his; a noble seate and strong castle, which was held by King Ch. I. but since dismanteled. Mem. Neer this castle was an oake, under which Sir Geoffrey was wont to sitt, called *Chaucer's-oake*, wch was cutt downe by ...... tpe Car. 1mi and so it was, that ...... was called into the starre chamber, and was fined for it. Judge Richardson harangued against him long, and like an orator, had topiques from the Druides, &c.† His picture is at his old house at Woodstock (neer the parke-

* From Mr. Roger L'Estrange.

† This information I had from an able attorney that was at the hearing.

gate), a foot high, halfe way: it has passed from proprietor to proprietor.

WILLIAM CHILLINGWORTH, D.D.

Was borne in Oxford, his father was a brewer. About A°. . . . . . he was acquainted with one . . . . . who drew him and some other scholars over to Doway, where he was not so well entertained as he thought he merited for his great disputative witt. They made him the porter (which was to trye his temper, and exercise his obedience,) so he stole over and came to Trinity coll. againe, where he was fellowe. W. Laud, A. B. C. was his godfather and great friend. He sent his grace weekly intelligence of what passed in the university. S^r. W^m. Davenant (poet laureat) told me that notwithstanding this doctor's great reason, he was guiltie of the detestable crime of treachery. Dr. Gill, F. D^ris Gill, schoolmaster of Paules school, and Chillingworth held weekely intelligence one with another for some yeares, wherein they used to nibble at state-matters. Dr. Gill in one of his letters calls King James and his sonne, the old foole and the young one, wch letter Chillingworth communicated to W. Laud, A. B. Cant. The poore young Dr. Gill was seised, and a terrible storme pointed towards him, which, by the eloquent intercession and advocation of Edward Earle of Dorset, together with the teares of the poore old Doctor, his father, and supplication on his knees to his ma^{tie}, were* blowne over. I am sorry so great a witt should have such a næve. He was a little man, blackish haire, of a Saturnine countenance. The Ld Falkland and he had such extraordinary clear reasons, that they were wont to say at Oxon, that if the great Turke were to be converted by naturall reason, these two were the persons to convert him. He lies buried in the south side of the cloysters at Chichester, where he dyed of the *morbus castrensis* after the taking of Arundel castle by the parliament. In his sicknesse he was inhumanely treated by Dr. Cheynell, who, when he was to be buried, threw his booke into the grave with him, saying, "Rott with the rotten; Let the dead bury the dead." This following inscription was made and set up by Mr. Oliver Whitby, his fellowe collegiate at Trin. coll. and now one of the prebendarys of this church:

Virtuti sacrum.
Spe certissima resurrectionis
Hic reducem expectat animam
GULIELMVS CHILLINGWORTH, S. T. P.
Oxonij natus et educatus,

* [Sic. EDIT.]

Collegij S[tæ] Trinitatis olim
Socius, Decus et Gloria.
Omni Literarum genere celeberrimus,
Ecclesiæ Anglicanæ adversus Romano-Catholicam
Propugnator invictissimus,
Ecclesiæ Sarisburiensis Præcentor* dignissimus ;
Sine Exequiis,
Furentis cujusdam Theologastri,
Doctoris Cheynell,†
Diris et maledictione sepultus:
Honoris et Amicitiæ ergò,
Ab Olivero Whitby,
Brevi hoc monimento,
Posterorum memoriæ consecratus,
Anno Salutis,
1642.

My tutor, W. Browne, hath told me, that Dr. Chillingworth studied not much, but when he did, he did much in a little time. He much delighted in Sextus Empericus. He did walke much in the College grove, and there contemplate, and meet with some *cod's-head* or other, and dispute with

* This is a mistake; he was not Chantor of the Church, but Chancellor of the Church of Sarum. Whose office was antiently to read a lecture in Latin, quarterly, in the pulpit in the library, either in Theologie or the Canon Lawe. Since the Reformation 'twas commuted into preaching on the Holy-dayes. He was never swore to all the points of the Church of England.

† Minister of Petworth.

him and baffle him. He thus prepared himselfe before hand. He would alwayes be disputing; so would my tutor. I thinke it was an epidemick evill of that time, wch I thinke now is growne out of fashion, as unmannerly and boyishe. He was the readiest and nimblest disputant of his time in the university, perhaps none hath equalled him since.

I have heard Mr. Tho. Hobbes, Malmesb. (who knew him) say, *that he was like a lusty fighting fellow that did drive his enemies before him, but would often give his owne party terrible smart back-blowes.*

When Dr. Kettle, (the president of Trin. coll.) dyed,* wch was in A^o^. . . . . . Dr. Chillingworth was competitor for the presidentship, with Dr. Hannibal Potter and Dr. Roberts. Dr. Han. Potter had been formerly chaplain to the Bp. of Winton, who was so much Dr. Potter's friend, that though (as Will Hawes hath told me) Dr. Potter was not lawfully elected, upon referring themselves to their visitor (Bp of Winton), the Bishop (Curle) ordered Dr. Potter possession; and let the fellowes gett him out if they could. This was shortly after the Lord Falkland was slaine, who had he lived, Dr. Chillingworth assured Will. Hawes, no man should have carried

* This cannot be; Dr. Kettle died after Chillingworth. [In the hand-writing of Anthony à Wood. Edit.]

it against him: and tho' he was so extremely discomposed and wept bitterly for the losse of his deare friend, yet notwithstanding he doubted not to have an after-game for it.

JOHN CLEVELAND

Was borne at . . . . . in Warwickshire. He was a fellow of St. John's colledge, in Cambridge, where he was more taken notice of for his being an eminent disputant, than a good poet. Being turned out of his fellowship for a *malignant*, he came to Oxford, where the King's army was, and was much caressed by them. He went thence to the garrison at Newark upon Trent, where upon some occasion of drawing of articles, or some writing, he would needs add a short conclusion, viz. "And hereunto we annex our Lives, as a labell to our Trust." After the K. was beaten out of the field, he came to London, and retired in Grayes Inne. He, and Sam. Butler, &c. of Grayes Inne, did hold a clubb every night. He was a comely, plump man, good curled haire, darke browne. Dyed of the scurvy, and lies buried in St. Andrew's church, in Holborne, An. D[ni] 165 . . .

THOMAS COOPER

(Magdalensis).

Dr. Edw. Davenant told me, that this learned man had a shrew to his wife, who was irreconcileably angrie with him for sitting up late at night compileing his *Dictionarie.* When he had halfe donne it she had the opportunity to gett into his studie, tooke all his paines out in her lap, and threw it into the fire, and burnt it. Well, for all that, that good man had so great a zeale for the advancement of learning, that he began it again, and went through with it to that perfection that he hath left it to us, a most usefull worke. He was afterwards made Bishop of Winton.

DR. CORBET.

Richard Corbet, D.D. was the son of Vincent Corbet (better known "by Poynter's name then by his owne,"*) who was a gardner at Twick-

* Here lies engaged till the day
Of raysing bones and quickninge clay:
No wonder, reader, that he hath
Two sirnames in one epitaph,
For this one doth comprehend
All that both families could lend.

nam,* as I have heard my old cosen Whitney say. He was a Westminster scholar; old parson Bussey, of Alscott, in Warwickshire, went to schoole with him, he would say that he was a very handsome man, but something apt to abuse, and a coward. He was a student of Christ Church, in Oxford. He was very facetious, and a good fellowe. One time he and some of his acquaintance being merry at Fryar Bacon's study (where was good beere sold), they were drinking on the leads of the house, and one of the scholars was asleepe, and had a paire of good silke stockings on: Dr. Corbet (then M.A. if not B.D.) gott a paire of cizers and cutt them full of little holes, but when the other awaked, and perceived how and by whom he was abused, he did chastise him, and made him pay for them.

After he was Dr. of Divinity he sang ballads at the crosse at Abingdon, on a market-day. He and some of his camerades were at the taverne by the crosse,† (which by the way was then the finest of England; I remember it when I was a freshman: it was admirable curious Gothique architecture, and fine figures in the niches: 'twas one of those built by King . . . . for his queene)

* V. in B. Jonson's "Underwoods," an epitaph on this Vincent Corbet, where he speakes of his nurseries, &c. p. 177.

† 'Twas after the fashion of the crosse in High-street, in Bristowe, but more curious worke. Qu. if not marble?

the ballad singer complained, he had no custome, he could not putt off his ballades. The jolly Doctor putts off his gowne, and putts on the ballad singer's leathern jacket, and being a handsome man, and had* a rare full voice, he presently vended a great many, and had a great audience. After the death of Dr. . . . . he was made deane of Christ Church. He had a good interest with great men, as you may find in his poems, and with the then great favourite, the D. of Bucks; his excellent witt was letter of recommendation to him. I have forgott the story, but at the same time that Dr. Fell thought to have carried it, Dr. Corbet putt a pretty trick on [him] to lett him take a journey on purpose to London for it, when he had already the graunt of it.

He preach't a sermon before the King at Woodstock (I suppose K. James), but it happened that he was out, on which occasion there were made these verses:

A reverend deane,
With his band starch't cleane,
  Did preach before the King;
In his band string was spied
A ring that was tied,
  Was not that a pretty thing?

* [Sic. Edit.]

If then without doubt,
In his text he was out
. . . . next,
The ring without doubt
Was the thing putt him out,
For all that were there,
On my conscience, dare sweare,
That he handled it more than his text.

His conversation was extreme pleasant. Dr. Stubbins was one of his cronies, he was a jolly fatt Dr. and a very good house-keeper. As Dr. Corbet and he were riding in Lob-lane, in wett weather, ('tis an ordinary deepe dirty lane) the coach fell, and Dr. Corbet sayd that Dr. Stubbins was up to the elbowes in mud, he was up to the elbowes in Stubbins. A^{o} D^{ni} 1628 he was made Bp. of Oxford, and I have heard that he had an admirable, grave, and venerable aspect. One time as he was confirming, the country people pressing in to see the ceremonie, sayd he, "*Beare off there, or I'll confirme yee with my staffe.*" Another time being to lay his hand on the head of a man very bald, he turnes to his chaplaine and sayd, "*Some dust, Lushington,*" (to keepe his hand from slipping). There was a man with a great venerable beard, sayd the Bp. "*You, behind the beard.*" His chaplaine, Dr. Lushington, was a very learned and ingeniose man, and they loved one another. The Bp. sometimes would take the key of the wine-cellar, and he and his chaplaine would goe and lock themselves in and be merry. Then first he layes downe his episcopall hat,—"*There lyes the Dr.*" Then he putts off his gowne,—"*There lyes the Bishop.*" Then 'twas,—"*Here's to thee, Corbet,*" and "*Here's to thee, Lushington.*"* He built a pretty house neer the Cawsey beyond Friar Bacon's studie. He married . . . . . . * * * * * * * *. She was a very beautifull woman, and so was her mother. He had a son (I think Vincent) that went to schoole at Westminster, with Ned Bagshawe; a very handsome youth, but he is run out of all, and goes begging up and downe to gentlemen.

He was made Bishop of Norwich, A^{o}. D^{ni}. 1632. He dyed . . . . . The last words he sayd were, "*Good night, Lushington.*" He lyes buried in the upper end of the choire at Norwich, on the south side of the monument of Bishop Herbert, the founder, under a faire gravestone of free-stone, from whence the inscription and scutcheon of brasse are stolen.

His poems are pure naturall witt, delightfull and easie.

* From Josias Howe, B.D. Trin. coll. Oxon.

TOM CORYAT.

Old Major Cosh was quartered at his mother's house at Sherburne, in Dorsetshire, her name was Gertrude. This was when Sherburne castle was besieged, and when the fight was at Babell hills, between Sherburne and Yeovill. The first fight in the civill warres that was considerable. But the first *brush* was between the Earle of Northampton (father to Hen. the Lord Bishop of London) and the Lord Brooke, neer Banbury : which was the latter end of July, or the beginning of August, 1642. I was sent for into the countrey to my great griefe, and departed the 9th of Aug. 'Twas before I went away, I beleeve in Aug. Quære de hoc ?

But to returne to T. Coryat: had he lived to returne into England, his travells had been most estimable, for though he was not a wise man, he wrote faithfully matter of fact.

ABRAHAM COWLEY.

He was borne in Fleet-street, London, neer Chancery-lane. His father was a grocer, at the signe of . . . . He was secretary to the Earle of St. Alban's (then Ld Jermyn) at Paris. When his ma^{tie} returned, the D. of Buckingham hearing that at Chertsey was a good farme of about . . . . lib. per annum, belonging to the queene-mother, goes to the E. of St. Alban's, at . . . . to take a lease of it. They answered that 'twas beneath his grace to take a lease of them. That was all one, he would have it, payd for it, and had it, and freely and generously gave it to his deare and ingeniose friend, Mr. Abraham Cowley, for whom purposely he bought it. He lies interred at Westminster Abbey, next to S[r] Jeoffrey Chaucer, where the D. of Bucks has putt a neate monument of white marble, viz. a faire pedestall, whereon the inscription was made by Dr. Spratt, his grace's chapellane. Above that a very faire urne, with a kind of ghirland of ivy about it.

Lines by Sir J. Denham :

Had Cowley ne'er spoke, nor Killigrew writt,
They'd both have made a very good witt.

A. C. discoursed very ill, and with hesitation.

EDWARD DAVENANT

Was the eldest son of . . . . . . Davenant, merchant of London, who was elder brother to the Right-reverend Father in God, the learned John

Davenant, Bishop of Sarum. I will first speake of the father, for he was an incomparable man in his time, and deserves to be remembered. He was of a healthy complexion, rose at 4 or 5 in the morning, so that he followed his studies till 6 or 7, the time that other merchants goe about their businesse, so that stealing so much and so quiet time in the morning, he studied as much as most men. He understood Greeke and Latin perfectly, and was a better Grecian then the Bishop. He writt a rare Greeke character as ever I sawe. He was a great mathematician, and understood as much of it as was knowen in his time. Dr. Davenant, his son, hath excellent notes of his father's, in mathematiques, as also in Greeke, and 'twas no small advantage to him to have such a learned father to imbue arithmeticall knowledge into him when a boy, at night times when he came from schoole (Merchant Taylors'). He understood trade very well, was a sober and good manager, but the winds and seas crost him. He had so great losses that he broke, but his creditors knowing it was no fault of his, and else that he was a person of great vertue and justice, used not extremity towards him; but I thinke gave him more credit, so that he went into Ireland, and did sett up a fishery for pilchards at Wythy Island, in Ireland, where in . . . . yeares he gott 10000lib. satisfied and payd his creditors, and over and above left a good estate to his son. His picture bespeakes him to be a man of judgement, and parts, and gravity extraordinary. There is written *Expecto*. He slipt coming downe the stone stayres at the palace at Sarum, which bruise caused his death. He lyes buried in the south aisle of the choire in Sarum Cath. behind the Bishop's stall. His son sett up and made an inscription for him.

Doctor Edward Davenant was borne at his father's house at Croydon, in Surrey (the farthest handsome great house on the left hand as you ride to Bansted Downes) Anno Domini . . . . I have heard him say, he thank't God his father did not know the houre of his birth; for that it would have tempted him to have studyed astrologie, for w[ch] he had no esteeme at all. He went to school at Merchant Taylors' school, from thence to Queen's colledge, in Cambridge, of which house his uncle, John Davenant (afterwards Bishop of Sarum), was head, where he profited very well, [and] was fellowe. When his uncle was preferred to the Church of Sarum, he made his nephew treasurer of the church, which is the best dignity, and gave him the vicaredge of Gillingham in com. Dorset, and then Paulsholt parsonage, neer the Devises, which last in the late troubles he resigned to his wife's brother . . . . Grove. He was to his dyeing day of great diligence in study, well versed in all kinds of learning, but his genius did most strongly encline him to the mathematiques, wherein he has written (in a hand as legible as print) MSS. in 4to. a foot high at least. I have often heard him say (jestingly) that he would have a man knockt in the head that should write any thing in mathematiques that had been written of before. I have heard Sr. Christopher Wren say, that he does beleeve he was the best mathematician in the world about 30 or 35 yeares agoe. But being a divine he was unwilling to print, because the world should not know how he had spent the greatest part of his time. He very rarely went any farther then the church, which is hard by his house. His wife was a very discreet and excellent huswife, that he troubled himselfe about no mundane affaires, and 'tis a private place, that he was but little diverted with visitts. I have writt to his executor, that we may have the honour and favour to conserve his MSS. in the Library of the R. Societie, and to print what is fitt. I hope I shall obtaine my desire. * * * He had a noble library, which was the aggregate of his father's, the bishop's, and his owne. He was of middling stature, something spare and weake, feeble leggs, he had sometimes the goute, was of great temperance; he alwayes dranke his beer at meales with a toast, winter and summer, and sayd it made the beer the better. He was not only a man of vast learning, but of great goodness and charity; the parish and all his friends will have a great losse in him. He tooke no use for money upon bond. He was my singular good friend, and to whom I have been more beholding then to any one beside; for I borrowed five hundred pounds of him for a yeare and a halfe, and I could not fasten any interest on him. He was very ready to teach and instruct. He did me the favour to informe me first in Algebra. His daughters were Algebrists. His most familiar learned acquaintance was Lancelot Morehouse, parson of Pertwood. I remember when I was a young Oxford scholar, that he could not endure to heare of the new (Cartesian, &c.) Philosophy; For, sayd he, if a new Philosophy is brought in, a new Divinity will shortly follow; and he was right. He dyed at his house at Gillingham aforesayd, where he and his predecessor, Dr. . . . . Jessop had been vicars one hundred and . . . . yeares, and lyes buryed in the chancell there.

He was heire to his uncle, J. Davenant, Bp. of Sarum.

Memorandum. When Bp. Coldwell came to this bishoprick, he did lett long leases, which were but newly expired when Bp. Davenant came to this see; so that there tumbled into his coffers vast summes. His predecessor, Dr. Tounson, maried his sister, continued in the see but a little while, and left severall children unprovided for, so the K. or rather D. of Bucks gave Bp Davenant the bishoprick out of pure charity. Sr. Anth. Weldon sayes* 'twas the only bishoprick yt he disposed of without symony, all others being made merchandise of for the advancement of his kindred. Bp. Davenant being invested, maried all his nieces to clergie-men, so he was at no expence for their preferment. He granted to his nephew (this Dr.) the lease of the great mannour of Poterne, worth about 1000lib. per annum, made him treasurer of the church of Sarum, of which the corps is the parsonage of Calne, wch was esteemed to be of the like value. He made severall purchases, all wch he left him; insomuch as the churchmen of Sarum say, that he gained more by this church then ever any man did by the church since the Reformation, and take it very unkindly that, at his death, he left nothing (or about 50lib.) to that church which was the source of his estate. How it happened I know not, or how he might be workt on in his old age, but I have heard severall yeares since, he had sett downe 500lib. in will for the Cath. Ch. of Sarum. He had 6 sonnes and 4 daughters. There was a good schoole at Gillingham: at winter-nights he taught his sonnes Arith. and Geometrie; his 2 eldest daughters, especially Mris. Ettrick was a notable Algebrist. He had an excellent way of

* In his Court of King James.

improving his children's memories, wch was thus: he would make one of them read a chapter or, &c. and then they were *(sur le champ)* to repeate what they remembered, which did exceedingly profitt them; and so for sermons, he did not let them write notes (which jaded their memorie), but give an account *vivâ voce*. When his eldest son, John, came to Winton-schoole (where the boyes were enjoyned to write sermon notes) he had not wrote; the master askt him for his notes—he had none, but sayd, "If I doe not give you as good an account of it, as they that doe, I am much mistaken."

SIR WILLIAM DAVENANT, KNIGHT,

(Poet Laureat,)

Was borne about the end of February, baptized 3 of March, A. D. 1605-6, in . . . . . street, in the city of Oxford, at the Crowne Taverne. His father, John Davenant, was a vintner there, a very grave and discreet citizen: his mother was a very beautifull woman, and of a very good witt, and of conversation extremely agreeable. They had three sons, viz. 1. Robert, 2. William, 3. Nicholas, (an attorney). Robert was a fellow of St. John's coll. in Oxon. then preferred to the parsonage of West Kington by Bishop Davenant, whose chaplaine he was: and two handsome daughters, one maried to Gabriel Bridges, B.D. of C. C. Coll. beneficed in the Vale of White Horse; another to Dr. Sherburne, minister of Pembridge, in Hereford, and a canon of that church. Mr. William Shakespeare was wont to goe into Warwickshire once a yeare, and did comonly in his journey lye at this house in Oxon. where he was exceedingly respected. * * * * * * * * * * * * * * Now S[r] W[m] would sometimes, when he was pleasant over a glasse of wine with his most intimate friends,—e. g. Sam. Butler, (author of Hudibras) &c.—say, that it seemed to him that he writt with the very spirit that Shakespeare,* and seemed contented enough to be thought his son * * * * * * * * * * * * * * He went to schoole at Oxon to Mr. Sylvester (Charles), where F. Degorij W. was his schoolefellowe, but I feare he was drawne from schoole before he was ripe enough. He was preferred to the first Dutchess of Richmond to wayte on her as a page. I remember he told me, she sent him to a famous apothecary for some Unicornes-horne, w[ch] he was resolved to try with a spider, w[ch] he empaled in

* [Sic. Edit.]

it, but without the expected successe; the spider would goe over, and through and through unconcerned. He was next a servant (as I remember a page also) to Sr Fulke Grevil, Ld Brooke, with whom he lived to his death, wch was, that a servant of his that had long wayted on him, and his lo^p^ had often told him that he would doe something for him, but did not, but still putt him off wth delayes, as he was trussing up his lord's pointes, * * * * * * (for then their breeches were fastened to the doubletts with pointes, then came in hookes and eies, wch not to have fastened was in my boy-hood a great crime) stabbed him. This was at the same time that the Duke of Buckingham was stabbed by Felton, and the great noise and report of the Duke's, Sr W. told me, quite drowned this of his lord's, that 'twas scarce taken notice of. This Sr Fulke G. was a good witt, and had been a good poet in his youth. He wrote a poeme in fol. wch he printed not till he was old, and then, as Sr W. said, with too much judgment and refining spoyld it, which was at first a delicate thing.

He writt a play or playes, and verses, wch he did with so much sweetnesse and grace, that by it he got the love and friendship of his two Mecænasses, Mr. Endymion Porter, and Mr. Henry Jermyn (since E. of St. Albans), to whom he has dedicated his poem called "*Madegascar.*" S^r^

John Suckling also was his great and intimate friend. After the death of Ben Jonson he was made in his place Poet Laureat. He gott a terrible .... of a black handsome wench that lay in Axe-yard, Westm. whom he thought on when he speakes of *Dalga* in "*Gondibert*," which cost him his nose, with which unlucky mischance many witts were too cruelly bold: e.g. S[r] John Menis, S[r] Jo. Denham, &c.

In 1641, when the troubles began, he was faine to fly into France, and at Canterbury he was seised on by the mayor.

"For Will had in his face the flawes
And markes received in countrey's cause:
They flew on him like lyons passant,
And tore his nose as much as was on't,
And call'd him superstitious groome,
And Popish Dog, and Cur of Rome
..... 'Twas surely the first time
That Will's religion was a crime."

In the civill warres in England he was in the army of William Marquess of Newcastle, (since Duke) where he was generall of the ordinance. I have heard his brother Robert say, for that service there was owing to him by King Charles ye First 10000lib. During the warre 'twas his hap to have two aldermen of Yorke his prisoners, who were something stubborne, and would not give the ransome ordered by the councell of warr. Sr William used them civilly, and treated them in his tent, and sate them at the upper end of his table, *à la mode de France,* and having donne so a good while to his chardge, told them (privately and friendly) that he was not able to keepe so chargeable guests, and bad them take an opportunity to escape, wch they did; but having been gon a little way they considered with themselves that in gratitude they ought to goe back and give S[r]. William their thankes, which they did; but it was like to have been to their great danger of being taken by the soldiers, but they happened to gett safe to Yorke.

The King's party being overcome, S[r]. Wm. Davenant (who rec[d] the honour of knighthood from the D. of Newcastle by comision) went into France, resided there, at Paris, where the Prince of Wales then was. He then began to write his romance in verse, called "*Gondibert,*" and had not writt above the first booke, but being very fond of it, prints it before a q[ter] finished, with an epistle of his to Mr. Th. Hobbes, and Mr. Hobbes' excellent epistle to him printed before it. The courtiers with the Prince of Wales could never be at quiet about this piece, w[ch] was the occasion of a very witty but satericall little booke of verses in 8o. about 4 sheetes, writt by G. D. of Buckes, S[r]. Jo. Denham, &c.

> "That thou forsak'st thy sleepe, thy diet,
> And wch is more then that, *our quiet.*"

This last word Mr. Hobbes told me was the occasion of their writing.

Here he layd an ingeniose designe to carry a considerable number of artificers (chiefly weavers) from hence to Virginia; and by Mary the Q. mother's meanes, he got favour from the K. of France to goe into the prisons and pick and choose, so when the poor dammed wretches understood what the designe was, they cryed *uno ore*—"*Tout Tisseran**!" *We are all Weavers!* Well [he took] 36, as I remember, and not more, and shipped them; and as he was in his voyage towards Virginia, he and his *Tisseran* were all taken by the shippes then belonging to the Parliament of England. The slaves I suppose they sold, but S^r. Wm. was brought prisoner to England; whether he was first a prisoner at Caresbroke-castle, in the Isle of Wight, or at the Tower of London, I have forgott. He was a prisoner at both. His "*Gondibert,*" 4to. was finished at Caresbroke-castle. He expected no mercy from the Parliament, and had no hopes of escaping [with] his life. It pleased God that the two aldermen of Yorke aforesayd hearing that he was taken, and brought to London to be tryed for his life, w^ch

* [Sic. Edit.]

they understood was in extreme danger, they were toucht with so much generosity and goodness, as upon their owne accounts and meer motion, to try what they could to save S^r. Wm.'s life, who had been so civill to them, and a meanes to save theirs, to come to London, and acquainting the Parliament with it, upon their petition, &c. S^r. Wm.'s life was saved.*

Being freed from imprisonment, because playes (scil. Trag. and Comœdies) were in those Presbyterian times scandalous, he contrives to set up an Opera *stylo recitativo,* wherein serjeant Maynard and severall citizens were engagers. It began at Rutland-house, in Charter-house-yard. Next (scil. A°. . . . .) at the Cock-pitt, in Drury-lane, where were acted very well *stylo recitativo,* S^r. Francis Drake . . . . and the Siege of Rhodes, 1st and 2d part. It did affect the eie and eare extremely. This first brought scenes in fashion in England; before, at playes, was only a hanging. A°. Dⁿⁱ. 1660 was the happy restauration of his ma^{tie}. Charles II. Then was S^r. Wm. made . . . . and the Tennis court, in Little Lincolnes-Inne fielde was turn'd into a

* 'Twas Harry Martyn that saved S^r Wm. Davenant's life in the House. When they were talking of sacrificing one, then said Hen.—"That in sacrifices they always offred pure and without blemish: now yee talke of making a sacrifice of an old rotten rascall." V. "H. Martyn's Life," where by this very jest, then forgot, the Ld. Falkland saved Martyn's Life.

play-house* for the Duke of Yorke's players, where Sr William had lodgeings, and where he dyed, April y^e . . . . . 166 . . . . I was at his funerall; he had a coffin of walnutt-tree. Sir John Denham saide 'twas the finest coffin that ever he sawe. His body was carried in a herse from the play-house to Westminster Abbey, where, at the great West dore, he was received by the singingmen and choristers, who sang the service of the church ("I am the Resurrection, &c.") to his grave,† which is in the south crosse aisle, on which, on a paving stone of marble is writt, in imitation of y^t on Ben Jonson, "*O rare Sr Will. Davenant.*" His first lady was Dr. . . . . daughter, physitian, ... by whom he had a very beautifull and ingeniose son y^t dyed above 20 yeares since. His 2d lady was the daughter of . . . by whom he had severall children, I sawe some very young ones at the funerall. His eldest is Charles Davenant, LL D. who inherits his father's beauty and phancy. He practises at Drs Commons. He writt a play called "*Circe,*" which has taken very well.

Sr William hath writt about 25 playes, the ro-

* It is now a Tennis court again, upon ye building of the duke's house in Dorset garden.

† Which is neer to the monument of Dr. Isaac Barrow. Mem. My hon^rd friend, Sr Robert Moray lies by him; but *sans* INS.

mance called "*Gondibert,*" and a little poeme called "*Madagascar.*"

His private opinion was, that Religion at last,—e. g. a hundred yeares hence,—would come to a settlement, and that in a kind of ingeniose Quakerisme.

JOHN DEE.

I left about 1674, with Mr. Elias Ashmole, 3 pages in folio concerning him. Mem. Mr. Meredith Lloyd tells me that his father was Roland Dee, a Radnorshire gentleman,* and that he hath his pedegree, which he hath promised to lend to me. He was descended from Rees, Prince of South Wales. My great grandfather, Will. Aubrey, LL.D. and he were cosins, and intimate acquaintance. Mr. Ashmole hath letters between them, under their owne hands, viz. one of Dr. W. A. to him (ingeniously and learnedly written) touching the "*Soveraignty of the Seas,*" of which J. D. writt a booke, wch he dedicated to Q. Eliz. and desired my gr. gr. father's advice upon it. Dr. A.'s countrey-house was at Kew, and J. Dee lived at Mortlack, not a mile distant. I have heard my grandmother say they were often together. Arthur Dee, M.D. his son, lived and

* J. Dee's father was a vintner in London, at ye signe of . . . . . in . . . . . From Elias Ashmole, Esq. who had it from his grand-sonne, sonne of Arthur.

practised at Norwich,* an intimate friend of S. Tho. Browne, M.D. who told me yt Sr William Boswell, ye Dutch ambassador, had all J. Dee's MSS. Qu. his executors for his papers. He lived then somewhere in Kent. Mem. Sr William Boswell's widowe lives at Bradburne, neer Swynoke, in Kent. Mem. Mr. Huke, of the Physitians' Colledge hath a MS. of Mr. John Dee's, wch see or gett.

Qu. A. Wood for the MSS. in the Bodleyan library of Doctor Gwyn, wherein are severall letters between him and John Dee, and Doctor Davies, of Chymistrey and of Magicall Secrets, which my worthy friend Mr. Meredith Lloyd hath seen and read : and he tells me that he hath been told that Dr. Barlowe gave it to the Prince of Tuscany.

Meredith Lloyd sayes that John Dee's printed booke of Spirits, is not above the third part of what was writt, wch were in Sr Rob. Cotton's library; many whereof were much perished by being buryed, and Sr Rob. Cotton bought the field to digge after it.

Mem. he told me of John Dee, c. conjuring at a poole in Brecknockshire, and that

* Arthur Dee (sonne of J. Dee), a physitian at Norwych, was born 13 Julij, 1579, mane hora 4. 30 fere vel potius 25 m̄. in ipso ortu solis, ut existimo. Thus I find it in his father's *Ephemerides*. Obijt Norwychi, about 1650.

they found a wedge of gold; and that theywere troubled, and indicted as conjurers at the assizes; that a mighty storme and tempest was raysed in harvest time, the countrey people had not knowen the like. His picture in a wooden cut is at the end of Billingsley's Euclid, but Mr. Elias Ashmole hath a very good painted copie of him from his sonne Arthur. He had a very fair, clear, sanguine complexion,* a long beard as white as milke. A very handsome man.

Old Good-wife Faldo (a natif of Mortlack, in Surrey), 80+ ætatis, did know Dr. Dee, and told me he dyed at his howse in Mortlack, next to the howse where the tapistry hangings are made, viz. West of that howse; and that he dyed about 60+,8 or 9 yeares since (January, 1672), and lies buried in the chancell, and had a marble stone upon him. Her mother tended him in his sicknesse. She told me, that he did entertain the Polonian ambassador at his howse in Mortlack, and dyed not long after; and that he shewed the Eclipse with a darke roome to the s[d] ambassador.† She beleeves that he

* As S[r] Hen. Saville.

† A Brief History of Muscovia, by Mr. Jo. Milton. Lond. 1682, pag. 100. sc. 1588. "Dr. Giles Fletcher "went ambassador from y[e] Queen to Pheodor then empe-"rour; whose relations being judicious and exact, are best "read entirely by themselves. This emperour, upon report "of the great learning the mathematician [possessed], invited "him to Mosco, with offer of two thousand pounds a-yeare,

was eightie years old when he dyed. She sayd, he kept a great many stilles goeing. That he layd the storme S[r] Everard Digby.* That the children dreaded him because he was accounted a conjurer. He recovered the basket of cloathes stollen, when *she* and his daughter (both girles) were negligent, she knew this.

He is buried (upon the matter*) in the middest* of the chancell, a little towards the South side. She sayd, he lies buried in the chancell between Mr. Holt and Mr. Miles, both servants to Q. Elizabeth, and both have brasse ISS. on their marble, and that there was on him a marble, but without any inscription, which marble is removed; on which old marble is signe of two or three brasse pinnes.* A daughter of his (I thinke Sarah) maried to a flax-dresser, in Southwarke. Qu. nomen.

He dyed within a yeare, if not shortly after the King of Denmark was here. V. S[r] Rich. Baker's *Chron.* and Capt. Wharton's *Alm.*

He built the gallery in the church at Mortlack. Goody Faldo's father was the carpenter that work't it.

A stone was on his grave, w[ch] is since removed. At the upper end of the chancell then were

" and from Prince Boris one thousand markes; to have his " provision from the Emperor's table, to be honourably re- " ceived, and accounted as one of the chief men in the " land. All which Dee accepted not."

* [Sic. Edit.]

steppes, which in Oliver's dayes were layd plaine by the minister, and then 'twas removed. The children when they played in the church would runne to Dr. Dee's grave-stone. She told me that he forewarned Q. Elizabeth of Dr. Lopez attempt against her. * * * *

He used to distill egge-shells, and 'twas from hence that Ben Jonson had his hint of the alchimist, whom he meant.

He was a great peace-maker; if any of the neighbours fell out, he would never lett them alone till he had made them friends.

He was tall and slender. He wore a gowne like an artist's gowne, with hanging sleeves, and a slitt.

A mighty good man he was.

He was sent ambassador for Queen Elizabeth (shee thinkes) into Poland.

Mem. His regayning of the plate for . . . . 's butler, who comeing from London by water with a basket of plate, mistooke another basket that was like his. Mr. J. Dee bid them* goe by water such a day and looke about, and he should see the man that had his basket, and he did so; but he would not gett the lost horses, though he was offered severall angells. He told a woman (his neighbour) that she laboured under the evill tongue of an ill neighbour (another woman), wch came to her house, who he sayd was a witch.

* [Sic. Edit.]

In J. David Rhesus' "*British Grammar*," p. 60. "Juxta Crucis amnem *(Nant y groes)*, in "agro *Maessyuetiano,* apud Cambro-brytannos, "erat olim illustris quædam Nigrorum familia, "unde *Joan Du,* id est, Johannes ille cognomento "*Niger,* Londinensis, sui generis ortum traxit: "vir certe ornatissimus et doctissimus, et omnium "hac nostra ætate tum Philosophorum tum Ma-"thematicorum facile princeps: monadis illius "Hieroglyphicæ et Propædeumatum aphoristico-"rum de præstantioribus quibusdam Naturæ vir-"tutibus, aliorumque non paucorum operum in-"signium autor eximius. Vir præterea ob tam "multam experientiam frequenti sua in tot trans-"marinas regiones peregrinatione comparatam, "rerum quamplurimarum et abditarum peritissi-"mus."

. . . . . DE LAUNE.

He was apothecary to Mary the Q. mother: came into England . . . . He was a very wise man, and as a signe of it left an estate of 80000lib. Sr W. Davenant was his great acq. and told me of him, and that after his returne into England he went to visit him, being then octogenary, and very decrepid with the gowt, but had his sight and understanding. He had a place made for him in the kitchen chimney, and no obstacle, he was master of such an estate. Sr W. sawe him slighted not only by his da.-in-lawe, but by the cooke-mayd, which much affected him. The misery of old age. He wrote a booke of prudentiall advice in quadrans in English verse, 8° which I have seen, and there are good things in it.

SIR JOHN DENHAM,

(Knight of the Bath),

Was borne at Dublin, in Ireland, A° D^ni . . . . . (Qu. Dr. Buzby* if he was a Westminster schollar, I have forgot.) A° . . . . he was admitted of Trinity colledge, in Oxford, where he stayed . . . His tutor there was . . . . . I have heard Mr. Jos. Howe say that he was the dreamingest young fellow; he never expected such things from him as he hath left the world. When he was there he would game extremely; when he had played away all his money he would play away his father's wrought cappes with gold. His father was Sr John Denham, one of the Barons of the Exchequer, he had been one of the Lords Justices in Ireland:† he maried Ellenor,‡ one of

* [Sic. Edit.]

† S^r Jo. told me his family was originally Westerne.

‡ She was a beautifull woman, as appears by her monument at Egham. Sir John, they say, did much resemble his father.

the daughters of S[r] Garret Moore, knight, Lord Baron of Mellifont, in y[e] kingdome of Ireland, whom he maried during his service in Ireland, in y[e] place of Chief Justice there. From Trinity colledge he went to Lincolnes-Inne, where (as Judge Wadham Windham, who was his countryman, told me) he was as good a student as any in the house. Was not supposed to be a witt. At last, viz. 1640, his play of "*The Sophy*" came out, w[ch] did take extremely: Mr. Edmund Waller sayd then of him, that he broke out like the Irish Rebellion—threescore thousand strong, when nobody suspected it. He was much rooked by gamesters, and fell acquainted with that unsanctified crew to his ruine. His father had some suspicion of it, and chid him severely, whereupon his son John (only child) wrot a little Essay in 8[o] printed .... *Against Gaming*, and to shew the vanities and inconveniences of it, w[ch] he presented to his father, to let him know his detestation of it: but shortly after his father's death* (who left 2000 or 1500lib. in ready money, 2 houses well furnished, and much plate) the money was played away first, and next the plate was sold. I remember about 1646 he lost 200lib. one night at New-cutt. An... (I ghesse 1642) he was high-sheriff of the countie of Surrey. At the beginning of the civill warre he was made governor

* January 6, 1638. sepult. at Egham, in Surrey.

of Farnham-castle for the king, but he was but a young soldier, and did not keepe it. In 1642-3 after Edghill fight, his poeme called "*Cowper's Hill*" was printed at Oxford, in a sort of browne paper, for then they could get no better. In 1646-7 he conveyed, or stole away the two Dukes of Yorke and Glocester from S[t] James's, (from the tuition of the Earle of Northumberland) and conveyed them into France to the Prince of Wales and Queen-mother. King Charles II. sent him and the Lord Culpepper envoys to the King of Poland. A° 1652, he returned into England, and being in some straights was kindly entertayned by the Earle of Pembroke at Wilton, where I had the honour to contract an acquaintance with him. Here he translated the . . . . . booke of *Virgil's Æneis,* and also burlesqu't it.* Qu. Mr. Chr. Wase who was then there, tutor to Wm. Lord Herbert. He was, as I remember, a yeare with my Lord of Pembroke at Wilton and London; he had then sold all the lands his father had left him. His first wife was the daughter and heire of . . . . Cotton, of . . . . in Glocestershire, by whom he had 500lib. per annum, one son and two daughters. His son did not *patrem sapere.* He was of Wadham college

* He burlesqued Virgil, and burnt it, sayeing that 'twas not fitt that the first poet should be so abused. From Mr. Chr. Wase.

in Dr. Wilkins's time: he died *sine prole*, I thinke there. One of his daughters is maried to . . . Morley, of Sussex, Esq. the other . . . . . He was much beloved by King Charles the First, who much valued him for his integrity. He graunted him the reversion of the surveyor of his buildings, after the decease of Mr. Inigo Jones; which place, after the restauration of King Charles II. he enjoyed to his death, and gott seaven thousand pounds, as Sr. Ch. Wren told me of, to his owne knowledge. Sr. Christopher Wren was his deputie. An. Dni. 166 . . . he maried his 2d wife, . . . Brookes, a very beautifull young lady, Sr John was ancient and limping. The Duke of Yorke fell deeply in love with her . . . . This occasioned Sr. John's distemper of madnesse in 166 . . wch first appeared when he went from London to see the famous free-stone quarries at Portland, in Dorset. When he came within a mile of it, turned back to London againe, and would not see it; he went to Hounslowe, and demanded rents of lands he had sold many yeares before; went to the king, and told him he was the Holy Ghost; but it pleased God that he was cured of this distemper, and writt excellent verses, particularly on the death of Mr. Abraham Cowley, afterwards. His 2d lady had no child, and was poysoned by the hands of the Co. of Roc. with chocolatte. At the coronation of King Charles II. he was made Knight of the Bath. He dyed at the house of his office, (which he built, as also the brick buildings next the street in Scotland-yard) and was buried An.º D.ni 1668-9, March the 23, in the south crosse aisle of Westminster Abbey, neer S.r Jeffrey Chaucer's monument, but (hitherto, 1680) without any memoriall for him.

Mem. the parsonage house at Egham (vulgarly called *The Place*) was built by Baron Denham; a house very convenient, not great, but pretty, and pleasantly situated, and in which his son, S.r John (though he had better seates), did take most delight in. He sold it to John Thynne, Esq. In this parish is a place called Cammomill-hill, from the cammomill that growes there naturally, as also West of it is Prune-well-hill, (formerly part of Sir John's possessions) where was a fine tuft of trees, a clear spring, and a pleasant prospect to the East, over the levell of Midd.x and Surrey. S.r John tooke great delight in this place, and was wont to say (before the troubles) that he would build a retiring place to entertaine his muses, but the warres forced him to sell that as well as the rest. He sold it to Mr. . . . Anstey. In this parish W. and by N. (above *Runney-Meade)* is *Cowper's Hill,* from whence a noble prospect, w.ch is incomparably well described by that sweet swan, S.r Jo. Denham.

Mem. He delighted much in bowles, and did bowle very well. He was of the tallest, but a little incurvetting at his shoulders, not very robust.

His haire was but thin and flaxen, with a moist curle. His gate was slow, and was rather a stalking, (he had long legges) which was wont to putt me in mind of Horace, *De Arte Poetica.*

"Hic dum sublimes versus ructatur, et errat,
"Si, veluti merulis intentus decidit auceps
"In puteum foveamve :"———

His eie was a kind of light goose-gray, not big ; but it had a strange piercingness, not as to shining and glory, but (like a Momus) when he conversed with you he look't into your very thoughts.

He was generally temperate as to drinking ; but one time when he was a student of Lincolnes Inne, having been merry at y[e] taverne with his camerades, late at night, a frolick came into his head, to gett a playsterer's brush and a pott of inke, and blott out all the signes between Temple-barre and Charing-crosse, w[ch] made a strange confusion the next day, and 'twas in Terme time. But it happened that they were discovered, and it cost him and them some moneys. This I had from R. Estcourt, Esq. y[t] carried the inke pott.

In the time of the civill warres, Geo. Withers, the poet, begged S[r] Jo. Denham's estate of the Parliament, in whose cause he was a captaine of horse. It [happened] that G. W. was taken prisoner, and was in danger of his life, having written severely against the King, &c. Sir John Denham went to the King, and desired his ma^tie not to hang him, for that whilest G. W. lived he should not be the worst poet in England.

Scripsit the Sophy: Cowper's Hill: Essay against Gameing: Poems, 8º printed Aº Dni . . . Cato Major, sive De Senectute, translated into English verse. London, printed by H. Heringman, in the New Exchange, 1669.

Mem. In the verses against Gondibert, most of them are Sir John's. He was satyricall when he had a mind to it.

MEUR RENATUS DES CARTES.

Nobilis Gallus, Perroni Dominus, summus Mathematicus et Philosophus, natus Turonum, pridie Calendas Apriles, 1596. Denatus Holmiæ, Calendis Februarij, 1650.* How he spent his time in his youth, and by what method he became so knowing, he tells the world in his treatise entituled, Of Method. The Societie of Jesus glorie in that theyr order had the educating of him. He lived severall yeares at Egmont (neer the Hague), from whence he dated severall of his bookes. He was too wise a man to encomber

* This inscription I find under his picture by C. V. Dalen.

himselfe with a wife; but as he was a man, he had the desires and appetites of a man, he therefore kept a good conditioned hansome woman that he liked, and by whom he had some children (I thinke 2 or 3). 'Tis pity but comeing from the loines of such a father, they should be well cultivated. He was so eminently learned that all learned men made visits to him, and many of them would desire him to shew them his . . . . . of instruments (in those dayes mathematicall learning lay much in the knowledge of instruments, and, as S^r. H. S. sayd, in doeing of tricks), he would drawe out a little drawer under his table, and shew them a paire of compasses with one of the legges broken; and then, for his ruler, he used a sheet of paper folded double. This from Alexander Cowper, (brother of Samuel) limner to Christina, Q. of Sweden, who was familiarly acquainted there with Des Cartes.

SIR KENELME DIGBY, KNIGHT.

He was borne at . . . . . . on the 11th of July. See Ben Jonson, 2d volume,

"Witnesse thy actions done at Scanderoon
Upon thy birth day, the eleaventh of June."*

* Mr. Elias Ashmole assures me from two or 3 nativities

He was the eldest son of Sr Everard Digby, who was accounted the handsomest gentleman in England. Sr Everard suffered as a traytor in the gunpowder treason; but K. James restored his estate to his son and heire. Mr. Fr. Potter told me that Sr Everard wrote a booke *De Arte Natandi.* I have a Latin booke of his writing in 8°.* His 2d son was Sr John Digby, as valiant a gent. and as good a sword-man as was in England, who dyed (or was killed) in the king's cause at Bridgewater about 1644. It happened in 1647, that a grave was opened next to Sir John Digby's (who was buried in sumer time, as it seemes), and the flowers on his coffin were found fresh, as I heard Mr. Harcourt (that was executed) attest that very yeare. S^r^ Jo. died a batchelour.

Sr Kenelme Digby was held to be the most accomplished cavalier of his time. He went to Glocester hall, in Oxon, A^o^ . . . The learned Mr. Thomas Allen, (then of that house) was wont to say, that he was the *Mirandula* of his age. He did not weare a gowne there, as I have heard my

by Dr. Napier, that Ben Jonson was mistaken, and did it for ye ryme-sake.

Mem. in the first impression in 8vo. it is thus, but in the fol. it is *my*, instead of *thy*.

* Everardi Dygbei de Duplici Methodo Libri Duo. In Dialogis inter Aristotelicum et Ramistam, in 8o.; the title page is torne out.

cosen Whitney say. There was a great friendship between him and Mr. Tho. Allen; whether he was his scholar I know not. Mr. Allen was one of the learnedest men of this nation in his time, and a great collector of good bookes, which collection S^r. Kenelme bought (Mr. Allen enjoyeing the use of them for his life) to give to the Bodlean Library, after Mr. Allen's decease, where they now are. He was a great traveller, and understood 10 or 12 languages. He was not only master of a good and gracefull judicious stile, but he also wrote a delicate hand, both fast hand and Roman. I have seen letters of his writing to the Earle of Pembroke,* who much respected him. He was such a goodly handsome person, and had so gracefull elocution and noble addresse, that had he been dropt out of the clowdes in any part of the world, he would have made himselfe respected. But the Jesuites spake spitefully, and sayd 'twas true, but then he must not stay there above six weekes.† He was well versed in all kinds of learning. And he had also this vertue, that no man *knew better how to abound, and to be*

* Father of this [the present. EDIT.]

† He was envoyé from Henrietta Maria, (then Queen-mother) to Pope . . . . . where at first he was mightily admired; but after some time he grew high, and hectored at his holinesse, and gave him ye lye. The Pope sayd he was mad.

abased, and either was indifferent to him. No man became grandeur better; sometimes againe he would live only with a lackey, and horse with a foote-cloath. He was very generous, and liberall to deserving persons. When Abr. Cowley was but 13 yeares old, he dedicated to him a comedy, called "*Love's Riddle,*" and concludes in his dedicatory epistle—"The Birch that whipt him then would prove a Bay." S^r^. K. was very kind to him. When he was at Rome one time, (I thinke he was envoyé from the Queen-mother to Pope . . . .) he contrasted* with his holinesse. A^o^. . . . . much against his mother's, &c. consent, he maried that celebrated beautie and courtezane, Mrs. Venetia Stanley, whom Rich. Earle of Dorset kept as his concubine, had children by her, and settled on her an annuity of 500lib. per annum; which after S^r^. K. D. maried was unpayd by the Earle; Sr Kenelme sued the Earle, after mariage, and recovered it. He would say that a handsome lusty man that was discreet might make a vertuose wife out of a brothel-house. This lady carried herselfe blamelessly, yet (they say) he was jealous of her.† She dyed suddenly, and hard-hearted

* [Sic. Edit.]

† Rich. Earle of Dorset invited her and her husband once a yeare, when, with much desire and passion he beheld her, and only kissed her hand; Sir Kenelme being still by.

woemen would censure him severely. After her death, to avoyd envy and scandall, he retired into Gresham colledge, at London, where he diverted himselfe with his chymistry, and the professor's good conversation. He wore there a long mourning cloake, a high cornered hatt, his beard unshorne, look't like a hermite, as signes of sorrowe for his beloved wife, to whose memory he erected a sumptuouse monument, now quite destroyed by the great conflagration. He stayed at the college two or 3 yeares. He was, 164 . . . prisoner for the king at Winchester-house,* where he practised chymistry, and wrote his booke of Bodies and Soule, wch he dedicated to his eldest son, Kenelme, who was slaine (as I take it) in the Earle of Holland's riseing. A°. 163 . . tempore Car. 1^mi^ he received the sacrament in the chapell at Whitehall, and professed the Protestant religion, wch gave great scandal to the Roman Catholiques ; but afterwards he *looked back*.† He

* The faire howses in Holbourne, between King's street and Southampton street, (wch brake off the continuance ot them) were built, about 1633, by Sr Kenelme; where he lived before the civill warres. Since the restauration of Ch. II. he lived in the last faire house westward in the north portico of Covent Garden, where my Ld Denzill Hollis lived since. He had a laboratory there. I thinke he dyed in this house—sed Qu.

† Mr. Thomas White, who wrote *De Mundo*, 1641-2,

was a person of extraordinary strength. I remember one at Shirburne (relating to the E. of Bristoll) protested to us, that as he, being a midling man, being sett in a chaire, S[r] Kenelme tooke up him, chaire, and all, with one arme. He was of an undaunted courage, yet not apt in the least to give offence. His conversation was both ingeniose and innocent. As for that great action of his at Scanderoon, see the Turkish Historie. S[r] . . . . Stradling, of Glamorganshire, was then his Vice-Admirall, at whose house is an excellent picture of his, as he was at that time: by him is drawen an armillary sphere broken, and undernethe is writt IMPAVIDUM FERIENT. See excellent verses of Ben Jonson (to whome he was a great patrone) in his 2d volume. There is in print in French, and also in English (translated by Mr. James Howell), a speech that he made at a Philosophicall assembly at Montpelier, 165 . . . *Of the Sympathetique Powder.* He made a speech at the beginning of the meeting of ye Royall Society *Of the Vegetation of Plants.* He was borne to three thousand pounds per annum. His ancient seat (I thinke) is Gote-herst, in Buckinghamshire. He had a faire estate also in Rutlandshire. What by reason of the civil warres, and

and Mr. . . . . Hall, of Liege, *è Societate Jesu,* were two of his great friends.

his generous mind, he contracted great debts, and I know not how (there being a great falling out between him and his *then* only son, John*) he settled his estate upon . . . Cornwalleys, a subtile sollicitor, and also a member of the house of commons, who did putt Mr. Jo. Digby to much charge in lawe. Qu. what became of it? Mr. J. D. had a good estate of his owne, and lived handsomely then, at what time I went to him two or 3 times, in order to your *Oxon. Antiqu.* and he then brought me a great book as big as the biggest Church Bible that ever I sawe, and the richliest bound, bossed with silver, engraven with scutchions and crest.† It was a curious volume. It was the history of the family of the Digbyes, which Sr Kenelme either did or ordered to be donne. There was inserted all that was to be found any where relating to them, out of Records of the Tower, Rolles, &c: all ancient church monuments were most exquisitely limmed by some rare artist. He told me that the compileing of it did cost his father a thousand pounds. Sr Jos. Fortescue sayd he did beleeve 'twas more. When Mr. Jo. Digby did me the favour to shew me this rare MS. "This booke," sayd he, "is

* He m...... sister to this present Henry Duke of Norfolke, no child living by her. His 2d wife ..... Fortescue, by whom he hath........ Quære the issue?

† An ostrich.

all that I have left me of all the estate that was my father's!" He was almost as tall and as big as his father: he had something of the sweetnesse of his mother's face. He was bred by the Jesuites, and was a good scholar. He dyed at . . .

V. in . . . . Lives when Sr Kenelme dyed.

Sr John Hoskyns informes me that Sr Kenelme Digby did translate Petronius Arbiter into English.*

* VENETIA STANLEY

Was daughter of Sr Edward Stanley, of Eynstoun, in com. Oxon, son of Sr Tho. Stanley, K^t. younger son to Edw. E. of . . . . .† She was a most beautifull desireable creature; and being *matura viro* was left by her father to live with a tenant and servants at Enston-abbey,‡ (his land, or the E. of Darby's) in Oxfordshire; but as private as that place was, it seemes her beautie could not lye hid. The young eagles had espied her, and she was sanguine and tractable, and of much suavity (wch to abuse was greate pittie). In those dayes Richard Earle of Dorset (eldest son and heire to the L^d treasurer) lived in the greatest splendor of any nobleman of England.§ Among other pleasures

† The words thus marked were inserted by Anthony à Wood.

‡ At the W. end of the church here were two towers as at Welles or Westminster Abbey, wch were standing till about 1656. The rooms of the abbey were richly wainscotted, both sides and roofe.

§ He lived in the greatest grandeur of any nobleman of his time in Engl. He had 30 gentlemen, and gave to each 30lib. per annum. besides keeping his horse. G. Villers (after Duke of Bucks) was a petitioner to have had a gentleman's place under him, and miss't it,

EARLE OF DORSET.

Epigram on the Earle of Dorset who dyed suddenly at the Council boord.

Uncivill death, that would'st not once conferre,
Dispute or parle with our treasurer,

that he enjoyed, Venus was not the least. This pretty creature's fame quickly came to his Lop's eares, who made no delay to catch at such an opportunity. I have now forgott who first brought her to towne, but I have heard my uncle Danvers say (who was her contemporary) that she was so commonly courted, and that by grandees, that 'twas written over her lodging one night *in literis uncialibus,*

PRAY COME NOT NEER,
FOR DAME VENETIA STANLEY LODGETH HERE.

The Earle of Dorset aforesayd, was her greatest gallant, who was extremely enamoured of her, and had one if not more children by her. He setled on her an annuity of 500lib. per annum. Among other young sparkes of that time, S[r] Kenelme Digby grew acquainted with her, and fell so much in love with her that he married her, much against the good will of his mother; but he would say "that a wise man and lusty could make an honest woman out of a brothell-house." S[r] Edm. Wyld had her picture, (and you may imagine was very familiar with her) which picture is now at Droitwich, in Worcestershire, at an inne, where now

and within a 12 mouth was a greater man himselfe; but the duke ever after bore a grudge to the E. of Dorset. From the Countesse of Thanet.

Had he been thee, or of thy fatall tribe,
He would have spar'd thy life, and ta'ne a bribe.

the towne keepe their meetings. Also at Mr. Rose's, a jeweller, in Henrietta-street, in Covent garden, is an excellent piece of hers, drawne after she was newly dead. She had a most lovely sweet-turned face, delicate darke browne haire. She had a perfect healthy constitution; strong; good skin; well proportioned; enclining to a *Bona Roba*. Her face, a short ovall; darke browne eie-browe, about w[ch] much sweetness, as also in the opening of her eie-lidds. The colour of her cheekes was just that of the Damaske rose, which is neither too hot nor too pale. She was of a just stature, not very tall.

S[r] Kenelme had severall pictures of her by Vandyke, &c.* He had her hands cast in playster, and her feet, and her face. See Ben Jonson's 2d volume, where he hath made her live in poetry, in his drawing of her both body and mind:—

> " Sitting, and ready to be drawne,
> What makes these tiffany, silks, and lawne,
> Embroideries, feathers, fringes, lace,
> When every limbe takes like a face !"—&c.

When these verses were made she had three children by S[r] Kenelme, who are there mentioned, Kenelme, George, and John. She dyed in her bed suddenly. Some suspected that she was poysoned. When her head was opened there was found but little braine, w[ch] her husband imputed to her drinking of viper-wine; but spitefull woemen would say 'twas a viper-husband who was jealous of her * * * *

* Her picture by Vandyke is now at Abermarleys, in Carmarthenshire, at Mr. Cornwalleys' sonne's widowe's (the Lady Cornwalleys' house), who was the da. and heire of . . . . Jones, of Abermarleys.

He that so often had, with gold and witt,
Injur'd strong lawe, and almost conquer'd it,

* * * * * * * I have heard some say,—e. g. my cos. Eliz. Falkner,—that after her marriage she redeemed her honour by her strickt living. Once a yeare the Earle of Dorset invited her and S[r] Kenelme to dinner, where the Earle would behold her with much passion, and only kisse her hand. S[r] Kenelme erected to her memorie a sumptuouse and stately monument at .... Fryars, Christ Church (neer Newgate-street), in the East end of the South aisle, where her body lyes in a vault of brick-worke, over which are three steps of black marble, with 4 inscriptions in copper gilt affixed to it: upon this altar her bust of copper gilt, all w[ch] (unlesse the vault which was onely opened a little by the fall) is utterly destroyed by the great conflagration. Among the monuments in the booke mentioned in S[r] Ken. Digby's life, is to be seen a curious draught of this monument, wth copies of the severall inscriptions. About 1676 or 5, as I was walking through Newgate-street, I sawe Dame Venetia's bust standing at a stall at the golden crosse, a brasier's shop. I presently remembred it, but the fire had gott off the guilding: but taking notice of it to one that was with me, I could never see it afterwards exposed to the street. They melted it downe. How these curiosities would be quite forgott, did not such idle fellowes as I am putt them downe!

Mem. At Goathurst, in Bucks, is a rare originall picture of S[r] Kenelme Digby, and his Lady Venetia, in one piece by the hand of S[r] Anthony Vandyke. In Ben Jonson's 2d volume is a poeme called "Eupheme, left to posteritie, of y[e] noble lady, the Ladie Venetia Digby, late wife of S[r] Kenelme Digby, K[t] a gentleman absolute in all numbers: consisting of these ten pieces, viz. Dedication of her Cradle; Song of her Descent; Picture of her Bodie;

At length, for want of evidence to shewe,
Was forc't himselfe to take a deadly blowe.

These verses I transcribed out of the collection of my hon[d] friend and neighbour, Tho. Tyndale, Esq.

Mem. The tryall was with this* S[r] Rich. Temple's gr. grandfather. The L[d] treas. had in his bosome some writings, w[ch] as he was pulling out to give in evidence, sayed, *"Here is that will strike you dead!"* and as soon as he had spoken these words, fell downe starke dead in the place. (Mem. An extraordinary perturbation of mind will bring an apoplexie. I know severall instances of it.) From S[r] Richard Temple.

'Twas this Lord that gott Salisbury house *cum*

Picture of her Mind; Her being chose a Muse; Her faire Offices; Her happy Match; Her hopefull Issue; Her ΑΠΟΘΕΩΣΙΣ, or Relation to the Saints; Her Inscription or Crowne."

Her picture drawn by S[r] Anth. Vandyke hangs in the queene's drawing-roome, at Windsor-castle, over the chimney.

Venetia Stanley was (first) a miss to S[r] Edmund Wyld, so he had her picture, w[ch] after his death, serjeant Wyld (his executor) had, and since y[e] serjeant's death hangs now in an entertaining roome at Droitwich, in Worcestershire. The serjeant lived at Droitwich.

Venetia Stanley's picture is at the E. of Rutland's, at Belvoir.

* [The present. Edit.]

appurtenantiis, juxta S[t] Bride's, in exchange for a piece of land, neer Cricklade, in Wilts, I thinke called Marston, but the title was not good, nor did the value answer his promise. From Seth Sarum, who sayes that all the parish of St. Bride's belonged to the Bp. of Sarum, as also all Shoe-lane.

MICHAEL DRAYTON, ESQ.

Natus in Warwickshire, at Atherston upon Stower. He was a butcher's sonne Was a squire, viz. one of the Esq[res] to S[r] Walter Aston, K[t] of the Bath, to whom he dedicated his Poeme. S[r] . . . . . B . . . was a great patron of his. He lived at the bay-windowe house next the East end of S[t] Dunstan's ch. in Fleet-street. Sepult. in N. of W. Abbey. The Countesse of Dorset (Clifford) gave his monument. Mr. Marshall, (the stone-cutter) who made it, told me. S[r] Edw. Bissh Clarenc. told me he asked Mr. Selden once (jestingly) whether he wrote the comment. to his "Polyolbion" and "Epistles," or Mr. Drayton made those verses to his notes.

In Westm. Abbey, neer Spencer.

MICHAEL DRAYTON, ESQUIER,
A memorable Poet of this age, exchanged his
Laurel for a Crowne of Glorie, A[o] 1631.

Doe pious marble, let thy readers knowe
What they, and what their children owe
To DRAYTON's name, whose sacred dust
We recommend unto thy trust.
Protecte his mem'ry, and preserve his storie,
Remaine a lasting monument of his glorye.
And when thy ruines shall disclame
To be the treas'rer of his name,
His name, that cannot fade, shall be
An everlasting monument to thee.

Mr. Marshall, the stone-cutter, of Fetter-lane, also told me, that these verses were made by Mr. Francis Quarles, who was his great friend, and whose head he wrought curiously in playster, and valued for his sake. 'Tis pitty it should be lost. Mr. Quarles was a very good man.

SAINT DUNSTAN.

I find in Mr. Selden's verses before Hopton's "Concordance of Yeares," that he was a Somersetshire gentleman. He was a great chymist. The storie of his pulling the devill by the nose with his tongues as he was in his laboratorie, was famous in church-windowes, picture, and poetrie.*

* V. Gazæi "*Pia Hilaria,*" delicately described.

He was a Benedictine monke at Glastonbury, where he was afterwards abbot, and after that was made A. B. Cant. He preached the coronation sermon at Kingston, and crowned King .... In his sermon he prophesied, wch the Chronnicle mentions. Mr. Meredith Lloyd tells me that there is a booke in print of his "De Lapide Philosophorum." Edwardus Generosus gives a good account of him in a Manuscript wch Mr. Ashmole hath. Mem. Lloyd had, about the beginning of the civill warres, a MS. of this Saint's concerning Chymistrey, and sayes that there are severall MSS. of his up and downe in England. Edwardus Generosus mentions that he could make a fire out of gold, with which he could sett any combustible matter on fire at a great distance. Mem. In Westminster library is an old printed booke, in folio, of the Lives of the old English Saints. Mem. Lloyd tells me that three or 400 yeares ago, Chymistrey was in a greater perfection much than now. The proces was then more seraphique and universall. Now they looke only after medicines. Severall churches are dedicated to him: two at London; Qu. if one at Glastonbury.

SIR EDWARD DYER,

Of Somersetshire, (Sharpham Parke, &c.) was a great witt, poet, and acquaintance of Mary Countesse of Pembroke, and S^r. Philip Sydney. He is mentioned in the preface of the "Arcadia." He had four thousand pounds per annum, and was left fourscore thousand pounds in money, he wasted it almost all. This I had from Captaine Dyer, his great grandsonne, or brother's gr. gr. son. I thought he had been the sonne of ye Lord Chiefe Justice Dyer, as I have inserted in one of these papers, but that was a mistake. The judge was of the same family the Capt. tells me.

SAINT EDMUND.

Seth Lord Bishop of Sarum tells me, that he finds S^t. Edmund was borne at Abington. He was A. B^p. of Cant. He built the college at Sarum, by St. Edmund's church. It is now Judge Wyndham's sonne's house. He resigned his archbishoprick, and came and retired hither. In S^t. Edmund's church here, were windowes of great value. Gundamore offered a good summe for them; I have forgott [what.] In one of them was the picture of God the Father, like an old man (as the fashion was), wch much offended Mr. Shervill, the recorder, who in zeale (but without knowledge) clambered up on the pewes to breake the windowe, and fell downe and broke his legg (about 1629), but that did not excuse him, for being questioned in the Star-chamber for it, Mr. Attorney Noy was his great friend, and shewed his friendship there. But what Mr. Shervill left undonne, the soldiers since have gonne through with, that there is not a piece of the glass painting left.

"Edmundus Cant. A. B. primus legit Elementa "Euclidis, Oxoniæ, 1290. Mr. Hugo perlegit "Lib. Aristotelis Analytic. Oxon. Rogerus "Bacon vixit A. D. 1292." This out of an old booke in the Library of University college, Oxon.

SIR THOMAS EGERTON, LORD CHANCELLOR,

Was the naturall sonne of Sir Rich. Egerton, of .... in Cheshire. He was of Lincolnes-Inne, and I have heard Sir John Danvers say, that he was so hard a student, that in three or 4 years' time he was not out of the house. He had good parts, and early came into good practice. My old father, Colonel Sharington Talbot,* told

* He had, I believe, 200 adopted sonnes.

me that . . . . . Earle of Shrewsbury desired him to buy that noble mannour of Ellesmer for him, and delivered him the money. Egerton liked the bargain and the seat so well, that truly he e'en kept it for himself, and afterwards made it his barony, but the money he restored to the Earl of Shrewsbury again.

His son and heir, since Earle of Bridgewater, was an indefatigable ringer.

DESID. ERASMUS, ROTERODAMUS.

He loved not fish, though born in a fish towne.* He was of the order of . . . . whose habit was the same that the Pest-house master at . . . .† in Italie wore, and walking in that town, people beckoned to him to go out of ye way, taking him to be the master of the Pest-house, and he not understanding the meaning, and keeping on his way, was there well basted. He made his complaint when he came to Rome, and had a dispensation for his habit.

His name was *Gerard Gerard,* which he translated into Desiderius Erasmus. He was *begot*

* From Sir George Ent, M.D. † I thinke, Pisa.

(as they say) *behind dores.** His father (as he says in his Life writt by himself) was the tenth and youngest son of his grandfather, who was therefore designed to be dedicated to God.† * *

His father took great care to send him to an excellent schoole, which was at Dusseldorf, in Cleveland. He was a tender chitt, and his mother would not entruste him as a boarder, but took a house there, and made him cordialls, &c. [From J. Pell, D.D.]

He studied sometime in Queen's colledge, in Cambridge, his chamber was over the water. He mentions his being there in one of his Epistles, and blames the beer there. One Long since wrote in the margent of the book in Coll. Libr. in which that is sayd—*Sicut erat in principio,* &c. and all Mr. Paschall's time they found fault with the brewer. He had the parsonage of Aldington, in Kent, which is about 3 deg. perhaps a healthier place then Dr. Pell's parsonage, in Essex. I wonder they could not find out for him better preferment; but I see that the ⊙ and ♑ being in the second house, he was not born to be a rich man. He built a schoole at Rotterdam, and endowed it, and ordered the institution. Sir George

* Vide an Italian booke in 8vo. de Famosi Bastardi. V. Anton. Possevini Apparatus.

† [A table containing the calculation of his Nativity is here omitted. Edit.]

Ent was educated there. A statue of brass is erected to his memory on the bridge in Rotterdam. Sir Charles Blount, of Maple-Durham, in com. Oxōn. (neer Reding) was his scholar, (in his Epistles there are some to him) and desired Erasmus to doe him the favour to sit for his picture, and he did so, and it is an excellent piece: which picture my cos. John Danvers, of Baynton (Wilts), has: his wife's grandmother was Sir Ch. Blount's daughter or grand-daughter. 'Twas pitty such a rarity should have been aliened from the family, but the issue male is lately extinct. I will sometime or other endeavour to get it for Oxford Library.

They were wont to say that Erasmus was interpendent between Heaven and Hell, till about the year 1655, the Conclave at Rome damned him for a heretique, after he had been dead . . . . yeares.

His deepest Divinity is where a man would least expect it: viz. in his Colloquies in a Dialogue between a Butcher and a Fishmonger, Ἰχθυοφαγία.

Vita Erasmi, Erasmo Autore, is before his Colloquies, printed Amstelodam. CIↃ IↃC XLIV. But there is a good account of his life, and also of his death, and where buried, before his Colloquies printed at London.

If my memory fails not, I have read in the first edition of Sir Rich. Baker's Chron. that ye Syntaxis in our English Grammar was writt by Erasmus.

Mem. Julius Scaliger contested with Erasmus, but gott nothing by it, for, as Fuller sayth, he was like a badger that never bitt, but he made his teeth meet. He was the Πρόδρομος of our knowledge, and the man that made the rough and untrodden wayes smooth and passable.

" The staires which rise up to his studie at " Queen's College, in Cambr. doe bring first into " two of the fairest chambers in the ancient " building; in one of them, which lookes into " the hall and chief court, the Vice-President " kept in my time; in that adjoyning, it was my " fortune to be, when fellow. The chambers " over are good lodgeing roomes; and to one of " them is a square turret adjoyning, in the upper " part of which is the study of Erasmus; and " over it leads. To that belongs the best pros- " pect about the colledge, viz. upon the river, " into the corne-fields, and countrey adjoyning. " So y[t] it might very well consist with the civility " of the House to that great man (who was no " fellow, and I think stayed not long there) to let " him have that study. His sleeping roome " might be either the Vice-President's, or, to be " neer to him, the next. The room for his ser- " vitor that above it, and through it he might " goe to that studie, which for the height, and " neatnesse, and prospect, might easily take his

" phancy." This from Mr. Andrew Paschal, Rector of Ched . . . in Somerset. June 15, 1680.

John Dryden, Esq. Poet Laureat, tells me that there was a great friendship between his great grandfather's father, and Erasmus Roterodamus, and Erasmus was godfather to one of his sonnes, and the Christian name of Erasmus hath been kept in the family ever since. The poet's 2d sonne is Erasmus, and at . . . . the seate of the family, is a chamber, called Erasmus's chamber. I ghesse that the Dreyden coate was graunted in K. Hen. 8th's time, by the odnesse of the charge.*

EARLE OF ESSEX.

Sr Charles Danvers advised the Earle of Essex, either to treat with the queen's hostages . . . . whom Sr Ferdinando Gorges did let goe ; or to make his way through the gate at Essex house, and then to haste away to Highgate, and so to Northumberland (the E. of Northumberland maried his sister), and from thence to the King of Scots ; and there they might make their peace ; if not, the queen was old and could not live long.

* [There is a page left for the Life of John Dryden, the poet, who promised to write it himself for Aubrey. This promise does not appear to have been performed. EDIT.]

But the Earle followed not his advice, and so they both lost their heads on Tower-hill. From my Lady Viscountesse Purbec.

. . . . . EARLE OF EXETER

Translated Monsieur Balsac's letters, as appeares by his Epistle to my Lord, in the 2d volume, Lib. V. lettre V, and vol. 2d. Lib. V. lettre VI.—" Et je suis sans doute beaucoup plus honnèste homme en Angleterre qu'en France, puisque j'y parle par vostre bouche."

THOMAS LORD FAIRFAX, OF CAMERON.

(Ld Generall of the Parliament armie.)

Mem. When Oxford was surrendred (24º Junij, 1646,) the first thing Generall Fairfax did was to sett a good guard of soldiers to preserve the Bodleian Library. 'Tis said there was more hurt donne by the cavaliers (during their garrison) by way of embezzilling and cutting-off chaines of bookes, then there was since. He was a lover of learning, and had he not taken this speciall care, that noble library had been utterly destroyed, for there were ignorant senators enough who would have been contented to have had it so. This I doe assure you from an ocular witnesse, E. W. Esq.

He hath a copie of verses before . . . . . in folio.

LUCIUS CAREY, SECOND LORD FALKLAND,

Was the eldest son of Sir Henry Carey, Lord Lieutenant of Ireland, the first Viscount Falkland. His mother was daughter and heir of Sir . . . . . Tanfield, Lord Chief Baron of the Exchequer, by whom he had Great Tue, in Oxfordshire (formerly the Rainsfords), and the Priory of Burford, in Oxfordshire, which he sold to , . . . Lenthall, the Speaker of the Long Parliament; and he was borne . . . . . had his University education at the University of Dublin, in Ireland; he travelled, and had one Mr. . . . . (a very discreet gent.) to be his governor, whom he respected to his dyeing days. He married Letice, the daughter of Sir . . . . Morison, by whom he had two sonnes: the eldest lived to be a man, dyed *sine prole*, the second was father to this Lord Falkland now living. This Lady Letice was a good and pious lady, as you may see by her life writt about 1649, or so, by . . . . Duncomb, D.D. But I will tell you a pretty story from Will. Hawes, of Trin. Coll. who was well acquainted with the governor aforesaid, who told him that my Lady was (after the manner of woemen) much governed by, and indulgent to, the nursery; when she had a mind to beg any thing of my Lord for one of her mayds, woemen, nurses, &c. she would not doe it by herselfe, (if she could helpe it) but putt this gent. upon it, to move it to my Lord. My Lord had but a small estate for his title; and the old gent. would say, "Madam, this is so unreasonable a motion to propose to my Lord, that I am certaine he will never graunt it;"—e. g. one time to lett a bargaine (a farm) twenty pound per ann. under value. At length, when she could not prevail on him; she would say, I warrant you for all this I will obtaine it of my Lord, *it will cost me but the expence of a few tears.* Now she would make her words good, and this great witt, the greatest master of reason and judgment of his time, at the long runne, being stormed by her *teares,* (I presume there were kisses and secret embraces that were also ingredients) would this pious lady obtain her unreasonable desires of her poor Lord. My Lord in his youth was very wild, and also mischievous, as being apt to stabbe, and doe bloudy mischiefs, but twas not long before he tooke up to be serious, and then grew to be an extraordinary hard-student. I have heard Dr. Ralph Bathurst say, that when he was a boy, my Lord lived at Coventry, (where he had then a house) and that he would sit up very late at night in his study, and many times came to the Library at the Schoole* there. The studies in fashion in those dayes (in England) were Poetrey, and Controversie with the Church of Rome. My Lord's mother was a zealous Papist, who being very earnest to have her son of her religion, and her son upon that occasion, labouring hard to find the Trueth, was so far at last from setling on the Romish church, that he setled and rested in the Polish (I meane Socinianisme) He was the first Socinian in England; and Dr. . . . . Cressey, of Merton Coll. (Dean of . . . . in Ireland, afterwards a Benedictine monke) a great acquaintance of my Lord's in those dayes, told me, at Sam. Cowper's, (1669) that he himself was the first that brought Socinus's bookes; shortly after, my Lord comeing to him, and casting his eie on them, would needs presently borrow them to peruse; and was so extremely taken and satisfied with them, that from that time was his conversion. My Lord much lived at Tue, which is a pleasant seat, and about 12 miles from Oxford; his Lordship was acquainted with the best witts at that University, and his house was like a Colledge, full of learned men. Mr. William Chil-

* There is Euclid's Harmoniques written with Philemon Holland's owne hand, in a curious Greeke character. He was school-master here.

lingworth, of Trinity Coll. in Oxford, (afterwards D.D.) was his most intimate and beloved favourite, and was most commonly with my Lord; next I may reckon (if not equall) Mr. John Earle, of Merton Coll. (who wrote the Characters); Dr. Aglionby, of Ch. Ch. was also in much esteem with his Lordship; his Chaplaine, Charles Gataker, F. . . . Gataker, of Redriff (a writer), was an ingeniose young gent. but no writer. For learned gent. of the Country, his acquaintance was Sir H. Rainesford, of * . . . . Sir Francis Wenman, of Caswell, in Witney parish; Mr. Sandys, the Traveller and Translator (who was uncle to my Lady Wenman); Ben. Jonson (V. Johnsonus Virbius, where he has verses, and 'twas his Lordship, Ch. Gataker told me, that gave the name to it), Edmund Waller, Esq. Mr. Th. Hobbes, and all the excellent witts of that peaceable time. In the civill warres he adhered to King Ch. I. who after Edge-hill fight made him Principal Secretary of Estate (with Sir Edward Nicholas), which he dischardged with a great deal of witt and prudence, only his advice was very unlucky to his Majestie, in persuading him (after the victory of Rowndway Downe, and the taking of Bristowe,) to sitt downe before Gloucester, which was so bravely defended by that incomparably vigilant governor Coll. . . . Massey,

* Neer Stratford-upon-Avon, now . . . .

and the diligent and careful soldiers and citizens (men and woemen), that it so broke and weakened the king's armys, that 'twas yᵉ procataretique* cause of his ruine. After this, all the King's matters went worse and worse; at the .... fight at Newbury, my Lord Falkland being there, and having nothing to doe, to chardge, as the 2 armies were engaging, rode in like a mad-man (as he was) between them, and was (as he needs must be) shott. Some that were your superfine discoursing politicians, and fine gent. would needs have the reason of this mad action of throwing away his life so to be his discontent for the unfortunate advice given to his master as aforesaid; but, I have been well informed, by those that best knew him, and knew intrigues behind the curtaine (as they say), that it was the griefe of the death of Mris Moray, a handsome lady at court, who was his mistresse, and whom he loved above all creatures, was the true cause of his being so madly guilty of his own death, as afore mentioned. (*Nullum magnum ingenium sine mixturâ dementiæ.*) The next day when they went to bury the dead, they could not find his Lordship's body, it was stript, and trod upon, and mangled; so there was one yᵗ waited on him in his chamber would undertake to know it from all other bodys, by a certaine mole his Lordship had on his neck,

* [Sic. Edit.]

and by that mark did find it. He lies interred in the . . . . . at Great Tue aforesaid, but I take it without any monument; Q. if any inscription. In the dining roome there is a picture of his at length, and like him ('twas donne by Jacob de Valke, who taught me to paint) he was but a little man, and of no great strength of body, he had blackish haire, something flaggy, and I thinke his eies black. Dr. Earle would not allow him to be a good poet, though a great witt; he writt not a smooth verse, but a great deal of sense. He hath writt . . . . .

He had an estate in Hertfordshire, at . . . . . . which came by Morrison (as I take it), sold not long before the late civill warres.

SIR MILES FLEETWOOD,

(Recorder of London),

Was of the Middle Temple, was Recorder of London, when King James came into England. Made his harangue to the City of London *ἀντανάκλασις*, "When I consider your wealth I doe admire your wisdome, and when I consider your wisdome I doe admire your wealth." It was a two-handed rhetorication, but the citizens tooke it in the best sense. He was a very severe hanger of highwaymen, so that the fraternity were resolved to make an example of his worship, w[ch] they executed in this manner: They lay in wayte for him not far from Tyburne, as he was to come from his house at .... in Bucks; had a halter in readinesse; brought him under the gallowes, fastened the rope about his neck, his hands tied behind him (and servants bound), and then left him to the mercy of his horse, w[ch] he called *Ball*. So he cryed "Ho, Ball! Ho, Ball!" and it pleased God that his horse stood still, till somebody came along, w[ch] was halfe a quarter of an hour or more.* He ordered that this horse should be kept as long as he would live, which was so; he lived till 1646. * * * * * *

His seate was at Missenden, in the county of Bucks, where his descendants still remaine.

He is buried at .....in com. Bucks.

MR. JOHN FLETCHER,

(Poet.)

In the great plague, 1625, a Knight of Norfolk or Suffolk, invited him into the countrey. He stayed but to make himselfe a suite of cloathes, and while it was makeing, fell sick of the plague and dyed. This I had from his tayler, who is now a very old man, and clarke of St. Mary Overy's.

* From Mr. Tho. Bigge, of Wickam.

END OF PART I.

Printed by Munday and Slatter, Oxford.

CPSIA information can be obtained at www.ICGtesting.com
Printed in the USA
LVOW11s0845220315

431427LV00001B/68/P